C000004520

The Later Heidegger

'A highly instructive and engaging guide through Heidegger's later writings, written in a lucid and accessible manner.'

Keith Ansell Pearson, *University of Warwick*

'... a lively, clear and engaging overview of the key ideas in Heidegger's later writings.'

Charles Guignon, *University of Vermont*

This Routledge Philosophy GuideBook guides the reader through the complexities of Heidegger's later works. The book offers a clear introduction to the main themes that preoccupied Heidegger in the second part of his career: technology, art, the history of philosophy and the exploration of a new post-technological way of thinking.

George Pattison explores many aspects of the later Heidegger, including the massive controversy surrounding his Nazism, as well as his readings of Nietzsche, the Presocratics and Hölderlin. Pattison also carefully investigates the difficult question of the nature of Heidegger's thought, together with its significance for philosophy today.

The Later Heidegger is essential reading for all students coming to Heidegger's later works for the first time.

George Pattison is Dean of King's College, Cambridge.

Routledge Philosophy GuideBooks

Edited by Tim Crane and Jonathan Wolff
University College London

The Later Heidegger
George Pattison

Hegel on History
Joseph McCarney

Hume on Morality
James Baillie

Kant and the *Critique of Pure Reason*
Sebastian Gardner

Mill on Liberty
Jonathan Riley

Mill on Utilitarianism
Roger Crisp

Wittgenstein and the *Philosophical Investigations*
Marie McGinn

Plato and the *Republic*
Nickolas Pappas

Locke on Government
D.A. Lloyd Thomas

Locke on Human Understanding
E.J. Lowe

Spinoza and the *Ethics*
Genevieve Lloyd

LONDON AND NEW YORK

Routledge Philosophy GuideBook to

The Later Heidegger

George Pattison

ROUTLEDGE

First published 2000
by Routledge
11 New Fetter Lane, London EC4P 4EE

Simultaneously published in the USA and Canada
by Routledge
29 West 35th Street, New York, NY 10001

Routledge is an imprint of the Taylor & Francis Group

© 2000 George Pattison

Typeset in Times and Gill Sans by Taylor & Francis Books Ltd
Printed and bound in Great Britain by Clays Ltd, St Ives PLC

British Library Cataloguing in Publication Data
A catalogue record for this book is available from the British Library

Library of Congress Cataloging in Publication Data
Pattison, George, 1950–
Routledge Philosophy GuideBook to The Later Heidegger / George Pattison.
(Routledge Philosophy GuideBooks)
1. Heidegger, Martin, 1889–1976. I. Title: Later Heidegger.
II. Title. III. Series.
B3279.H49 P39 2000
193–dc21 00-020572

ISBN 0–415–20196–9 (hbk)
ISBN 0–415–20197–7 (pbk)

Who laud and magnify with made, mutable and beggarly elements the unmade immutable beginnings and precessions of fair-height, with halting sequences and unresolved rhythms, searchingly, with what's to hand, under the inconstant lights that hover world-flats, that bright by fit and start the tangle of world-wood, rifting the dark drifts for the wanderers that wind the world-meander, who seek hidden grammar to give back anathema its first benignity.

Gathering all things in, twining each bruised stem to the swaying trellis of the dance, the dance about the sawn lode-stake on the hill where the hidden stillness is at the core of struggle ...

(From David Jones, *The Sleeping Lord and Other Fragments*)

Contents

Foreword

The text that follows explains itself, I hope. However, there is one point I should comment on. Different English renderings of Heidegger adopt different strategies with regard to capitalising the English 'Being' as a translation of Heidegger's German 'Sein'. The advantage of giving the lower-case 'being' is that it brings out the verbal aspect of the term and avoids misreading it as a hypostatised metaphysical concept. On the other hand, this could on occasion lead to it being read simply as a present participle and not as a distinctive philosophical term. In any case, the German word is a nominalisation of the infinitive, not the present participle 'seiend' (the nominal form of which, 'Seiendes', is usually translated 'beings' or 'entities'). Where I have quoted English translations that follow a different practice, I have, of course, kept to their usage.

Some measure of interpretation is unavoidable here, both on my part and on that of the reader. Perhaps, in the light of Heidegger's own comments on philosophy and translation, the best we can do is to remember to hear the German 'Sein' in the English 'Being'.

Acknowledgments

I have received help of various kinds from many friends and colleagues in preparing this volume, including those who have lent me books, discussed the argument as it developed and read the manuscripts. These include Don Cupitt, Istvan Hont, Clare Carlisle, Ulrich Knappe, Melissa Lane, Neil Pattison, Mike Weston and Espen Hammer. The genesis of the book owes a lot to Ulrich Fentzloff. I am particularly grateful to Utta Vinzent for her research on the reception of Van Gogh in the Nazi era. I was able to try out some of the ideas in a number of talks and seminars, and I would like to thank those who invited me: Simon Etheridge (Bishop's Stortford High School), Michael Wilcockson (Eton College), Brian Hebblethwaite (the 'D' Society, Cambridge Divinity School), John Lippitt (University of Hertfordshire) and Martin Kusch ('Philosopher King's' – the philosophy society of King's College, Cambridge). Thanks also to Sue Needham.

I am grateful to HarperCollins for permission to reprint extracts from *What is Called Thinking?* and *Poetry, Language, Thought*, and to the Trustees of the David Jones Estate for permission to reprint an extract from David Jones, *The Sleeping Lord and Other Fragments*.

And, chiefly, to Hilary.

Abbreviations used in the text

BT   *Being and Time*, followed by section and page number, giving the pagination in the German edition used by the translators
EGT   *Early Greek Thinking*
GA   *Gesamtausgabe* (1978–), followed by volume and page number
HCT   *History of the Concept of Time*
N   *Nietzsche* (followed by volume number)
PLT   *Poetry, Language, Thought*
QT   *The Question Concerning Technology and Other Essays*
WT   *What is a Thing?*
WCT   *What is Called Thinking?*

For full details of these titles, see the Bibliography.

Chapter 1

Is there a later Heidegger?

The danger and the turning

In December 1949 Martin Heidegger, banned from lecturing in the University of Freiburg on account of his involvement with Nazism, gave a series of four addresses to 'The Club' in Bremen, a gathering of business and professional people who, for the most part, had no great interest in or understanding of philosophy, but who were happy to turn out to hear a man known as their country's most influential living philosopher. In these lectures Heidegger spoke of the danger hanging over the present age. This was already the era of the Atomic Bomb and the beginning of the Cold War, in which the possibility of a catastrophic nuclear exchange was a continuous threat to the peoples of the world, and especially to those of Central Europe. Perhaps Heidegger's non-philosophical auditors may have heard in his words a reference to that situation, and perhaps he was himself happy to use the rhetorical force of such an allusion to win a hearing for his argument, but the danger with which Heidegger was chiefly concerned operated on another level altogether. This danger was neither Russian Communism, nor American capitalism, nor the prospect of all-out war between them, but, in Heidegger's own formulation 'The coming to presence of Enframing is the danger.' (QT: 41) What did he mean? In order to answer this question, let us look, firstly, at what Heidegger means by the odd-sounding term 'enframing'.

'Enframing', in Heidegger's sense of the word, is not unconnected with the world of technology for whose darker possibilities the Atomic Bomb was, at that time, the most potent symbol. Nevertheless, as Heidegger many times insists, enframing is not itself anything technological. Very provisionally, we may say that it is something like the mind-set underlying modern technology. However, 'enframing' is not only manifested in such things as atomic bombs, televisions or washing-machines, but is equally present in culture and everyday life. When we talk of 'the culture industry' or 'quality time' or of being 'consumers of the countryside' we are revealing the influence of enframing on our way of thinking. And, quite apart from such threats as nuclear war and environmental degradation, the 'danger' of which Heidegger spoke would still, in his terms, remain. For the danger is in enframing itself, not in the success or failure of the technology that it sustains or in the malign application of that technology.

As the mind-set that underlies the rise of technology and that permeates our daily habits of speech and thought, enframing is Heidegger's term for a way of objectifying our world and our experience (including our experience of ourselves) in such a way as to make what is enframed available for our use, manipulable and transformable in the service of designated goals and purposes. Put like this, it may sound as if enframing is merely shorthand for the human ambition of achieving dominion over nature. That is how it may seem both to those who are the agents of enframing and to many of those who see themselves as its enemies. However, as Heidegger understands it, the roots of enframing in some sense precede 'man', and certainly precede 'man' as conceived by post-Renaissance humanism. Humanism, with its slogan 'Man, the measure of all things', is not the cause of the situation but its expression. The origin of enframing does not lie in any human act, but, Heidegger says, hails from a destining of primordial Being.

With this enigmatic assertion we are already confronted with two of the key terms of the later Heidegger, 'destining' and 'Being', and we are already face to face with the problems of translation that have dogged the reception of Heidegger in the English-speaking world. 'Destining' translates the German term *Geschick*, which has the twofold meaning of 'destiny' and 'suitability' or 'capacity' – and Heidegger intends both of these meanings to be heard in his use of the word. 'Destining' is therefore not simply a destiny or fate imposed on the world from outside, but suggests a self-adaptation on the part of Being to the way the world is, making its self-giving and self-disclosure suitable to the capacities of those who receive it. It is therefore a two-way process. But what is 'Being' that is the source of this destining? Being is, of course, a key word in the Western philosophical vocabulary, the meaning of which has been widely debated and contested. For some philosophers it has been virtually a synonym for God, whilst others have spoken of it more as the substratum of the world, or the most abstract of all possible categories. I shall look more closely at Heidegger's use of the term in the following section, noting for now only the general point that, for Heidegger, the question of Being is the question that most of all needs to be thought about by philosophers, the question that decides how things are for us and for our world.

But if enframing is a destining of Being, and is therefore a self-adaptation of Being to our capacities, where does the danger lie? Surely whatever comes to us from Being must reflect the way things are and, therefore, be in some sense true? So it may seem; yet, whilst Heidegger says that enframing comes from or is an event within Being, he also says that it shrouds Being in oblivion. In other words, when we are immersed in seeing the world as enframed, there is a real possibility that we fail to see or to understand what it is for Being truly to be.

What then is to be done?

Such a question may seem like a natural response to any perceived danger – but what if it already betrays a humanistic, action-oriented perspective that is itself an expression of enframing?

However, if waking up to the danger we're in is not a call to action – what is it? A call to thinking, maybe: and, if the danger is ultimately rooted in Being, that must mean a call to attend thinkingly to what is going on in Being itself. Heidegger liked to quote some words of Hölderlin: 'Where danger is, grows also that which saves'. The implication of these words is that, if becoming aware of the danger of the oblivion of Being directs us to attend more urgently to the question of Being, then, paradoxically, the danger itself may in the long term prove to be of service to Being. The paradox is that precisely because enframing prevents us from seeing Being, Being is protected from us. Neglected, even abandoned, Being is left to itself. Yet, Heidegger's argument continues, for this to happen, or for the situation to be understood in this way, enframing will have to be seen for what it really is, and therefore the danger will have to be seen for the danger that it is. However, because this cannot occur as the result of human planning, willing or doing (since these are already compromised by their entanglement in enframing), it can only occur as the outcome of an event within Being itself, and 'When and how it will come to pass … no one knows. Nor is it necessary that we know.' (QT: 41) Our task is not to secure for ourselves a clear and distinct knowledge of Being but 'to be the one who waits, the one who attends upon the coming to presence of Being in that in thinking he grounds it. Only when man, as the shepherd of Being, attends upon the truth of Being can he expect an arrival of a destining of Being' (QT: 42).

What is to be looked for, then, is a turning, a reversal, that is both a turning in Being and a turning in humanity: in Being in that its oblivion is transformed into a safekeeping, in humanity in that we are transformed from *homo faber*, man the maker, Lord of creation and Master of the Universe, into the Shepherd of Being, the one who waits. 'Perhaps,' Heidegger muses, 'we stand already in the shadow cast ahead by the advent of *this* turning' (QT: 41).

What the business and professional people of Bremen made of this we do not know, but, if there is a single issue that can be said to constitute the centre around which the thinking of the later Heidegger revolves, then the question and expectation of this 'turning' would have a good claim to consideration. For, from the 1930s onwards, Heidegger is continually preoccupied with the danger that he sees as threatening modern civilisation and with the hope that there might yet be a new event within the history of Being itself that would, in some as yet undefined way, save us from the danger and from ourselves.

In focusing on this theme of the turning we have already run on ahead of ourselves. In arriving so quickly at 'the centre' of the later Heidegger we have put in play terms and topics that remain unexplained, and we have, inevitably, left much out. Nothing has been said so far about the later Heidegger's paramount concern for language, or about the role of language in enabling the turning of which he speaks to come to pass – yet some commentators would say that the philosophy of the later Heidegger is nothing if not a philosophy of language. And there are other themes, too, that we have not broached, or that lie submerged and unremarked in what has been said thus far. There is, then, a lot to do in terms of clarifying and amplifying these few introductory pages, and such clarification and amplification is, in essence, the burden of the remainder of this book. At the same time it is worth remembering that, at one level, the heart of Heidegger's later thinking *can* be reached quite quickly and stated quite simply (if not exactly perspicuously). For it is important to Heidegger that the kind of waiting upon Being to which we are called is not something that can only be reached or constructed as the result of a protracted and complex chain of reasoning or by the acquisition of new knowledge. Instead, he aims to make us look again at what we already know, to see what is already within the compass of our possible experience, but to which, intoxicated by the fantastic results achieved by enframing, we fail to attend. As Heidegger said many times, it is the simplest things that are hardest to think, and the nearest things that are most remote – yet it is just these to which his philosophy wishes to lead us.

The motif of the 'turning' is, I have claimed, central to the thought of the later Heidegger. But does the thought of the later Heidegger itself represent a 'turning': a turning-away from the existential analysis of Dasein that was the focus of *Being and Time*, and a turning towards the kind of ruminations upon the history of Being to which the lecture on 'The Turning' has already introduced us? And, if we are justified in speaking of such a turning in Heidegger's own career, what exactly does that mean? Does it mean that at a certain point Heidegger simply abandoned the complex of questions and methods that found their fullest expression in *Being and Time*? Or does it mean that the same questions were carried over but subordinated to other, newer questions, or were subjected to different methodological treatment? How much continuity, and how great a discontinuity is there between the earlier and the later Heidegger? Are we in fact justified in talking about the later Heidegger at all? Or should we be ultra-cautious and follow those scholars who speak of an early, a middle and a late Heidegger? In any case, are these divisions, breaks and paradigm-shifts things that can be dated precisely or tied to particular works? So just what is meant by the later Heidegger?

Since an adequate answer to such questions would presuppose a substantive interpretation of Heidegger's work as a whole, I shall for now simply sketch some of the reasons why I believe that we are justified in speaking of the 'later Heidegger'. These amount to the view that there is a complex of themes, methods, topics and even stylistics that, taken together, define a distinctive body of writing that can be read and studied in relative independence from the Heidegger of *Being and Time*, and that this body of writing constitutes in its own right a particular (and a particularly important) position in the twentieth-century philosophical landscape. There are those, of course, who contest whether these writings can genuinely be called philosophical at all, a challenge to which I shall return in the final section of this book.

The earlier and the later Heidegger

In attempting to define more closely what is meant by the later Heidegger, we must identify both the continuities and the discontinuities that shape Heidegger's philosophical career. But we also have to ask why Heidegger 'turned', and to say what the philosophical motivations were that led him to direct his thought in the new ways opened up by his 'turn'. Let us take these points one at a time, beginning with the question as to the discontinuities that separate the later from the earlier Heidegger.

As Heidegger himself and many of his commentators since have stated, one crucial area of discontinuity concerns the way in which the question of Being is addressed.

Being and Time opened with a clarion call to philosophy to reopen the question of Being, a question that, Heidegger claimed, had been forgotten by contemporary philosophers. In such a situation, in which the question of Being is no longer asked, the very first challenge facing anyone seeking to reopen it is: where to begin? How can one ask such a big question without any kind of philosophical context in which to ask it?

True, says Heidegger, philosophy as it is now studied and taught in universities is not engaging with this question and can give us very little by way of a direct lead, but this does not mean that we are entirely without resources. After all, even philosophers still participate in the average, everyday discourses in which human beings talk amongst themselves about themselves. Now, human beings are precisely those beings for whom their own being is an issue, who can ask what it is for them to be, what their being *means*, and who are thus, essentially, describable as *Da-sein* (literally: 'there-being'), beings in whom the question of Being is brought out into the open, brought out 'there' into the public space of the world. Now even though human beings, Dasein, are for the most part immersed in the daily round and common task and are caught up in the idle chatter of average everydayness, what they say about themselves, their hopes, fears, plans and projects, does reveal to an appropriately attuned listener what their being means to them. Even if Dasein's everyday self-understanding is only the expression of the mumbling confessions of unfulfilled lives, we can deduce from these confessions what it is that Dasein considers would count as full and authentic Being, what Dasein has it in itself to be – even if, for the most part, it falls far short of realising its own possibilities. The disclosure of authentic Being that occurs when Dasein confronts its own finitude and death and resolutely accepts its utter immersion in the raging flux of time that carries it inescapably towards its death provides philosophy with a basis from which to sketch a horizon for the interpretation of Being as such.

This account became definitive for what became known in Germany as the philosophy of existence and subsequently played a decisive role in the shaping of French existentialism. In the most popular version of existentialism, as propounded by Jean-Paul Sartre, Heidegger's Dasein was identified more or less unproblematically with the individual human subject, becoming an angst-ridden version of the Cartesian ego – 'Existentialism is a Humanism' as the title of one of Sartre's popularising works put it. The human subject, in this view, is defined by the fact that his existence precedes his essence. Rather than being determined by some pre-existing 'human nature' (as both Christian theology and scientific anthropology would have it), the individual is simply the sum of his own actions, actions issuing from a radical and undefinable freedom. Everything – absolutely everything – in our lives is what it is as the outcome or expression of a free act – 'there are no accidents', Sartre declared. Fairly obviously, despite humanism's long-standing affirmation of human freedom, such an account goes well beyond anything traditional humanism had dared to say. Sartre is uncompromising in his rejection of any objectivising or essentialising interpretation of the human situation, whether theological, scientific, sociological, psychological or philosophical. Our freedom – and that means our very identity – is rooted solely in an upsurge of nothingness, a vortex of indeterminacy in the midst of the congealed mass of Being-in-itself that is the world. However, this passionate advocacy of the primacy of freedom not only leads Sartre to oppose conventional theories of human identity, it also brings him into conflict with everyday moral discourse. Like Heidegger, Sartre regards human beings as typically evasive in face of their own possibility for free self-affirmation. We characteristically talk about our own behaviour and that of others in terms that blunt the razor edge of radical freedom. We ascribe our conduct or our attitudes, our achievements or our failures, to our nationality, our class, our gender, our upbringing or our lack of a private income. We might, for example, dismiss Sartre's whole philosophy as the expression of a pampered male bourgeois intellectual occupying a particular time and place in French cultural life. That, we might think, 'explains' Sartre. And if we catch ourselves behaving badly, we always have a set of mitigating circumstances to hand: I was drunk, I was tired, I was frightened, I was seduced, we say – meaning: I didn't mean it, it wasn't my fault. But that, says Sartre, is fake, or, as he put it, acting 'in bad faith'. The truth is that we are always responsible for everything, and even the Resistance fighter who has been tortured beyond the point of endurance is responsible for betraying his comrades. There are no excuses. We decide, by our actions, each for ourselves, who we are and the values we live by.

Given that, in the popular imagination at least, Sartre owed his central insights to Heidegger, this seemed to be the outcome of Heidegger's own phenomenological analysis of the human situation in *Being and Time*. However, Heidegger himself did not see it that way. Although he was personally interested in the possibility of meeting Sartre, his repudiation of Sartrean existentialism was spelt out in the 1947 *Letter on Humanism*, a title deliberately referring to Sartre's own *Existentialism is a Humanism*, published the previous year.

Like Sartre, Heidegger is prepared to see the human situation in terms of ontological homelessness, meaning that on this earth we have no abiding home, since we are not embedded in the world as a part of nature. Instead we are, as it were, thrown into the world, into a life we did not choose but which, now we are here, we must choose or, in one of a myriad ways, evade. However, as Heidegger tells the story in 1947, this does not lead to the apotheosis of individual subjective freedom. For Heidegger, it seems, man's thrownness is part of a larger story: 'The human being is ... "thrown" by being itself into the truth of being,' he writes (1998: 252). Our abandonment is not an arbitrary fact, but is to be understood in terms of our abandonment *of* Being and, conversely, of our abandonment *by* Being. This situation confronts us with a certain danger, as we have seen, but it also contains the possibility of a kind of salvation. If, as Heidegger has it, existence is ek-sistence, Dasein's standing-out from a world, it is not simply standing out into the nothingness of freedom (as for Sartre), it is ek-sisting into the nothingness of *Being*, 'ecstatic inherence in the truth of being' (1998: 251).

Sartre had doomed us to the absurd situation of continually seeking to be the ground or foundation of our own Being, to act 'as if a man were author of himself' – although it is impossible to *be* our own self-author, since our freedom, because it is grounded in nothing, cannot establish anything objective. It is neither deducible from any chain of causality nor can it influence any chain of causality. Thus, for Sartre, man is 'a useless passion', whose freedom is bought at the price of absurdity. In contrast to Sartre, Heidegger now sees our distinctiveness within nature, our radical freedom and the nothingness that is interconnected with it, as issuing in a more positive-sounding possibility: namely, to take upon ourselves the obligation to 'guard the truth of being, in order that beings might appear in the light of being as the beings they are.' (1998: 251) Our standing-out opens a possibility for us to become 'the shepherd of Being.' (1998: 251) At its simplest, then, the outcome is this: 'that in the determination of the humanity of the human being as ek-sistence what is essential is not the human being but being' (1998: 254).

In comparison with the global reversal in our customary philosophical and everyday ways of thinking that this turning from man to Being requires, Sartre's reversal of the priority of existence and essence seems somewhat regional and can be portrayed simply as a bid to replace the objectivising metaphysics of scholastic tradition with a metaphysics of subjectivity, or, to put it crudely, to replace God with humanity. Heidegger's call to us to become 'shepherds of Being', however, points (or so he claims) beyond traditional oppositions of subject vs. object, of humanity vs. God.

In thus drawing a line between his own thought and that of French existentialism, Heidegger is also drawing a line between the concerns that now govern his thinking and what preoccupied him in the days when he could be seen as the principal philosopher of existence. Then it was Dasein that stood in the centre of the picture, and it was as an issue in Dasein's self-understanding that the question of Being was asked. Now it is Being that stands at the centre, and Dasein is 'there' for the sake of Being.

In this way the question of Being, the guiding thread of Heidegger's whole philosophical labour, is transposed into a new key, and we hear of a 'history of Being', a sequence of destinings bestowed upon us from a more-than-human origin that lies beyond everything hitherto known to philosophers as 'Being'. In order to emphasise this Heidegger adopts the archaic spelling 'Seyn' for 'Sein'[1] or writes the term under erasure: ~~Being~~. Such usages emphasise that Being–*Seyn* ~~Being~~ is not a concept or substance, but belongs to a dimension that precedes all conceptualisation and all knowledge.

However, if the *Letter on Humanism* was the most concise and, outside Germany, the most rapidly disseminated testimony to Heidegger's turning, it can by no means be regarded as its beginning. Throughout the 1930s and early 1940s Heidegger had been giving series of lectures in which the trajectory of his changing path of thinking is, at least with hindsight, plainly discernible. Very important here is what was eventually published in 1950 as *On the Origin of the Work of Art*, whilst Heidegger himself placed particular emphasis on his Nietzsche lectures, given in the 1930s and 1940s (although, again, these were not published till 1961). Perhaps most significant of all is the work *Beiträge zur Philosophie: Vom Ereignis* (*Contributions to Philosophy: Concerning the Event*), written between 1936 and 1938, which, together with its companion volume, *Besinnung* (*Mindfulness*), might lay claim to be a 'summa' of the later Heidegger.[2]

Noting, then, that the critique of the philosophy of existence (justifiably or unjustifiably associated with *Being and Time*) in the *Letter on Humanism* was giving expression to a shift that was already well-established in Heidegger's thought, can we identify other differences between the earlier and the later Heidegger in addition to the reordering of priorities as between humanity/Dasein and Being?

Certainly we can discern a fairly clear and fairly widespread shift of thematic focus. *Being and Time* offered a phenomenological analysis of the human situation in terms of 'falling': idle chatter, anxiety, care, resolve, death, guilt and the decisive 'moment of vision' in which past, present and future are repeatedly synthesised into a horizon that enables *Dasein* to project itself upon Being. The later philosophy, by way of contrast, speaks less heroically, its pathos is that of resignation and expectation, and the human subject is no longer the existential hero, riven by angst and confronting nothingness, but the wanderer on forest paths, shepherd of Being, attuned to the joyous hymning of a spiritual homeland, bounded by the fourfold of earth, sky, death and the gods.

In the spirit of such changes Heidegger repeatedly redefines his own task, so that whereas in *Being and Time* and *What is Metaphysics?* (his inaugural lecture in Freiburg in 1929) he seems to be setting about a relaunch of metaphysics, by the early 1930s 'metaphysics' is itself being seen as part of the problem, and Heidegger prefers to talk simply of 'philosophy'; however, philosophy too turns out to be problematic and by the late 1930s and early 1940s he is experimenting with the term *Besinnung*,[3] until, in *What is Called Thinking?*, he resolves on the simple 'thinking'.

Throughout all these changes, Heidegger's strategy is one of progressive self-critique and defamiliarisation, and yet there seems to be a constant, steady purpose: to break the grip of an over-technical 'school' philosophy that is permeated by the presuppositions of what Heidegger came to call 'enframing' and to provoke the student into a new and original encounter with the matter under consideration. And there are other, no less significant, continuities.

Earlier, we took at face value the rough-and-ready categorisation of *Being and Time* as belonging to the 'philosophy of existence' and, as such, a philosophical forerunner of Sartrean existentialism. However, already in the 1930s Heidegger himself is arguing that it was a mistake to read *Being and Time* in those terms. His project there, he claimed, was not an exercise in the philosophy of existence, nor was it intended as a nihilistic self-affirmation of twentieth-century alienation. Instead it was directed towards a fundamental ontology, i.e., towards Being, not towards humanity. Similarly, in the *Letter on Humanism*, Heidegger argues that the account of ek-sistence given in *Being and Time* was already conceived in terms of Dasein standing out ecstatically into the truth of Being, rather than into the empty abyss of existential freedom.

It is likewise easy to see an analogy between the later Heidegger's preoccupation with the oblivion of Being in an age of technological enframing and the effort made in *Being and Time* to re-open the question of Being in an age dominated intellectually by positivism and absorbed at an everyday level in the various modes of 'falling' (idle chatter, etc.). In each case the aim is a reawakening of the encounter with Being, even if this is seen from the point of view of the human subject in the one case and from the point of view of the history of Being in the other.

But there are other affinities and analogies between *Being and Time* and the later Heidegger. Take, for example, what Heidegger does with the expression 'there is' (German: 'es gibt', literally: 'it gives'), and the relation between time and Being.

Heidegger's interpretation of this everyday expression shows how our conscious, conceptualising representation of the world relies upon an assumed, background familiarity with Being – that 'there is' something at all – that is never itself thematised in non-philosophical consciousness. The 'there is', he suggests, points directly to just this prereflective acquaintance with Being, and to the situation that the world, that whole realm of beings that concerns us in our scientific enquiries and in our everyday lives alike, is given to us from a source that always eludes the penetrating gaze of rational enquiry.

It is precisely with reference to this expression that the *Letter on Humanism* argues that the germ of the whole later development of the understanding of Being is already present in *Being and Time*. Heidegger acknowledges that in *Being and Time* itself he wrote that 'Only so long as Dasein is, is there [*gibt es*] Being.' However, he now claims that 'the sentence does not say that Being is the product of man'. The Being that 'is there' only in and through Dasein is, he asserts, already conceived as essentially transcendent in relation to Dasein. Being is only 'illumined for man' in the light cast by man's own projects: i.e., it is our questioning and our doing that determine how Being will appear and give itself to us. 'But this projection does not create being' (1998: 257). Furthermore, since *Being and Time* understands Dasein in terms of its thrownness, such that Dasein is never the ground of its own Being, and since also it is only on the basis of this thrown being that Dasein generates its own projects, practical or theoretical as the case may be, 'What throws in such projection is not the human being but being itself, which sends the human being into the ek-sistence of Da-sein that is his essence' (1998: 257).

However, if in such ways we are able to trace lines of continuity running back from the later work to *Being and Time*, such that the later work appears more as deepening or taking further what was begun in *Being and Time* rather than as a 180° turn-about, it does not follow that what may indeed be latent in *Being and Time* is directly stated there as such. Again, Heidegger himself acknowledges that 'For all that, being is thought [in *Being and Time* – GP] on the basis of beings, a consequence of the approach – at first unavoidable – within a metaphysics that is still dominant.' (1998: 256) In other words, the revolution in philosophy that began in *Being and Time* had to start with the conceptual situation bequeathed to it by the tradition itself. The apparent 'humanism' of *Being and Time* may, then, be understood as a concession to the presuppositions of Heidegger's audience, or, perhaps (if we are to believe the *Letter on Humanism*) to the fact that, although the deeper implications of *Being and Time* pointed beyond humanism, Heidegger himself did not fully grasp this, and first had to work through what he had inherited from the past before he could move beyond it.

Time, death and the rhetoric of superiority

A similar picture of continuity/discontinuity emerges if we look at the way in which Being and time are reciprocally defined in the earlier and in the later work respectively.

In 1962 Heidegger gave a lecture 'On Time and Being', the title of which intentionally reverses that of *Being and Time*. The implications of this reversal are not hard to see in the light of what has been said about Heidegger's shift towards a less anthropocentric view. In *Being and Time* itself Being is approached exclusively through historicity, that is, through Dasein's all-pervading temporality. Dasein's view on Being is given only in and through time itself in the form of a 'moment of vision' that enables Dasein to will the synthesis of past, present and future and so (and only so) 'to be'. Being, consequently 'is' for us only insofar as it is grasped from within the radical historicity of the moment of vision. Being is dissolved into time. Reversing the terms, however, yields a very different picture. If we think 'time and Being', then we are taking as our starting point a thoroughly temporalised understanding of the world – that of Heraclitus, perhaps, for whom we can never step twice into the same stream, since all things are perpetually in flux and for whom war is the father of all, meaning that conflict, contradiction and the lack of a conclusion are fundamental features of the world. To think *Being* within such a vision of the world, however, would be to introduce a restraint, to prevent temporality from dissolving into the kind of mere flux propounded by a pupil of Heraclitus who drew the conclusion that it is not even possible to step into the same stream once. It is, in other words, to refuse to allow temporality to be experienced or interpreted as meaningless: time is not mere time because 'there is' (*es gibt*: it gives) time, such that time itself comes to us as a gift, as a way of being. Thus, whereas the hypothesis of radical historical relativism seems to result in an oblivion of Being, a dissolution of Being into pure flux (a standpoint identified with *Being and Time* on a nihilistic reading of that work), temporality is now conceived as revealing the possibility of a guarding and a protecting, a shepherding of Being.

Yet, if the thrust of 'time-and-Being' seems to be the opposite of 'Being-and-time', there is a certain correspondence between the two formulations. For both are concerned with how Being and time (or time and Being!) can be thought together without distorting or falsifying either. It is not so much a matter of establishing an order of precedence, but of finding a way of thinking both in the unity of their divergence and convergence. Both ways of putting the question show a concern with how meaning can be affirmed when existence is seen in thoroughly temporal terms, and how truth can be affirmed in the face of the consequent threat of historical relativism. It is important, therefore, that when the later Heidegger speaks, as we have heard him speak in the Bremen lectures, of the expectation of a new destining of Being, the fulfilment of this expectation and the advent of such a new destining would not mark the end of history in the sense of bringing history to a stop. At no point does Heidegger even suggest that any future destining of Being would exhaust the possible ways of Being's self-revolutions. Even if it has been a peculiar feature of modern Western thought to conceive of the world historically, and to conceive of history itself as a linear, teleologically determined process, the 'end' of our historical and historicising epoch would not be the end of time itself. Non-historical peoples and cultures also, and in a very real sense, live 'in' history. If – and we shall return to this question later – Heidegger really does believe in the advent of some kind of post-historical utopia, he never conceives of this eschatologically, i.e., as history arriving at some final state, as in some Marxist and Christian versions of the 'end of history'. Obviously, whatever follows such a utopia chronologically can be of very little immediate concern to us, especially as Heidegger speaks of the technological era we inhabit as being likely to continue for a long time to come. The theoretical possibility of the continuation of history after the advent of such a utopia, however, is important for our understanding of Heidegger's thought, since it underlines the point that Being is not being thought in simple opposition to temporality, as when 'Being' is opposed to 'becoming', but Being is itself temporalised and has itself a history.

We find a similar pattern of continuity and discontinuity if we turn to a topic intimately connected with that of temporality, namely, death. The question of death is undoubtedly one of the pivotal moments in the thought of the early Heidegger. Certainly the popular impact of *Being and Time* owed a great deal to the sheer force of Heidegger's summons to a 'preparedness for death' as the key to authentic existence. In the *Contributions to Philosophy*, however, in the course of repudiating an anthropological or psychological reading of *Being and Time* (which he nevertheless acknowledges has a certain plausibility), Heidegger specifically rejects seeing the burden of that work as a 'philosophy of death' (GA 65: 283). All the same, the question of death remains central. In the *Contributions to Philosophy* itself Heidegger also insists that 'Only humanity "has" the distinction of standing and facing death, because the human being is earnest about Being (*Seyn*): death is the supreme testimony to Being (*Seyn*)' (GA 65: 230). Death opens up the question of Being (GA 65: 284).

It is therefore no surprise when we read that 'death' (or the vision of humanity as 'mortals') is one of the pillars of the fourfold of earth, sky, death (or mortals) and gods that is itself one of the most characteristic envisionings of Being in the later Heidegger.

The role of death in the later Heidegger is well represented by a talk he gave in 1961, when he returned to his native town of Meßkirch and gave a talk on the theme of 'home'. The climax of the talk came when Heidegger asked rhetorically *where* we should go to in order best to reflect on the mystery of our origin, our 'home' in the deepest of senses. His answer was that we should go to the graveyard, 'God's acre': *There* is where we may best practise a remembrance of things past that collates meaning out of the dispersion of temporal existence and the distractedness of modern city life. But such a call to reflective, recollective meditation is very different in tone from the summons to heroic resoluteness in the face of annihilating death found in *Being and Time*, although in each case the encounter with death is what most profoundly highlights the question of Being.

Moving away from substantive theoretical issues, we can also discern significant continuity in many characteristic features of Heidegger's general approach to philosophy.

Thus, Heidegger typically develops his own thought through a stated or implied opposition to what is taken to be a general and virtually unquestioned set of intellectual, indeed metaphysical, assumptions. For, as Heidegger sees it, the apparent oppositions of modern thought and culture betray an underlying unity. Such contraries as scientific positivism/philosophy of life, Aristotelian metaphysics/Christian theology, Americanism/Communism turn out to share hidden presuppositions of which their various proponents are, for the most part, entirely unaware. Over against this profound uniformity, Heidegger's ever-repeated tactic is to question, to challenge, to provoke, to demand that we 'stop and think', that we question our presuppositions and that we abandon the assumption that we know what reality, truth, Being, human existence are and mean. Often Heidegger proceeds by means of revisionist rereadings of major figures of the tradition, presenting their thought in a new and unexpected light. At other times he resorts to vivid phenomenological descriptions of everyday situations and objects that startlingly defamiliarise our customary view of how things are. Also, notoriously, he conducts experiments with neologisms, etymologies and retranslations of Greek texts that often strike both naive and philosophically sophisticated readers alike as strange and even bizarre. Yet, if this is madness, there is method in it, for Heidegger himself points out that if the question really is how to break out of the constrictions of the prevailing metaphysical tradition, then we cannot argue our way out, since all the forms of argument we could possibly use are familiar to the tradition. We cannot argue our way out, we can only leap – and it is entirely consistent with the discontinuity introduced by such leaps that we land in strange and unfamiliar surroundings. On the far side of the leap, the world looks different.

Yet if all of this is most obviously true of the later Heidegger, it applies no less to *Being and Time*. Perhaps, for us, the shock of the new has in this case subsided, and *Being and Time* has aged into a defining classic of modern continental philosophy. Nevertheless, we should not blind ourselves to the extraordinary originality of that work, a work that, formally and in terms of content, involves a head-long assault on the conventions of philosophical writing no less radical than the assault by Expressionistic art on the conventions of academic painting, or of Eliot's *The Waste Land* on the prevailing canons of British poetry.

Now, it is, of course, open to question whether the tradition is as uniform or as closed to new possibilities as Heidegger represents it. Nor is this just a matter of being fair to the tradition. It is also a question as to whether Heidegger is in fact making his task easier than it really is. Is his assumption regarding the almost monolithic uniformity of contemporary thought, culture and society a piece of corner-cutting on Heidegger's part, a piece of rhetorically brilliant but intellectually deceptive misrepresentation that facilitates Heidegger's own self-representation as the forerunner of a new epoch of thinking? Do the earlier and the later Heidegger's great simplicities cover up real, and philosophically important, complexities? We shall need to revisit this question at a number of points in what follows, but for now it stands simply as a question put to the earlier and the later Heidegger alike.

Not unconnected with this is the continual polemic running though Heidegger's entire intellectual career against what he sees as the vulgar, derivative, secondary understanding of philosophy and of life typical of his contemporaries. In his recent, influential biography, R. Safranski points out how easy it was for someone of Heidegger's conservative Catholic upbringing and education to see the whole modern world, the world shaped by Enlightenment values and ideas, as decadent and corrupt. However, this attitude of philosophical disdain for the multitude is shaped by many other sources in Heidegger's early development and subsequent career. There was, for example, his intensive reading of Luther, for whom the 'normal' life of the world, even when swinging along in a happy, comfortable way, was 'really' nothing but the expression of smug, self-satisfied, sinful humanity. And there was his encounter with Kierkegaard, who depicted 'the present age' as an age of mediocrity, of prudential reflec-tiveness and moral cowardice, an age of levelling, dominated by the will to conformity and the subservience of the individual to public opinion as mediated by press and the academy and passed on in the idle chatter that perpetually belittles all greatness and originality. And, of course, the distinction of the philosophical way of life from that of the multitude, and the understanding of the philosophical vocation as an attempt to break loose from the customary and taken-for-granted but essentially unthinking discourse of the market-place, goes back to the earliest sources of Western philosophy and is very much to the fore in Heidegger's own exegetical lectures of the 1920s on Plato's *Sophist*.

When such sources are fed into the atmosphere of cultural pessimism following the First World War, an era when Spengler's *Decline of the West* became one of the most influential works in the German-speaking world, the ground is laid for a stance of contempt for modern mass society that was typical both of Heidegger and of many of his contemporaries. We shall occasionally touch on the question as to whether Heidegger was essentially a modernist or an anti-modernist thinker, and we should note now that the attitude being described is one that, in this era, was found amongst both modernists and anti-modernists. If Safranski emphasises the conservative Catholic strand in Heidegger's negative reaction to the contemporary world, similar complaints as to its mediocrity, conformity and general meaninglessness are no less frequent in the avant-garde artistic circles to which Heidegger's early work also spoke.

In *Being and Time* itself, Heidegger is careful to emphasise that when he speaks of the average, everyday understanding of existence as 'falling' he is not speaking in the manner of a Christian moralist or invoking any dogmatic idea of the fallenness of human beings. Yet it is hard not to hear something like a tone of moral judgment in Heidegger's account of 'das Man', especially, indeed precisely, because of the possibility of choosing instead the way of authentic existence.

Heidegger's contempt for the crowd is not, however, unqualified. At least, it is not simply a matter of the intellectual élite versus the unlettered many. More decisive, particularly from the 1930s onwards, is the contrast between the rootless, cosmopolitan life of the city and the profound but simple wisdom to which the thinker indeed aspires but that is also shared by, e.g., the Black Forest farmer. The contemporary city man is the 'ape' or 'dupe' of civilisation (1995: 6) yet Heidegger says of his own work that it is 'of the same kind' as that of the farmers. Complementing this valorisation of simple peasant life is Heidegger's characteristic use of ordinary non-technical German terms or figures of speech, bringing out overlooked or forgotten aspects of their meaning in order to throw light on philosophical problems.

The farmers are, nevertheless, not philosophers, no matter how greatly Heidegger esteems their intuitive wisdom. And, farmers apart, the later Heidegger is no less insistent than the earlier Heidegger, that 'essential thinkers' are 'rare' – so rare perhaps that there can be only one in any generation? (Certainly, Heidegger's closest rivals to the crown of German philosophy, Cassirer and Jaspers, are not regarded by him as essential thinkers, and still less could any of his theological contemporaries, Barth, Bultmann or Tillich, come into the reckoning.)

The combination of elements we have been considering gives Heidegger's philosophy a distinctive stamp, for all the variations of themes, topics and vocabulary throughout his work. Some would regard this stamp as that of a wisdom deeper than that of a merely academic thinker or manager of knowledge. Others, however, are likely to see it as flowing from and contributing to an élitist and authoritarian, not to say pretentious, view of the task of the philosopher, couched in a grandiose rhetoric of superiority whose promises cannot be delivered – Plato's philosopher king, but without the discipline of logic or dialectic. On this view, any claim that might be made by or for Heidegger as a philosopher is spurious. At best he might be counted a kind of secular prophet or quasi-mystical poet, whose words speak only to those who like that sort of thing. Or, simply, a latter-day sophist.

Whether this is too harsh, and whether Heidegger's pathos of superiority fatally undermines the credibility of his thought, are questions to which we shall return, when we have been prepared for them by a more extensive exposition of that thought itself. However, by flagging such criticisms at this point, I hope to pre-empt the suspicion that, in attempting to expound Heidegger in his own terms, I am walking blindfold into the trap set by this most seductive of thinkers.

How, then, can we set about understanding the later Heidegger? How, when so much about his philosophical style might seem to discourage further engagement – and, certainly, to militate against any kind of straightforward introductory 'guidebook' – how can his work be made accessible without eliminating everything that is distinctively Heideggerian from it?

And there is a further problem arising from the nature of the texts themselves. If the 'early' Heidegger can, more or less justifiably, be identified with one major work, *Being and Time*, the 'later Heidegger' is scattered across a range of works of different types on varied topics. Many of these are lectures and addresses of an occasional nature, not necessarily given to university audiences – although there are also university lecture courses, such as the lectures on Nietzsche of the 1930s and 1940s – and there are the two extraordinary books *Contributions to Philosophy* and *Besinnung*. What, then, should we take as most representative of the later Heidegger? And why?

I have chosen to focus this study on two principal texts. The first originated in a lecture which was subsequently expanded into a series of three lectures (1935–6) and then reworked as a book entitled *On the Origin of the Work of Art* (first published 1950). The lectures provided one of the earliest manifestations of the later Heidegger and, in a highly condensed form, do much to set out the agenda that was to dominate his course for the subsequent decades, providing important insights into the understanding of the relationship between philosophy and art and introducing important elements of the characteristic vocabulary and style of the later work. I have complemented this with the lectures given in Freiburg University in the Winter Semester of 1950–51, published as *What is Called Thinking?* These lectures have a singular place in Heidegger's career, in that they were the first lectures he gave in the university after the ban imposed by the denazification programme but also the last he gave as a salaried professor before his retirement. They therefore mark the final moment of his formal academic career and offer both a retrospective over what has concerned him in the preceding decade-and-a-half and also adumbrate what will continue to concern him in the 1950s and through to his death in 1976.

Yet neither of these texts, nor the two of them taken together, covers every single aspect of the later Heidegger, and to confine our view to what is contained in these texts in a strict sense would result in a very limited understanding of what is going on in his later thought.

Heidegger himself insisted that the standard edition of his collected works should bear the motto 'ways not works', a motto that evokes the supremely Heideggerian metaphorics of endless wanderings along forest paths: paths that trail off into impenetrable undergrowth, requiring us to retrace our steps, or that unexpectedly debouch onto clearings flooded with light, from where we are able to look around and take our bearings. In the spirit of such metaphorics I am not taking these texts as compendia that 'contain' the whole of the later Heidegger, but as paths on which we not infrequently encounter sign-posts leading to other paths, indicating questions, topics and aspects of the history of philosophy not immediately present in the texts themselves. In this way I hope both to have a sufficiently firm grounding in the texts to help the student using them as textbooks, and also to open a larger perspective for those with a more general interest in the later Heidegger.

It is, I believe, important in reading the later Heidegger to attempt such a larger perspective, and not to allow a single topic, passage or even word to be elevated to the status of interpretative be-all and end-all, as if what he did with the expression 'there is' or the word 'event' ('Ereignis') provided a single, simple key to the burden of the later philosophy. George Steiner once wrote that music could well serve to illustrate some of the fundamental traits of Heidegger's thought, and, although (as Steiner admitted) Heidegger himself did not claim this, the suggestion is useful, if we understand it in a very precise way. It certainly should not be taken as meaning that we are to allow the later Heidegger to work on us as an emotive and intoxicating wave of sound, a current of pure feeling, as some romantic theories of music might understand it. We should rather understand it in accordance with terminology that Heidegger himself does use, although not with particular emphasis on its musicological associations. This is the terminology derived from the German term 'Fuge'. This word does not have the exclusively musical connotations of the English 'fugue', but suggests a range of terms and meanings, such as the verb 'fügen' (to fit together, join, unite, ordain, will, direct, dispose, add), and the noun 'Gefüge' (joining, fitting together, structure, system, frame, articulation, joints, texture, stratification), that Heidegger uses to describe the overall organisation of his later thought. Applying the musical analogy, I suggest that the diverse writings that make up the later Heidegger are connected fugally. This, as I understand it, not only undermines any attempt to read these writings as merely emotive-expressive, it also points to a kind of structure that resists incorporation into any linear progression in which the various parts are ordered hierarchically and in which discord and conflict are resolved into a final unity. Such a sequential, harmonic model might, arguably, be applicable to Hegel, and, given the analogies between harmonic progression and dialectic that are already hinted at in Plato, we might be tempted to think of this as the most relevant of all musical analogies for any work of philosophy. In the case of Heidegger, at least, this would be misleading. We cannot assume any final resolution of the varied elements of his later thought, but, equally, we should not conclude that it is therefore lacking in coherence. We should instead be looking for a coherence of a different kind.

These comments give rise to a reflection that may seem accidental and literary, rather than philosophical, yet which, nevertheless, indicates with utter precision a problem that any attempt to come to terms with Heidegger, early or late, must face. The reflection is provoked by the sub-title of the German edition of R. Safranski's ground-breaking biography of Heidegger: *A Master from Germany*. This alludes to the poem 'Fugue of Death' by Paul Celan, a Holocaust survivor. Celan and Heidegger admired each other's work, but when Celan sought an understanding with Heidegger concerning the latter's attitude to the Holocaust, all that was forthcoming was a painfully inconclusive visit. If death came, in the camps, as a fugally poetised 'Master from Germany', how did such death concern a philosopher for whom death was what supremely brings humanity to the encounter with Being? The force of this question is, inevitably, compounded by the biographical fact that, for a crucial period in his life, Heidegger was not merely a member of the Nazi Party but very publicly endorsed the way of Adolf Hitler as the way of the future for German academic life.

Before proceeding to our texts, then, we must pause to confront the bitter question of Heidegger's complicity in Nazism and, in particular, the question as to how significant his political error is for the philosophical understanding of his later work.

Chapter 2

1933 and after

Heidegger's silence

Heidegger's philosophical career is controversial for the same reasons that all philosophical careers are controversial: the interpretation and evaluation of his work remain debated in the same sorts of ways as in the case of a Wittgenstein, a Sartre or a Russell. But there is a further dimension of controversy in the case of Heidegger that is virtually unique amongst modern philosophers, owing to the fact that in May 1933 he very publicly joined the Nazi Party, was elected Rector of Freiburg University, and set about enthusiastically promoting the policy of *Gleichschaltung* (or 'co-ordination'), whereby, in the cause of national unity, the traditional independence of the university was to be subordinated to the policies of the Hitler regime. Although Heidegger resigned from the rectorship a year later and gradually drifted away from the Party, to the point where his lectures were monitored by Party officials, he never decisively repudiated the Nazi regime and, after the War, never made more than the most enigmatic of comments on the Holocaust nor acknowledged his own responsibility as a public servant for helping to create the climate in which the totalitarian state could take root and flourish.

We shall return to the question of the nature and extent of Heidegger's involvement in National Socialism, but first we have to ask whether – apart from the fact that it has been one of the most hotly debated points of Heidegger studies in the last ten years – this is an issue that should concern us in a study devoted to the philosophical aspects of Heidegger's thought and, especially, to his later thought. After all, ever since Thales fell down a well while looking up at the stars it has been customary to regard philosophers as rather impractical characters whose absorption in 'higher things' often blinds them to the realities of everyday life, including the realities of social and political life. Consequently, if Heidegger is not primarily a political philosopher in the narrow sense (though this is not, of course, a question we have yet addressed, let alone decided), do his personal political views and actions really matter philosophically? Can we not just, regretfully, shrug our shoulders and say 'What a pity that such a great philosopher was such a political ass'?

Now, unless one is committed to the kind of Marxist approach to philosophy that sees every nuance of theory as charged with ideological significance, this is perhaps in many cases a possible line of argument. If we were to ransack the biographies, private papers and correspondence of many great philosophers we would almost certainly come up with a great number of peculiar and even distasteful opinions on various aspects of political and moral life, including gender, race, democracy, crime and punishment and many other issues, in addition to evidence of appalling or idiotic personal conduct. In many cases, however, we could (or, at least, we usually do) hold such shortcomings at arm's length and refuse to allow them any significance with regard to our philosophical evaluation of the author concerned.

Such a separating-out of the personal from the philosophical may seem appropriate in the case of Heidegger also. Certainly there is some evidence that, if not politically innocent, he was politically inept. The rapid failure of his rectorship and his hasty retreat from active political involvement, together with anecdotal evidence as to the more ludicrous aspects of his behaviour in 1933–4 could well suggest the image of a head-in-the-clouds philosopher getting worsted in the rough-and-tumble of real political life, and being driven back into the seclusion of his study. On this view the episode of the rectorship was no more than a bout of madness, a momentary aberration that does not disclose anything about Heidegger the thinker.

It would be possible to go further in support of this view by emphasising the need for a more than usual level of historical imagination and sensibility in trying to make judgments about the conduct of German citizens in 1933. Above all, we have to remember that no one then knew what we know about the final outcome of the whole Nazi misadventure. Germans who voted for Hitler in 1933 were not voting for the Holocaust, they were voting for a right-wing, nationalistic party, with clearly illiberal and anti-Semitic tendencies, that was prepared to define and to defend what it regarded as the territorial integrity of the nation with military force. None of that, however, made it obviously a party of genocide. If Heidegger erred, many others also erred, their desire for strong leadership and national renewal (powerful rallying-calls even in mature democracies) blinding them to the true nature of the beast they were about to unleash. It was not impossible – foolish perhaps, but not impossible – to believe that anti-Jewish violence was a fringe phenomenon that would be curbed once the Party was securely settled in power. Even some German Jews, including prominent academics, expressed enthusiasm for the new regime (see Safranski 1998: 230). Karl Jaspers, whose wife was of Jewish origin and who was generally held to have conducted himself during the Hitler years in such a way as to be beyond reproach, responded positively to Heidegger's inaugural address as Rector, despite the fact that its rhetoric was richly imbued with Nazi images and associations. Outside Germany there were many admirers of the new regime. It is a sign of the times that Albert Speer's design for the approach avenue to the Nuremberg Stadium where Nazi Party rallies were held won the Grand Prix at the 1937 Paris World Fair.

Heidegger erred, foolishly, we might conclude, but understandably – and to understand is, of course, to forgive.

Nevertheless there are several points we should consider before settling for this relatively comfortable solution.

Firstly, and most importantly, we cannot but take into account the sheer enormity of the crimes committed by the Nazi regime. As I have already said, the German public at large did not vote 'for' the 'Final Solution' in 1933, and perhaps few in the Party envisaged anything like that as a clearly defined goal at that point. We cannot blame Heidegger for not foreseeing that outcome. However, it is deeply troubling that after the War, and after the evidence of the Holocaust had been made public, Heidegger said little or nothing to show either that he grasped the import of what had taken place or that he had any deep regrets relating to it. The occasions when he was faced with the question did not elicit anything like a clear and distinct response. When Herbert Marcuse, a former student, wrote to him in 1947 requesting a clarification of his position, Heidegger replied that the charge of genocide could only be justified if, at the same time, one made the same charge against the victorious Allies' treatment of the East Germans (Wolin 1993: 152ff; Ott 1994: 192–3).[1]

Two crucial texts come from Heidegger's lectures to the Club in Bremen in 1949. In the lecture 'The Enframing' Heidegger drew an analogy between the death camps and industrial production in general: 'Agriculture is now a motorised food-industry – in essence the same as the manufacturing of corpses in gas chambers and extermination camps, the same as the starving of nations, the same as the manufacture of hydrogen bombs' (Young 1997: 172). This, though brief, is a complex assertion and brings into play some of the fundamental assumptions about the nature and the threat of technology that are so important for the whole thinking of the later Heidegger and that we shall be examining in more detail in the next chapter. One way of taking it would be to see in it a simple – and gross – failure to recognise the unique enormity of the Holocaust. Thus Miguel de Beistegui in his study *Heidegger and the Political* describes it as 'a failure of thinking itself' because it ignores the singularity of Auschwitz, 'this gap in history, this black hole from which we must learn to rethink light and reinvent the day' (de Beistegui 1998: 154). Instead, according to de Beistegui, Heidegger integrates Auschwitz into a class of events that, properly seen, just aren't on the same scale.

More sympathetically, Julian Young has argued that such a 'damning' reading of the text ignores what is most obvious in it, that 'the force of the linkages in the passage is not to minimise the moral horror of the Holocaust, but rather to maximise, to render vivid, a sense of horror at the contemplated means of winning the Cold War and at modern methods of food production' (Young 1997: 187). Young goes on to point out that Heidegger is not, as a casual reading might suggest, asserting the moral equivalence of modern methods of food production and the Holocaust, but is suggesting that both are manifestations (and this does not mean identical or morally identical manifestations) of the same essence of technology that is the metaphysical truth of modernity. If we were to push the defence of Heidegger further, and this is a point that Young also makes, we might read the passage as implying that, so long as the danger concealed in the essence of technology remains unrecognised and unnamed, further Holocausts will recur. If this reading is sustained, then Heidegger could indeed be said to be taking the Holocaust seriously as a decisive warning from history.

In another Bremen lecture, 'The Danger', Heidegger said the following: 'Hundreds of thousands die *en masse*. Do they *die*? They succumb. They are done in. They become mere quanta, items in the business of manufacturing corpses. Do they die? They are liquidated inconspicuously in extermination camps ... But to die is to endure death in its essence' (Young 1997: 172). Again the reference is ambiguous. Heidegger's critics argue that he here endorses the executioners' dehumanisation of their victims, that it reduces the Jews murdered in the camps to items on an industrial conveyor belt. Again, Young offers an interpretation that says almost the opposite. In revealing that this is indeed the executioners' perspective, Young claims, Heidegger in fact subjects that view to the most extreme censure. Not only do we need the context of Heidegger's whole critique of technology to understand what is being said here, we also need to be aware of the significance of death, of being able to die, for Heidegger – and death, as we saw in the previous chapter, was a central theme in early and in later Heidegger alike. Already in *Being and Time* he had declared that only Dasein, only human individuals can *die* in the fullest sense, by deliberately choosing to take upon themselves the burden of their mortality. Plants and animals, by way of contrast, only perish. (BT: 47/240–1) Not dissimilarly, the later Heidegger speaks of death as 'the shrine of Nothing' and, as such, 'the shelter of Being'. If we hear Heidegger's words about the extermination camps in this context, then, we might well hear them as an indictment of the desecration of this shrine by the managers of the liquidation process and therefore an ultimate denial of the humanity and dignity of their victims – compared, say, to some 'traditional' forms of execution that allow the victim the consolation of religion, the opportunity to deliver a last word, to say or to write a last farewell or time to smoke a final cigarette. In this light, Heidegger is deepening rather than trivialising our understanding of the crimes of the perpetrators.

Yet, even on the most generous readings of these pivotal texts, many of Heidegger's philosophical admirers might wish that he had named and repudiated the crimes of the Party to which he at one time belonged in simpler, clearer, unambiguous words. In this respect one might compare his attitude with that of his Japanese contemporary, Hajime Tanabe (1885–1962). Tanabe played a highly influential role in Japanese philosophy in the 1930s, but in the closing stages of the war arrived at a vivid sense of his own culpability with regard to the catastrophe brought upon his country by the imperialist policies to which he had given philosophical legitimacy. This realisation led him to completely recast his philosophical position and to practise 'philosophy as metanoetics' (deriving from the New Testament Greek term 'metanoia', meaning 'repentance').[2] But there is nothing analogous to this in the case of Heidegger. Even Heidegger's defenders have found themselves embarrassed and chagrined, experiencing what Paul Celan, perhaps the most significant poet to have endured and survived the camps, experienced when he visited Heidegger in July 1967, writing in the visitors' book of his hope 'of a word to come in my heart.' Yet neither on this or on their subsequent meeting did any word come.[3]

1933

We have run on ahead of the actual events of 1933–4, and the question of Heidegger's post-war silence does not of itself decide the question as to the extent either of his active involvement in Nazism or, more importantly to us, of the entanglement of his philosophy in Nazi ideology.

There is much in these years that remains debated. Heidegger's own version of events, at best extremely sketchy, has been extensively challenged by recent literature, most notably in the biographical study *Heidegger: A Political Life* by Hugo Ott. What is, however, not in doubt is the fact of the rhetorical tone and, in some cases, the overt political content of many of Heidegger's public statements in these crucial years.

Most notorious, precisely because most public, is the *Rektoratsrede*, Heidegger's inaugural address as Rector of Freiburg University, delivered on 27 May 1933. Heidegger himself had been involved in preparing the programme of events, in which the 'German Greeting' ('Heil Hitler') was prescribed and the Horst Wessel song was to be sung – a popular Nazi marching song that included such verses as 'Raise high the flag, stand rank on rank together! / Stormtroopers march with firm and valiant tread. / Comrades gunned down by Red Front and reaction / March on in spirit, swelling still our ranks' (Ott 1994: 152).

Heidegger was to contest the interpretation of the address as a political statement, asserting that it was simply a development of the 'fundamental questions of thinking' that had been broached in *Being and Time*. 'The question which concerned me directly as a teacher in the university was the question concerning the meaning of the sciences and, in connection with this, the question of the determination of the task of the university' (Wolin 1993: 95). Now clearly the address *is* concerned with the nature of the university and the meaning of the sciences and can, as de Beistegui has interestingly demonstrated, be contextualised in an ongoing debate about the nature and organisation of academic life in Germany that reaches back to the early years of the nineteenth century and beyond (de Beistegui 1998: 35ff.). However, the manner in which this concern is articulated in the address exploits the characteristic rhetoric of Nazi speechifying, curiously fused with the language of *Being and Time*, and issues in a call to heroic confrontation with a singular moment of decision.

The teachers and students who constitute the rector's following will awaken and gain strength only through being truly and collectively rooted in the essence of the German university. This essence will attain clarity, rank, and power, however, only when the leaders are, first and foremost and at all times, themselves led by the inexorability of that spiritual mission which impresses onto the fate of the German Volk the stamp of their history ... Does this essence truly have the power to shape our existence? It does, but only if we *will* the essence fully ... The will to the essence of the German university is the will to science as the will to the historical spiritual mission of the German Volk as a Volk that knows itself in its state ... [Teachers and students must] stand firm in the face of German fate extreme in its extreme distress

(Wolin 1993: 29–30)

This will to the essence of science must, Heidegger continues, be developed in relation to the original beginning of science amongst the Greeks, but it is also what creates for the German *Volk* today 'a truly *spiritual* world': 'And the *spiritual world* of a Volk is not its cultural superstructure, just as little as it is its arsenal of useful knowledge and values; rather, it is the power that comes from preserving at the most profound level the forces that are rooted in the soil and blood [*Boden und Blut*] of a Volk' (Wolin 1993: 33–4). These forces have awoken amongst the German students who are now resolutely and fatefully 'on the march', with Heidegger, their rector, at their head. But what is to be achieved by this march? Firstly, that 'the much praised "academic freedom" is being banished from the German university, for this freedom was false, because it was only negating' (*ibid.*: 34). Instead, academic life will put itself under the threefold constraint of the essential bonds of society: ethnicity and nationhood, as realised in the obligation of work for the state; the bond of mutual defence, realised in the obligation of military service; and the bond that lies in the spiritual mission of the *Volk*, the service of knowledge.

In upbeat mode, Heidegger concluded 'it is our will that our Volk fulfil its historical mission ... "All that is great stands in the storm"' (*ibid.*: 39).

Even apart from its rhetorical invocation of such favourite Nazi themes as struggle, will, hardship, blood and soil and *Volk* (people),[4] it is clear that Heidegger's address is a massive refusal of the Enlightenment conception of the university. The first obligation of the academy is not to the universal, disinterested pursuit of knowledge but to the people, the 'ethnic and national community'. Of course, Heidegger does not understand this in terms of subordinating academic enquiry and debate to the dictates of politics but in terms of positive participation in the collective life of the people as a necessary precondition of academic work. Yet the policy of *Gleichschaltung* ('co-ordination') between university and state that Heidegger promoted as the practical expression of such participation did, inevitably and even obviously, open the door to direct political influence on academic life. Moreover, Heidegger took entirely seriously the idea that military and labour service should be an integral part of university life and actively promoted military training amongst students. Military training, labour and the pursuit of knowledge came together in a work-and-study camp Heidegger led near his Black Forest home, to which the students marched in a body, and for which they were encouraged to wear Nazi uniforms (which was hardly surprising, given that the purpose of the camp was 'The lively inculcation of the aim of a National Socialist revolution in our university system' [Ott 1994: 229]). Nor is it entirely incidental that memoirs of those attending the camp agree that Heidegger's own presentations were characterised by an extremely aggressive attack on Christianity.

Unfortunately, the rectorial address is by no means the most directly Nazistic of Heidegger's public speeches in this period. The day before, he had called upon the students of Freiburg to emulate the student Leo Schlageter, who had been executed by the French occupying forces in 1923 for sabotage. In a speech in June Heidegger declared that '*A fierce battle* must be fought' against the present university situation 'in the national Socialist spirit, and this spirit cannot be allowed to be suffocated by humanising, Christian ideas that suppress its unconditionality' (Wolin 1993: 44). The struggle 'will be fought out of the strengths of the new Reich that Chancellor Hitler will bring to reality' (*ibid.*: 45). In November 1933 Heidegger issued a flurry of appeals to the German students to support Hitler in the plebiscite that was decisively to confirm his grip on power. The message was, simply, that 'The Führer alone *is* the present and future German reality and its law.'

> The German people has been summoned by the Führer to vote; the Führer, however, is asking nothing from the people. Rather, he *is giving* the people the possibility of making, directly, the highest free decision of all: whether it – the entire people – wants its own existence [Dasein] or does *not* want it … This ultimate decision reaches to the outermost limit of our people's existence … [because it concerns] the most basic demand of all being [Sein] that it preserve and serve its own essence.
>
> (Wolin 1993: 47)

> The Führer has awakened this will in the entire people and has welded it into a single resolve … And so we, to whom the preservation of our people's will to know shall in the future be entrusted, declare: the National Socialist revolution is not merely the assumption of power as it exists presently in the State by another party … Rather this revolution is bringing about *the total transformation of our German existence* [Dasein].
>
> (Wolin 1993: 49, 51–2)

Apart from depressingly demonstrating how unqualified was the support Heidegger gave to the Nazi cause in 1933, what is most striking in all these speeches is the way in which the language of existence, Being, essence, decision and resolve that Heidegger had developed in *Being and Time* is put so directly to political use. Thus far we can say that Heidegger himself was justified in his retrospective claim that the topic of the rectorial address had grown out of his purely philosophical concerns in *Being and Time*. As he also commented (to Karl Löwith in 1936), his whole involvement in Nazism could be traced back to the concept of historicity in *Being and Time*, i.e., that authentic decision concerning its own essence could only be accomplished by Dasein on the basis of insight into its own thoroughly temporal, historical nature and thus in the power of a 'moment of vision' that enables Dasein to seize the time in unblinking recognition of his utter temporality and finitude.

It is for such reasons that it is impossible to dismiss Heidegger's Nazism as simply a personal foible that does not concern Heidegger the philosopher. But what is the nature of the connection between his Nazism and his philosophy? Does the evidence suggest that the existential analyses of *Being and Time* are themselves inherently fascistic?

There are a number of reasons to hesitate before drawing such a conclusion. Not the least of these is the fact that a number of Heidegger's own pupils and contemporaries who had been decisively influenced by *Being and Time* or who embraced it as mirroring their own philosophical vision (Hannah Arendt, Karl Jaspers, Herbert Marcuse and Paul Tillich are obvious examples) set themselves on a completely different political course. The philosophy of existence was by no means the preserve of the right. The case of Tillich is particularly instructive. A Christian socialist who held a chair in philosophy in Frankfurt and was one of the founding figures of the neo-Marxist 'Frankfurt School' of social theory, Tillich was also one of the first university teachers to be dismissed by the new regime. Most interestingly, his book, *The Socialist Decision*, which was in the process of publication when Hitler came to power, argued in terms closely analogous to those used by Heidegger for an anti-nationalist Marxist resolution of the German crisis. The 'socialist decision' advocated by Tillich is a matter of seizing the crucial moment of decision in the power of a courageous resolve that is also, simultaneously, a self-revelation of Being.

But if the philosophy of existence did not necessarily lead directly to Nazism, does it follow that it was essentially apolitical, adaptable to whatever prejudices and commitments its various proponents held dear?

Importantly, Heidegger himself had drawn a distinction in *Being and Time* between what he called the ontic and the *existentiell* on the one hand and the ontological or existential on the other. In terms of this distinction he categorises Kierkegaard as a Christian psychologist who operated on the 'merely' ontic level, analysing and describing how individuals lived through the crises of religious faith and the encounter with their individual deaths. By way of contrast, Heidegger understood his own project as existential and ontological, that is, as concerned with the deep structures of Being that underlie the kind of specific, individual situations with which Kierkegaard is preoccupied. Now it is not easy to make this distinction absolutely clear-cut, since the data of ontic, existentiell life are themselves the phenomena that reveal the deeper ontological structures, the existentialia. Indeed, at several points Heidegger catches himself on the edge of coming up from the ontological depths to the surface of individual life. In speaking of the joy that accompanies Dasein's resolute readiness-for-action, he quickly adds that 'the analysis of these basic moods would transgress the limits which we have drawn for the present Interpretation by aiming towards fundamental ontology' (BT: 62/310).

In terms of *Being and Time*, however, what we generally call political life operates on the plane of the merely existentiell, no less than individual life. The crucial division is not that between individual and community, or between private and public, but between the surface appearance or phenomenality of beings, individual and communal, and that which the phenomena disclose and which actually determines how they disclose themselves. In this perspective it could be argued that the 'mistake' of 1933 was simply that Heidegger forgot his own self-limitations and applied the ontological categories in a directly ontic, existentiell way.

1933 and the later Heidegger

This study is, of course, primarily concerned with the later Heidegger, and it might be said that none of this is relevant. For what has the connection between *Being and Time* and the events of 1933 to do with the later philosophy which, however one dates it, is definitely post-1933? This query might seem to receive added force from the observation that Heidegger's own post-war comments on his involvement in Nazism were very few and extremely reticent. If the later Heidegger left the events of 1933 in a fog of reticence, should we not also leave things there and limit ourselves to the question of reticence itself and the implications of the philosopher's failure to take responsibility or to show remorse for the crimes in which, however marginally, he was implicated?

The connection between Heidegger's Nazism and *Being and Time* –

however one understands this connection – is clear, but, precisely in the light of the reflections in Chapter 1 on the continuities and discontinuities of Heidegger's thought, it is impossible simply to confine the question of Heidegger's Nazism to the 'early' Heidegger. This might seem attractive – after all, isn't the highly subjectivist rhetoric of decision, resolve and struggle precisely what the later Heidegger repudiated or strongly qualified in his turning away from the philosophy of existence to the task of becoming a shepherd of Being?

However, this already suggests one way of seeing the importance of the Nazi episode for Heidegger's later thought: that the 'mistake' of 1933 brought into focus for Heidegger what was wrong, or, at least, unsatisfactory, in his work thus far. The later development would then be an attempt by Heidegger to reconstruct his thought from within in such a way as to make it resistant to the kind of temptation to which he succumbed in 1933. One way of understanding this is represented by Tom Rockmore.[5] Essentially Rockmore takes his bearings from a much-quoted line in a 1935 lecture 'Introduction to Metaphysics', where Heidegger speaks of 'The works that are being peddled (about) nowadays as the philosophy of National Socialism' as having 'nothing whatever to do with the inner truth and greatness of this movement (namely, the encounter between global technology and contemporary man)' (see Wolin 1993: 103). His argument is that although Heidegger turned away from actual National Socialism relatively early, what he never renounced was 'an ideal form of Nazism' (Rockmore 1992: 123–4), i.e., a Nazism that preserved the 'inner truth and greatness' of the movement without being contaminated by its actual history. Nevertheless, this 'ideal form of Nazism' is still a 'form of Nazism', and, unless one holds the line between the ontological and the ontic, the ideal and the real, with an extraordinary degree of tenacity, the ideal form of Nazism that is professed by the later Heidegger is chronically liable to give ideological aid and comfort to actual Nazism. But is it adequate to say that Heidegger simply elevates his Nazism to an ideal level? Does this really do justice to what is going on in the gradual transformation of his thought that is indicated, perhaps over-simplistically, by reference to 'the turning'? Another way of looking at it, then, might be to say that, in the light of his 'mistake', Heidegger undertook a re-examination of the philosophical commitments that had led to it. Such a re-examination brought about a recognition of the excessive subjectivism of *Being and Time* (or, at least, of the failure of *Being and Time* to guard against a subjectivist reading) and of the need to define more closely the relationship between the ontological and the ontic, between Being and beings. This is, of course, a shift that would have been possible with or without the Nazi episode and can arguably be said to represent a line of development that genuinely takes further the trajectory of Heidegger's own internal development. In this light there is a convergence between the philosophical development and the personal disappointment over the failure of his rectorship and the concurrent recognition that Nazism was not what he had taken it to be. On this view the thought of the later Heidegger is not an ideal or spiritual Nazism but a genuine alternative – albeit at an ideal rather than at a political level – to Nazism (amongst other things). Whether, in that case, it is not only a genuine but also an effective alternative is another question.

Either way, it will not be surprising to find resonances between the later Heidegger and aspects of Nazi ideology, although, as I have been arguing, we might hear these resonances in quite diverse ways. Let us, then, briefly examine these, bearing in mind that a number of them will already have been adumbrated in the earlier Heidegger.

Beginning with the rectorial address itself we can already see some of the themes that will continue to characterise the later philosophy. Negatively, these include the repudiation of the Enlightenment model of universal reason and the liberal political values derived from it. More positively, it hints at an axis linking the original metaphysical thought of the Greeks with the contemporary crisis of knowledge – and, as we shall see, this is to become one of the pillars of the later Heidegger.

Moving beyond the rectorial address we might note Heidegger's continual privileging of the values of the world of the Black Forest over against the world of the 'city man' and his technology. In 1936, when Heidegger was offered a chair in Berlin, he justified his decision not to accept in a radio broadcast entitled 'Creative Landscape: Why do we remain in the Provinces?' In the broadcast he describes how, working at philosophy in the solitude of his mountain hut, he shares the world of the farmers. Whereas 'the city man believes that he is going "amongst the people" the moment he condescends to have a long conversation with a farmer', Heidegger pictures himself just sitting with the locals through long evenings, smoking their pipes together, saying nothing, except every now and then to pass comment on a cow that's about to calve or the weather. The climactic conclusion arrives when Heidegger relates a meeting with a seventy-five-year-old farmer who has read about the 'call to Berlin' in the papers, and, looking the Herr Professor in the face, puts his 'trusty and concerned hand' on Heidegger's shoulder and simply, silently shakes his head. Heidegger realises at once that he belongs with the farmers, as one of them (GA 13: 9–13).

Such 'folksiness', anticipated in the Leo Schlageter speech when Heidegger relates the young hero's clarity of vision and firmness of will to the skies and mountains of the Forest, sets Heidegger in a long tradition of German national and nationalist writing. This tradition is summarised by Simon Schama as

> organised around a series of oppositions between those aspects of the land shaped by the engine of the market and those which has escaped its force. The 'road' connected producers and consumers while the 'path' connected villagers and citizens. The most strongly opposed countryside worlds were those of the open field and the forest – respectively, commercialised agriculture and the wilderness – the forests were 'the heartland of [German] folk culture' ... the home of community, the absolute opposite of a Germany made over into one vast overupholstered, department-store-manufactured bourgeois parlor. If in this scheme, the rootless Jew was the purveyor of this corrupted, citified society, the forester was his antithesis – the embodiment of ethnic authenticity, rooted like his trees in the ancient earth of the Fatherland.
>
> (Schama 1995: 114)

Heidegger's susceptibility to this tradition famously drew the fierce contempt of Adorno, for whom it marked the degeneration of the philosopher's 'reflected unreflectiveness' 'into chummy chit-chat ...

the description of the old farmer reminds us of the most washed-out clichés in plough-and-furrow novels ... Philosophy which is ashamed of its name, needs the sixth-hand symbol of the farmer, as a way of acquiring some otherwise unavailable distinctiveness' (Adorno 1986: 55–6).[6]

One-sided as Adorno's criticism is, it is painfully close to the mark. Fortunately, the folksy tone of 'Creative Landscape' is rarely laid on quite so heavily elsewhere in the later work. Nevertheless the whole of the later philosophy is pervaded by images drawn from the forest life, from the world of craftsmen and woodcutters and the landscape of river and mountain.

If this puts the later Heidegger in a certain proximity to images and values exploited by Nazism, it does not of itself make the later Heidegger a Nazi: it merely indicates that his world was that of a conservative, patriotic countryman – and we must remember that many conservative, patriotic countrymen died in Germany as opponents of Nazism. Moreover – and the remark about the encounter between humanity and technology is very important here – it is clear that, from the mid-1930s onwards, the later Heidegger did not regard Nazism as justified in representing itself as the true guardian of those values, since Nazism, like Communism and Americanism, is also seen as merely one more agent of planetary technology.

We can pursue the significance of these issues further by following Julian Young in his study *Heidegger, Philosophy, Nazism*, in which he attempts to reconstruct the ideology that guided Heidegger's political misadventure. Young emphasises what he calls the 'ideas of 1914', and he sees Heidegger's ideology of 1933 as essentially a repetition of those ideas.[7] What, then, were they? Fundamental was the idea of *Volk*. Typically, the *Volk*, the people, was conceived in terms of an organic whole, as opposed to an artificial assemblage held together by a merely external contract. A *Volk* could be conceived naturalistically, as a kind of living entity, a conception of which the Nazi ideology of race was an extreme development. But this was only one way of conceiving the *Volk*. Heidegger himself, in his Nietzsche and Hölderlin lectures of the 1930s and 1940s, repeatedly attacked the biologistic, pseudo-Darwinian thinking that lay behind such a view. More mainstream, at least amongst the intellectuals of 1914, was a conception of

Volk in '*geistig* (spiritual-intellectual) terms'. This meant seeing the *Volk* 'as, essentially, a person; an entity endowed with a distinctive set of historically revealed virtues, talents and character traits and with, accordingly, a distinctive task or "mission", a role in world-history, assigned, uniquely, to it. So far as the German *Volk* is concerned, its chief characteristic was taken to be *Innerlichkeit* ... 'inwardness', spirituality.' (Young 1997: 14) This inwardness was connected with the German genius for music and, as epitomising 'culture', was contrasted with the superficiality of French 'civilisation'. At the same time, this justified the German people in warfare aimed at securing the economic and social foundations necessary for culture to flourish. In doing so, however, they are not acting merely selfishly but vicariously, on behalf of the world, because culture is a necessary bulwark against nihilistic levelling, the empty, technological materialism of the Anglo-Saxon world and, after 1917, of Russian communism. The heroic spirit of the German *Volk* was needed against the mercantile spirit of England. In the light of this mission the *Volk* must take priority over the individual. Its social form was that of *Gemeinschaft*, community, over against *Gesellschaft*, society, 'a nation of atomic individuals standing in a fundamentally competitive relation to each other and lacking authentic meaning in their lives'.[8] Not only did this conception of *Volk* call for loyalty and self-sacrifice on the part of individuals, it also encouraged a negative attitude towards democracy. As Young quotes Wilhelm Wundt, one of the spokesmen for the 'ideas of 1914', '"Between democratic and German thought no accommodation is possible"' (*ibid.*: 22). This does not necessarily mean a dictatorship of the right, since it could also be understood as endorsing the co-operative values of socialism. Moreover, class and privilege are relativised in favour of the needs of the whole.

Now, these attitudes were shared by many opponents of Nazism, as well as by some Nazis – nor are they without some parallel in contemporary forms of communitarianism of the centre-left variety, where they are promoted as the basis of a gentle or caring alternative to the rigours of unrestrained free-market neo-liberalism.

However, as Young points out, a further distinction needs to be made between the various adherents of *Volk* ideology. On the one hand are those – Goebbels is the example given by Young – who embraced technology and the military-industrial complex as a means by which to realise the destiny of the *Volk*, and those – like Heidegger, Young suggests – who saw such an embrace as profoundly antithetical to the whole world of the *Volk*. In these terms, Young argues, Heidegger is an anti-modernist, akin to the 'Nazi Greens' whose ideal was to recreate 'an agrarian, *völkisch*, premodern society' for which the 'conquest of *Lebensraum* in the East [was] precisely that which would make possible the significant de-urbanisation and de-industrialisation of German society' (Young 1997: 34). This was, for example, the position of Himmler.

Now this is a deeply unpleasant twist to the concept of *Volk* but, as far as Heidegger is concerned, somewhat speculatively runs on ahead of the evidence. For, if Young's account very broadly captures the overall cultural frame of reference within which Heidegger (including the later Heidegger) operated, there is no evidence that he actively endorsed an unprovoked conquest of the Eastern territories or looked to settle them with German farmers. Indeed, such a policy would run against Heidegger's continual preoccupation with the specificity of the southern German landscape and the intimate bond between a people and its original land. Nevertheless, the split between those Young describes as modernist and anti-modernist Nazis does throw some light on Heidegger's disaffection with the Party. Although some of the reasons for the failure of the rectorship were personal and are connected with Heidegger's lack of political savvy, as well as with the mismatch between his enthusiasm to serve and the Party's lack of eagerness to accept him wholeheartedly, we can begin to see how precisely the question of technology could provide the focus for this disaffection. If, in 1933, Hitler might, to someone as politically unaware as Heidegger, plausibly seem to be offering an escape from the world-historical dominion of technology, all such hopes were eclipsed fairly early on. As we have seen, Heidegger was already drawing a contrast in 1935 between the 'inner truth and greatness' of National Socialism and what was being 'peddled about' as Nazi philosophy – the latter, fairly clearly, being what was endorsed by the Party itself. Moreover, this 'inner truth and greatness' was precisely to do with the question of technology.

Now Heidegger's critique of technology was, as we shall see in the next chapter, intimately connected with his critique of science and metaphysics, the basic outlines of which were already apparent before 1933.[9] Indeed, in his earliest phenomenological writings Heidegger is already setting his face against the then dominant positivism that characterised the philosophy of science. However, the explicit critique of technology and the search for an alternative vision of the world was to provide one of the unifying threads of Heidegger's later thought. This concern with technology goes well beyond the question of Heidegger's politics in the narrow sense, but it is important to see the profound interconnection between the development of this critique and the disillusionment with Nazism. In this sense, the critique of technology and the positive attempts to think 'beyond' technology may be said to constitute an 'inner emigration' from or an 'inner resistance' to Nazism, rather than, as Rockmore sees it, a simple spiritualisation of Nazi values. Even if this falls short of hailing Heidegger as a 'resistance fighter' (as in his son's introduction to the 1990 edition of the *Rektoratsrede*) the concept of inner emigration implies an element of reserve or critique in face of the claims of the regime.

These reflections help us to make sense of the way in which, for example, Heidegger links the death camps with the industrialisation of agriculture. In Heidegger's own perspective this is not a trivialisation of what happened at Auschwitz but the assertion of the world-historical significance of this event as the ultimate outworking of the levelling, dehumanising process of modern technology and mass production.

Also relevant here is the emergence of the question of art in Heidegger's thinking during the 1930s. In terms of the dominant cultural paradigms of post-Industrial-Revolution societies, art acts as a 'natural' counterpoint to science and technology, and it might seem almost inevitable that, in sharpening his critique of technology Heidegger should turn to art. However, this too is connected with the issue of Heidegger's Nazism in complex ways. Philippe Lacoue-Labarthe, following the insights of the German film-maker Hans Jürgen Syberberg (especially in the latter's film *Hitler – A Film from Germany*), has drawn attention to the aesthetic dimension of Nazism itself and suggested that Heidegger's turn to poetry and art is itself deeply congruent with his Nazism (Lacoue-Labarthe 1990). Again, however, I shall argue that we can see this development as an outworking of Heidegger's inner emigration.[10]

Yet doubts remain. Is Heidegger's inner emigration characterised by the kind of moral passion that events of such enormity should inspire? We do not need to subscribe to the view that Auschwitz was an event without parallel in history, 'planet Auschwitz', in order to demand that any discussion of the circumstances of its occurrence be conducted with an appropriate seriousness and, above all, an appropriate sense of responsibility. Did Heidegger say enough? He may have retreated and resisted, but did he repent? Isn't the whole business of his critique of technology conducted in a way and on a level that obscures the moral dimension that is, in this case, a *sine qua non* of authentic discourse?

Again, the question is not merely a personal one. It is also philosophical.

As suggested in the previous chapter, the holy grail of Heidegger's entire philosophical quest was the question of Being. It is, in the last resort, the way in which it covers up the question of Being that requires us to take metaphysics and its progeny, technology, to task.

In the view of Richard Wolin it is precisely this concern with the question of Being that provides the key to Heidegger's political thought and also to what is wrong with it. Wolin's position is condensed into his comment that 'In his political thought, Heidegger wilfully sacrifices the plurality and difference of human practical life on the altar of an atavistic Eleatic totem – the totem of "Being"' (Wolin 1990: 14). If Heidegger's actual Nazism, according to Wolin, is the putting into practice of what has already been prepared in *Being and Time* and the transformation of the question of Being from a genuinely philosophical question into the first principle of a world-view, the later, less subjective, less humanistic conception of Being is no great help. Wolin comments that '… one might be justified in interpreting [Heidegger's] later doctrine of the history of Being as an involuted rationalization of his own failed National Socialist involvement' (*ibid.*: 133). Heidegger's later privileging of 'earth' and the values associated with it against technology is, according to Wolin, one result of this, since earth (rather than Dasein) is now identified with Being (a comment I regard as completely misleading, since, as we shall see, 'earth' is only one dimension of the 'fourfold' in which Being manifests itself and behind which thought cannot penetrate). This critique of technology is, Wolin remarks, 'almost' fruitful, but, precisely because it is conducted on the plane of ontology (which Wolin refers to as 'the mystified perspective of neo-ontology' [*ibid.*: 163]), it avoids historical concretion. Similarly Heidegger's characteristic doctrine of truth leads him to deny any fundamental difference between truth and error, but this renders him incapable of formulating any intellectual or moral argument against genocidal evil, or, indeed, contributing anything to any serious political issue (*ibid.*: 117ff.). There is no significant place for the human other, since only Being, physis, etc. are allowed to matter (*ibid.*: 149).

For reasons that will become clearer as we proceed, Wolin's account of Heidegger's later view of Being is too one-sided and limited to do complete justice to the situation. Yet his words suggest a caution that is worth heeding: that whatever our philosophical commitments may be, they should not be such as to blind us to the claim of the local, particular, concrete other; that philosophers cannot and should not use their philosophy to hide from their own moral responsibility.

This missing dimension of Heidegger's thought, perhaps especially of the later Heidegger's thought (although, as previously indicated we can also connect this with the distinction between the ontological/existential and the ontic/existentiell as found in *Being and Time*) is well described by R. Safranski:

> the problem of [Heidegger's] silence is not that he was silent on Auschwitz. In philosophical terms he was silent about something else: about himself, about the philosopher's seducibility by power. He too ... failed to ask the one question: Who am I really when I am thinking? ... The contingency of one's own person disappears in the thinking self and its great dimensions. The ontological long-distance view lets the ontically nearest become blurred. There is a lack of acquaintance with oneself, with one's time-conditioned contradictions, biographical accidents, and idiosyncrasies. He who is acquainted with his contingent self is

less likely to confuse himself with the heroes of his thinking self, or to let the little stories drown in great history. In short: knowledge of self protects against seduction by power.

(Safranski 1998: 421)

Yet if that failure is not merely personal but is also, in whatever measure, conditioned by the philosophy, what does it mean for those who seek to go a certain stretch of the way with Heidegger in their own philosophising? Can one go any way at all 'with' Heidegger without falling under his spell and becoming vulnerable to analogous seductions, even if they will only rarely have as terrible outcomes as the events of 1933? But perhaps such a question is unanswerable unless or until we have set out along Heidegger's path and taken a larger view as to what that involves than has so far been possible. If, then, despite the spectre of Heidegger the Nazi, we do set out on this path, we do so with a certain caution, a certain fear and trembling, lest we too, for all our philosophising – or perhaps precisely because of all our philosophising – become blind to what is humanly most important.

Chapter 3

Technology

Technē and truth

The question of technology is central to the body of
texts that have come to be known as 'the later
Heidegger'. The topic is the main focus of such essays
as 'The Question Concerning Technology', but, even
when not directly addressed, it is rarely far from the
surface.

Thus, in the lectures *On the Origin of the Work of
Art* the discussion of 'the thing' and of the way in
which 'the thing' has been conceptualised in the
history of Western thought contains important hints
concerning the question of technology.[1] In this discussion Heidegger claims that the conceptual schema of
matter-and-form, coupled with the Christian idea of
the world as 'made' by God, has defined the Western
view of the thing and, in doing so, has defined it in
relation to 'equipment' and 'usefulness'. Noting the
derogatory way in which we speak about 'mere' things,
Heidegger suggests that the 'mere' thing is what a thing

is or becomes when abstracted or removed from the sphere of equipment and use: the mere thing that can't be used for anything, the piece of equipment that doesn't work, the broken radio, the flat battery. Although the realm of equipment and usefulness is nothing if not material, the way in which we speak about the mere thing suggests that the material element in it is not valued in its own right but solely in terms of whatever use it is being put to. As Heidegger says 'In fabricating equipment – e.g., an ax – stone is used, and used up. It disappears into usefulness. The material is all the better and all the more suitable the less it resists perishing in the equipmental being of the equipment' (PLT: 46). In other words, in using the stone axe I am not primarily interested in the stone as an object of geological interest – its kind or age or site of origin – nor as an object of aesthetic admiration – whether it has a matt or a shiny surface, whether it glitters, is veined or pocked. All I am interested in is whether it does the job of cutting, cleaving or severing, for which I have made or acquired it. The point is all the more clear if, with Heidegger, we contrast this with the way in which a work of art relates to its materials. Thus, in writing about a Greek temple, Heidegger describes how, by means of the presence of the Temple, nature is made visible in its very materiality as if for the first time. 'The luster and gleam of the stone, though itself apparently glowing only by the grace of the sun, yet first brings to light the light of the day, the breadth of the sky, the darkness and the night … metals come to glitter and shimmer, colors to glow, tones to sing, the word to speak' (PLT: 42, 46).

So far, nothing specific has been said about technology in the modern sense, but later in the lectures Heidegger does turn to discuss the meaning of *technē* and, as so often, takes his bearings from an interpretation of the Greek understanding of the term. His argument, however, sets out to contest a set of assumptions common to various forms of idealist aesthetics in the nineteenth and early twentieth centuries. These assumptions especially concern the distinction between the mechanical and the fine arts, a distinction in which, inevitably, the fine arts are estimated as 'higher' or 'nobler' on account of their relation to the truth or the moral values they are intended to convey. By way of contrast, mechanical arts, including crafts such as pottery, joinery, weaving, etc., are not regarded as capable of telling us important truths or instructing us in moral ideals. The most they can do is to adorn our domestic and public environments. As such they may have a certain value, but they are clearly secondary – merely background scenery, not what the art is about. Even if fine art needs a craft element (such as dexterity in drawing) it is essential that this is subordinated to the artistic end, to the expression of the artist's vision of beauty, truth and goodness.

This kind of division has been repudiated by many twentieth-century artists and critics, and, according to Heidegger, it is also alien to the Greeks, who, as he put it, 'knew quite a bit about works of art' (PLT: 59). The Greeks used the same word, *technē*, for art and craft alike, and, similarly, the same word, *technitēs*, is used for craftsman and artist.

Is this simply a matter of etymological curiosity? It may look like that to us, but, for Heidegger, language, and especially the Greek language, is never a matter of mere curiosity, since it reveals the fundamental experience of a people. The fact is, Heidegger says, that *technē*, understood in the Greek sense, means neither art nor craft nor anything 'technical' (in the modern sense) at all. Instead, *technē* is 'a mode of knowing'.

At this point Heidegger calls upon one of his most characteristic and influential reinterpretations of fundamental philosophical terms: truth. Again, Heidegger's interpretation depends on taking the term back to its Greek form, *alētheia*, a term composed, he claims, of the privative prefix 'a-' (as in 'a-political' or 'a-moral') and a form of the verbal stem – *lath* – 'to be concealed'. The 'original' meaning of 'truth', then, is 'being unconcealed'. This revision of the concept of truth plays a crucial role at many points in the later Heidegger, being sometimes linked to the image of a clearing into which the wanderer emerges from out of the twilight of a forest path, a place in which one can look around, take one's bearings and see out over the landscape in which one has been rambling. In fact, Heidegger's distinctive concept of *alētheia*/truth is already clearly developed in *Being and Time*, where he also links it to another fundamental philosophical term: phenomenon. Once more he finds the Greek term instructive. He notes that the underlying verb *phainesthai* signifies 'to show itself', '[t]hus *phainomenon* means that which shows itself, the manifest' (BT: 7/28). But this is not all, since the verb itself can be further traced back through the active form, *phaino*, 'to bring to the light of day, to put in the light' (*ibid.*), to a stem, *pha-*, that is related to *phos*, light (as in 'phosphorescence'), which as Heidegger glosses it means 'that wherein something can become manifest, visible in itself' (*ibid.*). 'Phenomenon', then, signifies '*that which shows itself in itself*, the manifest' and '[a]ccordingly the *phainomena* or "phenomena" are the totality of what lies in the light of day or can be brought to the light – what the Greeks sometimes identified with *ta onta* (entities)' (*ibid.*). Thus, truth, understood as *alētheia* and, according to Heidegger, already identified by Aristotle with *phainomena* means 'things themselves', 'things that are', 'what shows itself – *entities in the "how" of their uncoveredness*' (BT: 44/219).

Now, *technē*, if it is understood primarily as a way of knowing and not merely as a certain kind of practical aptitude or a way of 'making', must also belong within the orbit of *alētheia*/truth. For, as a way of knowing, it is a way of bringing beings, entities, things '*out of* concealedness and specifically *into* the unconcealedness of their appearance' (PLT: 59). Putting it like this, Heidegger suggests, helps us to see why the artist is understood primarily in terms of *technē*. This is not because art is a kind of making but because it actively uncovers, actively brings beings forth into unconcealedness, into the openness of disclosure, and thereby enables us to see things for what they are, to see metals glitter and shimmer and colours to glow.

There are two aspects to Heidegger's concept of truth which it is particularly important to be aware of. Firstly, truth is conceived as profoundly dynamic, and, secondly, although truth is defined as unconcealment it is at the same time a form of concealment. Let us take these in turn.

Firstly, the dynamic aspect of truth.

The conventional view, as Heidegger sees it, centres on the correspondence of idea (word/proposition) and thing (object, thing signified) and thus implies that each side of the equation has a certain fixity in itself outside or apart from their relationship. The proposition is the same whether or not there is a state of affairs corresponding to it (when there is not it is false, but nevertheless its notional content is the same as if it had turned out to be true), and the things that make up the world are what they are whether or not we talk about them. A proposition is either true or it is not. It cannot be more or less true. Thinking of truth in terms of the metaphor of unconcealment, on the other hand, opens a way to understanding the possibility of something being more or less unconcealed, more or less uncovered, like a landscape seen in the half-light of dawn or through a mist. In such instances clarity and distinctness emerge only gradually – first we see only an indistinct outline, then, slowly, colour and detail appear, and objects that had been indistinguishable come to stand out in their separate individuality.

The work of art, then, as an instance of *technē*, of bringing-forth from unconcealment, is not the presentation of a finished product with a determinate significance (as if it were the case that 'the work means *this* and nothing else') but an active bringing-forth, a process of unconcealment. Consequently, the truth of the work, that which is unconcealed in it, always stands in a determinate relation to the prior state of concealment from which it emerges. It comes with an accompanying penumbra, and, beyond that, with a relation to what is not at all unconcealed in it, a darkness beyond and behind it. Even when the sun has come fully out, and we are able to admire the landscape in all its beauty, we should not forget that daylight itself is not an absolute, static element. The colour of the sky is at all times conditioned by the unillumined space beyond, and even the brightest summer sky has a residual background darkness that makes it possible for it to be light at all, as we understand it. Pure light would have no colour. Our normal experience of daylight is, of course, of a constantly shifting pattern of light and shade, and our perception and appreciation of the visual field is inseparable from the fluctuating process of illumination.[2]

To take an example that is extremely important for the later Heidegger, it is not hard to understand that the meaning of a poem is not exhausted by the fact that I understand it to a certain extent on a first reading – on the contrary, the more deeply true the poem is, the more there is concealed behind what reveals itself on a first, superficial, reading; indeed, if it is a truly great poem (or picture or piece of music or even, perhaps, a well-wrought earthenware vessel), then it will be inexhaustible in its capacity to reveal new depths, new aspects, new meanings to me. Just to emphasise the point: it is precisely to the degree that I sense that there is more to the work than initially meets the eye, that behind what I read there is an undisclosed reservoir of hidden truth, that I am moved to make the judgment that this is a truthful work of art. As Heidegger puts it 'there belongs to [truth] the reservoir of the not-yet-uncovered, the un-uncovered' (PLT: 60).

But Heidegger goes further than this. It is not just that truth is, as it were, always under way, always in the process of uncovering what is still concealed but never reaching an end. Truth itself, he says, is a form of concealment. Given the equivalence of truth and unconcealment, this means that Heidegger is able to come up with what, on the conventional view of truth is the shocking assertion that 'Truth is untruth'. Clearly, on the conventional view, this is not merely shocking, but absurd, since, as we have seen, a proposition must be considered to be either true or false. So how can what is true be at the same time and in the same respect what is untrue? How can truth be untruth? Understood in Heidegger's sense, however, the statement makes perfect sense, for, as he explains (in the full form of the quotation given in the previous paragraph), 'Truth is un-truth, insofar as there belongs to it the reservoir of the not-yet-uncovered, the un-uncovered, in the sense of concealment' (PLT: 60). Yet if Heidegger is saying more than that unconcealment is always in process and never arrives at a point of complete transparency, and is pushing towards the position that truth, what is unconcealed, has an *internal relation* to what is not unconcealed in it, it has to be said that his formulation 'Truth is untruth', taken by itself, is something of a deliberately provocative overstatement.

Truth, in Heidegger's sense, is, untruth, in that it is inseparable from the penumbra of what is not yet unconcealed in it. Any particular bringing-forth by art in the sense of *technē* – a temple, a painting, or a piece of pottery – is what it is as a particular configuration of this duplicitous relationship. But the relationship is not merely duplicitous, it is downright conflictual. Thus, in each work a particular domain of beings is set forth in unconcealment but, by that very act, something is also, and necessarily, concealed. In taking the jug into my hands, I turn away from the plate. In taking the jug and admiring it as a beautiful jug, I overlook the clay from which it was moulded and see only its formal perfection. I stop dancing to look at the painting.

In looking at the glass I ignore the light streaming through it. In my dealings with such works the world is presented to me in a particular way, in a particular and necessarily singular, and therefore also exclusive, aspect. This characteristic particularity, Heidegger says, is the work's figure, its Gestalt, a term which he interprets in the light of the verb *stellen*, to place, and the noun *Ge-stell*, a 'framing' or 'framework' that provides a location or context for what is thus 'framed' and which we have already heard translated as 'enframing'.

Again Heidegger notes the distinction between a piece of equipment and a work of art. Equipment 'frames' its material as ready for use, and thus reduces the material to its usefulness or serviceability. The work of art, on the other hand, allows the material, the thingliness of the thing-element in the work, to permeate and be tangibly present in the figure. It is not 'used up' or reduced to 'usefulness' but is re-presented in a new aspect.

Now Heidegger does not develop the concept of *Ge-stell* further in *On the Origin of the Work of Art* itself. Nevertheless, the foundations have been laid for much of his later critique of technology.

Technology

I shall follow through the further development of the concept of enframing in one of the later essays where it plays a leading role, *The Question Concerning Technology*.

In this essay Heidegger moves directly from reflecting on *technē* in terms essentially identical to those we have been considering to a discussion of technology. 'Technology,' he writes, 'is a mode of revealing. Technology comes to presence [*west*[3]] in the realm where revealing and unconcealment take place, where *alētheia*, truth, happens' (QT: 13). He acknowledges that there might seem to be a quantum leap from the Greek sense of *technē* to the world of modern physics and its accompanying technology (he is now writing after the explosion of the Atom Bomb). Nevertheless, the Greek understanding *does* show us something essential about modern technology. For this too, Heidegger says, 'is a revealing' and it is '[o]nly when we allow our attention to rest on this fundamental characteristic ... [that] that which is new in modern technology shows itself to us' (QT: 14).

However, Heidegger not only accepts, he also insists that the kind of revealing that occurs in technology is very different from the kind of bringing-forth that we encounter in the work of art. Technology does not so much 'bring forth', but 'challenges forth' [*herausfordert*]. Unlike art, technology does not let what is to be made show itself, but places a demand upon its product that it answers to a predetermined purpose. In the interaction with nature that occurs in technology, nature is no longer allowed to function or to become manifest on its own terms, but is transformed into a quantifiable resource, into energy that can be abstracted from and stored and disposed of independently of its originating context. Whereas the sails of the windmill are also a means of harnessing natural energy for human purpose, they 'work' only as and when the air itself flows into them, making them move. The hydroelectric turbine, however, is no longer dependent on the force or flow of the river in the same way. Electricity 'produced' by hydroelectric turbines is no different from electricity produced by coal, gas, nuclear or, it has to be said, wind power or solar panels (see GA 15: 391). What is important in technology is not that wind or water is made to serve a particular purpose but that a particular product – in this case electricity – is made available in a quantifiable and usable way. 'The work of the peasant does not challenge the soil of the field. In the sowing of the grain it places the seed in the keeping of the forces of growth and watches over its increase.' By way of contrast, modern agriculture 'is now the mechanized food industry' – and so on: 'Air is now set upon to yield nitrogen, the earth to yield ore, the ore to yield uranium, for example; uranium is set upon to yield atomic energy, which can be released either for destruction or for peaceful use' (QT: 15).

Modern technology, then, enacts a very specific kind of revealing, a revealing that Heidegger speaks of as a 'challenging' or a 'setting upon', in which the powers of nature are indeed unlocked, transformed, stored up, distributed and redistributed, but always and only within the frame, the 'Ge-stell', that the human requirement of usefulness places upon it. Nature, as the totality of what is deemed 'knowable' by modern science, is thereby conceived from the outset in terms of equipment, instrumentality, becoming what Heidegger calls 'Bestand' – usually translated as 'standing reserve' but perhaps more loosely (and certainly less awkwardly) translatable as 'resource'. As 'resource' nature is no longer an object, a realm of beings standing over against us in its own right, but is what it is solely in terms of its function as 'resource' for technological exploitation.

In the next chapter we shall see how Heidegger understands the crucial role of Newton's epochally innovative theorisation of motion and the concomitant privileging of mathematics as the definitive language of science. This, for Heidegger, is decisive for the re-envisioning of the world that comes to its fullest expression in modern technology. However, if we are to grasp the overall shape of Heidegger's thinking at this point, it is absolutely essential to recognise the order of priority between theory and practice in science. In terms of historical development Heidegger is very well aware that the theoretical foundations of modern physics were laid long before its technological application was fully developed. This might seem to argue for the priority of theory and to suggest that the technological application is merely a kind of accidental outcome, something that might – or, equally, might not – have resulted from the theory. In reality, however, Heidegger claims, it is the other way round. 'Within the complex of machinery that is necessary to physics in order to carry out the smashing of the atom lies hidden the whole of physics up to now' (QT: 124). Although subsequent to theory in the order of historical progression, technology is prior in the order of aims and purposes: technology is the *telos*, the final cause of theoretical science. That theoretical physics is from the very start oriented towards its application, towards the realm of usefulness and thus towards grasping nature as nothing but resource, is indicated by the way in which it 'sets nature up to exhibit itself as a coherence of forces calculable in advance' (QT: 21).

But is Heidegger really saying anything in all this other than reformulating in a provocatively idiosyncratic way the kind of anti-technological rhetoric of a certain kind of ultra-right-wing agrarian conservatism, a kind that, as we have seen, found expression in one wing of Nazism? Putting it at its crudest, is Heidegger simply a philosophically articulate Luddite?

I think not – but to see why he is doing more than this we need to take note of a number of qualifications to his critical remarks concerning technology.

In the first place, none of this is directed exclusively against what we conventionally call 'science' and 'technology'. In an age such as ours, an age in which (as Heidegger sees it) enframing is the dominant mode of unconcealment, i.e., of representing the world, this dominance is not only expressed in the construction of nuclear power stations or the omnipresence of television screens. Enframing is not something that comes into play only when we enter into a laboratory, press a switch or turn a handle, something we can leave behind us when we go home or go for a stroll in the hills. It is no less influential in the realms of culture and leisure than in those of high tech and IT. Where, for example, art is conceived in terms of its ability to provide 'aesthetic experiences', then, according to Heidegger, we are also in the domain of enframing, because we have already determined the realm of art in advance as the site of a specific kind or range of experiences, experiences that, as modern aesthetics understands it, have nothing to do with 'truth'. Heidegger would not have been at all surprised by the recent fashion for speaking about the arts in terms of 'the culture industry', because this, as he sees it, is where even, perhaps especially, the most refined aestheticism is already heading.

Indeed, there is no dimension of life in which enframing is not at work. We see it in theology when God is conceived in terms of 'a cause-effect coherence', as the God of the philosophers, the God of 'representational thinking' who has lost 'all that is exalted and holy, the mysteriousness of his distance' (QT: 26). Or, equally but conversely, when in the religious life itself faith is conceived in terms of 'religious experience', analogous to aesthetic experience, then, Heidegger says, 'the gods have fled' (QT: 117).

Thus the distinction between 'arts' and 'sciences' has little or nothing to do with what is decisive in enframing. For it is characteristic of the arts no less than of the sciences that research and teaching are organised on the basis of a predetermining projection of a field of enquiry that both prescribes and precludes particular methods or topics.

For every procedure already requires an open sphere in which it moves. And it is precisely the opening up of such a sphere that is the fundamental event in research. This is accomplished through the projection within some realm of what is – in nature, for example – of a fixed ground plan of natural events. The projection sketches out in advance the manner in which the knowing procedure must bind itself and adhere to the sphere opened up. This binding adherence is the rigor of research.

(QT: 118)

Heidegger speaks here of nature, but it is clear from the context that it could just as well be history, literature or modern art. Indeed, Heidegger goes on to make just this point in a comment on academic life that is certainly not less pertinent now than in 1938.

[H]istoriographical or archeological research that is carried forward in an institutionalized way is essentially closer to research in physics that is similarly organized than it is to a discipline belonging to its own faculty in the humanistic sciences that still remains mired in mere erudition. Hence the decisive development of the modern character of science ... also forms men of a different stamp. The scholar disappears. He is succeeded by the research man who is engaged in research projects. These, rather than the cultivating of erudition, lend to his work its atmosphere of incisiveness. The research man no longer needs a library at home ... he is constantly on the move. He negotiates at meetings and collects information at congresses. He contracts for commissions with publishers. The latter now determine along with him which books must be written. *The research worker necessarily presses forward of himself into the sphere of the technologist in the essential sense. Only in this way ... is he real.*

(QT: 125 (emphasis added))

How, then, can any discipline – even philosophy – remain immune to the spirit of enframing? And why should any discipline want to cut itself off from a procedure that is so effective in getting things done?

Of what value is scholarly erudition in relation to the 'results' of well-organised research?

But if nuclear power, medicine and research are all able to vouch for themselves on the basis of 'results', Heidegger does not forget that the unconcealment that occurs in enframing is also, as we have seen, necessarily a concealing, a continuous closing-down or covering-over of other possibilities of representing and living in the world. Despite the prodigious explanatory and technological success of science, it is, Heidegger believes, an essentially limiting, one-sided, and one-track way of approaching the world. In terms of the aims of enframing itself, this self-limitation is necessary, but when we forget that there is just such a limitation, that science's truth is also untruth, imagining that our one-sidedness is omnicompetence, then we are en route to a rapid impoverishment of the world, of experience, of language.

> Everything is leveled to one level. Our minds hold views on all and everything, and view all things in the identical way. Today every newspaper, every illustrated magazine, and every radio program offers all things in the identical way to uniform views ... The one-sided view ... has puffed itself up into an all-sidedness which in turn is masked so as to look harmless and natural. But this all-sided view which deals in all and everything with equal uniformity and mindlessness ... reduces everything to a univocity of concepts and specifications the precision of which not only corresponds to, but has the same essential origin as, the precision of technological process.
>
> (WCT: 33–4)

Symptomatic of this 'growing power of one-track thinking' is the multiplication of acronyms and abbreviations. When we talk about the 'Uni' or the 'UL', Heidegger says, we unwittingly disclose the situation that our academic way of life is under the spell of a quantifying, instrumentalising and trivialising set of attitudes and practices. We are reducing education to a resource, an object of consumption, rather than a process of induction into a humanistic way of life. And, we might add, perhaps something similar is going on at the level of political life, when nations, alliances and groups of nations become known by their acronyms – USA, UK, EU, NATO, etc. And is it any wonder that as the acronyms fragment or coalesce (USSR, DDR, BRD) nations re-emerge: Russia, Lithuania (etc.), Germany?

Certainly, a Heideggerian perspective could find virtually endless material in the domain of popular culture and current affairs to illustrate the advancing hegemony of one-track thinking. As previously remarked, people who enjoy visiting the countryside are now sometimes referred to as 'consumers of the countryside' and are, as such, part of the 'leisure industry'. The 'sport of kings' has become the 'racing industry', and the 'recreational use' of drugs provides prepackaged 'Ecstasy' – something quite different from the opium dreams of a Coleridge or de Quincey or even the 'heaven or hell' sought by Aldous Huxley.

These comments, however, do nothing to prove the truth of Heidegger's analysis. Indeed, as they drift towards the level of journalistic comment they might seem simply to confirm the view that Heidegger is merely an out-and-out fogey who has the ability to dress his reactionary views in portentous phraseology. Does he really have anything to offer other than an unrealisable nostalgia for a past that probably never was, neither amongst ancient Greeks nor amongst German peasant farmers?

Heidegger is sensitive to the charge. He acknowledges that 'a haughty contempt' (WCT: 34) is not enough to break the spell of 'the imperceptible power of the uniformly one-sided view'. Moreover, it is clear that he does not regard the advent of the technological era as a short-term aberration. Technology is here to stay, probably for a very long time. Nor is this simply a reflection of its *de facto* effectiveness. Rather – and as we shall explore further in the following section – technology draws its power from the fact that it is essentially rooted in a destining of Being, from an event that is prior to any act of human willing, and, perhaps, prior to humanity itself.[4]

Illustrative of Heidegger's acceptance of the actuality of technology is the talk he gave when, in 1961, he returned to his home town of Meßkirch on the occasion of the 700th anniversary of its founding. In 1933 Heidegger had straightforwardly contrasted the simple virtues of the Black Forest farmers with the ape-like 'civilisation' of the city man. By 1961, however, the contrast was no longer so clean-cut. Heidegger's talk, appropriately enough, was on the meaning of 'home', and, he remarks, coming home to Meßkirch today, the first thing one notices is the forest of television and radio aerials on every roof-top. He sees in this a potent symbol of what the future holds in store for Meßkirch and the world. What these aerials show is that 'human beings are, strictly speaking, no longer "at home" [*zu Hause*] where, seen from outside, they "live"'. I may be sitting in my living room, but 'really', thanks to television, I'm in the sports stadium or on Safari or being a bystander at a gunfight in the Old West. Television, as the most immediate, most visible 'sign' of the dominion of technology is, as such, the solvent of everything meant by 'home'.

> Spellbound and pulled onward by all this, humanity is, as it were, in a process of emigration. It is emigrating from what is homely [*Heimisch*] to what is unhomely [*Unheimisch*]. There is a danger that what was once called home [*Heimat*] will dissolve and disappear. The power of the unhomely seems to have so overpowered humanity that it can no longer pit itself against it. How can we defend ourselves against the pressure of the unhomely? Only by this: that we continually enable the bestowing and healing and preserving strength of what is homely to flow, to create proper channels in which they can flow and so exert their influence.
>
> (GA 7: 61)

Despite this, Heidegger is prepared to contemplate the possibility that humanity as a whole is embarked upon a process of collective migration 'into a condition of homelessness' (GA 7: 63). In this situation it may even be that the relation to and the bonds with 'home' and 'homeland' are disappearing.

In these remarks Heidegger hints at what he elsewhere makes explicit: that enframing is not simply something man does to the world. It is a process that intimately and totally concerns humanity itself. In the age of technology humanity is itself set upon and challenged forth by enframing and is drawn into the web of calculation and exchange that is the world-as-resource.

The forester who, in the wood, measures the felled timber and to all appearances walks the same forest path in the same way as did his grandfather is today commanded by profit-making in the lumber industry, whether he knows it or not. He is made subordinate to the orderability of cellulose, which for its part is challenged forth by the need for paper, which is then delivered to newspapers and illustrated magazines. The latter, in their turn, set public opinion to swallowing what is printed, so that a set configuration of opinion becomes available on demand.

(QT: 18)

Humanity itself is thus reduced to the status of resource, even if we may say that, as the provider and distributor of all other resources, it is also the supreme resource.

Here, as at many points in his discussion of technology, Heidegger reveals the influence of the writings of Ernst Jünger.[5] Jünger, originally renowned as a war hero and novelist, developed a highly influential theory of contemporary culture. Unlike Heidegger, Jünger embraced the world of modern technology enthusiastically. Reflecting on his own war experience, he pointed out that, whereas traditional warfare involved a monarch despatching a more or less large army to take the field against his foes, modern warfare involves a 'total mobilisation' of society. War is no longer the prerogative of a warrior caste but is a matter for a nation in arms in which industry, agriculture and all aspects of national life are equally involved. Everything and everyone in society is brought together in a co-ordinated war effort. What Jünger now anticipates is the normalisation of this mode of social organisation, such that it becomes as characteristic of peace as it is of war. In this regard, the Soviet Union, with its Five-Year Plans, represents a tendency that is not confined to the Soviet Union itself.

It suffices simply to consider our daily life with its inexorability and merciless discipline, its smoking, glowing districts, the physics and metaphysics of its commerce, its motors, airplanes, and burgeoning cities. With a pleasure-tinged horror, we sense that here, not a single atom is not in motion – that we are

profoundly inscribed in this raging process. Total mobilization is
far less consummated than it consummates itself: in war and
peace, it expresses the secret and inexorable claim to which our
life in the ages of masses and machines subjects us. It thus turns
out that each individual life becomes, ever more unambiguously,
the life of a worker ...

(Wolin 1993: 128)

The worker (the title of a subsequent book by Jünger) emerges as
the archetypal figure of contemporary humanity. But what is important here is precisely this: that what is decisive about the age is not its
technical capacities in terms of technology, narrowly understood, but
what Jünger calls its *readiness* for action'. What really characterises
the modern age is not its machinery but the type of man it produces
and, who, in turn, produces it. That Germany lost the (First World)
war was therefore not so much a matter of military failure or of technological inferiority, but the lack of readiness in German society for
total mobilization. Jünger expressed the view that, contrary to
popular opinion, Anglo-Saxon democracy actually provided a more
fertile milieu for the onset of total mobilization, because the democratic process ensured the genuine popularity of any war effort,
thereby heightening the moral claim upon each citizen to participate
in executing the common will. As total mobilization throws its net
ever wider in order to draw it in ever tighter, Jünger suggests, it
becomes increasingly clear that the only option for human beings is to
embrace the process.

If people, then, are both the primary agents and the primary
objects of total mobilization, or, in Heidegger's terms, of the transformation of reality into a resource for technological manipulation
(what he calls *Machenschaft*), what can the future hold but an ever
greater homelessness, a homelessness that encompasses us even when
we are sitting 'at home' watching television?

However, Heidegger does not go all the way with Jünger. It is clear
that he could not endorse this process as something we should heroically embrace. Nor, on the other hand, does he succumb to the
cultural pessimism of someone like Spengler, who foresaw the inevitable 'downfall of the West'. Rather, whilst recognising the inexorability

of total mobilisation and the accompanying state of homelessness, Heidegger aims at 'a new relation to what is homely [that] is preparing itself even in the midst of the pressure exerted by the unhomely' (GA 7: 63).

We shall return in later chapters to different aspects of what this 'new relation' might mean, and there is a sense in which we might understand the whole of the later Heidegger as an attempt to articulate this new relation in such a way as to defend it against being drawn back into the domain of enframing and neutralised by being reduced to just one more fashion in one-track thinking. Here is, precisely, the key to many of the difficulties associated with the later Heidegger. Like Kierkegaard's Johannes Climacus who, looking out upon the modern city in which inventions, encyclopaedias and the promoters of public works were making life easier and easier for everybody, resolved, contrariwise, to make something (in his case Christianity) more difficult, so the thought of the later Heidegger is deliberately expressed in such a way as to resist instant comprehension and easy understanding. To seek to reinstate the homely in the midst of our collective homelessness is to go against the most deeply engrained and most characteristic patterns of thought of the modern world, the enframing that holds sway in atomic physics and glossy magazines alike. Nor was Heidegger forgetful of what Jünger had already noted – that behind every presumed exit from the world of total mobilization lurks 'pain and death' (Wolin 1993: 138), the ostracism and punishment that befall the deserter.

Let us recall that we have been considering how we might defend Heidegger against the charge that he is merely offering an intellectual justification for gut-reaction Luddism, a philosopher's 'haughty contempt' for progress and democracy. Our argument has taken the following steps. Firstly, it was shown that Heidegger's decisive category of enframing is not restricted to science and technology in the everyday sense, but makes its influence felt no less in the arts and in aesthetic experience, in theology and religious life, in the humanities and in innumerable phenomena of popular life, from acronyms to 'the leisure industry'. Secondly, we saw that the kind of contrast between city and country, technology and traditional agrarian life, that was characteristic of 'Creative Landscape' is undermined by the realisation that the country, no less than the city, is now in the grip of technology. Thirdly, what is most characteristic of enframing, the transformation of the world into a totalised network of resources, is not merely something humans do to the environment or do with machines but, first and foremost, is a demand, a requirement, they place upon themselves, their self-transformation into the 'human resources' necessary for total mobilisation. On the basis of these considerations we have suggested that the later Heidegger's strategy is not simply one of refusal, nor yet of agrarian revolt, but of cohabitation, the necessarily difficult quest for 'a new relation' to the homely in the midst of the unhomely – and thereby a reconfiguration of humanity itself in relation to being as a whole.

However, in the light of everything that has been said directly and indirectly about the totalising tendencies of enframing it is indeed difficult to see where, even in his own terms, Heidegger might hope to find an avenue of escape from the all-consuming grip of technology, or where he might hope to find a domain that has not been colonised by technology. All this, Heidegger acknowledges – and, in doing so, acknowledges the complaint that those who inhabit the scientific world-view will inevitably make against him: that all he can offer is a non-scientific, emotive, meaningless gesture of refusal.

The essence of technology

Despite Heidegger's instinctive and frequently expressed preference for the world of windmills over against nuclear power plants, we have at several points seen that the question raised by technology points beyond technology in the normal sense of the word. In this respect, the danger that chiefly preoccupies Heidegger is not the danger that humanity might destroy itself in a nuclear war or render the planet uninhabitable by means of industrial pollution or the exhaustion of natural resources. Although Heidegger himself says things like 'Everywhere we remain unfree and chained to technology, whether we passionately affirm it or deny it' (QT: 4), he also insists that what matters is not, in the last resort, technology itself, but the *essence* of technology, and this, he says quite explicitly, 'is by no means anything technological' any more than the 'essence of "tree" ... is ... itself a tree that can be encountered among all other trees' (QT: 4).

This distinction between technology and the essence of technology invites being understood in terms analogous to the distinction between the ontic and the ontological that was so important for *Being and Time*. In the light of previous comments about how that distinction problematised the relevance of Heidegger's ontological thought for practical action in the world, this might seem to detach his reflections on the essence of technology from any possible application to the concrete problems of technology. However, as we shall see, Heidegger claimed that only reflection on the essence of technology would prepare us for an adequate response to the phenomenon of technology itself. What, then, is this essence, and where are we to seek it?

If the question seems unnerving, especially after having spent so long discussing what we had thought was the question of technology, the answer has in fact already been substantially given in what was said about enframing. For enframing itself is not a form of technology. Equally, however, it is not a way of representing the world that just happens to be exemplified in the world of technology. Enframing is not itself a piece of technology but it is intrinsically connected with the world of technology. As the remark about the relationship between the equipment for smashing the atom and theoretical physics showed, the technological outcome is what enframing itself demands, and theoretical science, as a way of enframing the world in terms of its calculability, already determines the world as a resource for technological manipulation.

The question of the essence of technology is a question concerning our own relation to technology, and whether we are able to be free in our relation to the essence of technology (QT: 3). A necessary condition of such freedom is that we are able to see the essence of technology for what it is. Otherwise – whether we are research scientists, captains of industry or eco-warriors – we are plunged into an all-pervasive fog in which we wrestle with we know not what.

Now we already know that, whatever else it is, the essence of technology is a certain kind of unconcealment, and it follows that the essence of technology belongs to truth. It is not simply a misconstrual of the world, but an unconcealing of the world in a certain aspect or dimension of its being. The practical and theoretical knowledge we have of the world in and by means of enframing is not false: what is false is its claim to totality. For, as we have seen, enframing is not even the only kind of bringing-forth facilitated by *technē*. There is also the way of art, and perhaps there are other ways not yet considered. We shall return to this in a later chapter, but now the question is how enframing, the peculiar kind of challenging-forth of being that Heidegger calls *Ge-stell*, arises on the basis of Greek *technē*? Whence comes enframing? Is it itself a 'discovery', a methodological orientation devised at a certain point in history by Newton, perhaps, or Pythagoras? Is the advent of enframing itself an event in the history of ideas or the history of science?

Once we put the question in this way, it soon becomes clear that, for Heidegger at least, the answer cannot be a simple affirmative. Enframing is not something we opt for as individuals, nor is it something thought up by one of the great thinkers of the past. Enframing is not something we do, since it already involves a determination of who 'we' are and what our 'world' is. Caught up in and defined by enframing, we do not so much direct it as operate within it or on the basis of it. It is something that befalls us, a kind of destiny. More precisely, insofar as we are agents of enframing, serving it, perpetuating it and ever extending its dominion, we are so on the basis that we are ourselves already 'framed', already determined in our essence by enframing. Just as human beings turned out to be the prime resource of technology, so the question as to the essence of technology turns out to be a question as to who we ourselves are in our being.

This has the appearance of a paradox: that in the era of technology man (and there is a case for retaining the gender-specific noun in this context) arrogates to himself the role of Lord of Creation, Master of the Universe, ruler of all he surveys. But that which enables him to exercise such mastery is not, in the final reckoning, anything of his own devising. Reiterating his definition of enframing as 'the way in which the real reveals itself as standing-reserve [resource: *Bestand* – GP]', Heidegger asks 'Does this revealing happen somewhere beyond all human doing? No. But neither does it happen exclusively *in* man, or decisively through man' (QT: 24). And, he adds, 'As the one who is challenged forth in this way, man stands within the essential realm of Enframing' (QT: 24). More strongly still, in 'The Turning', Heidegger writes 'it seems time and time again as though technology were a means in the hand of man. But in truth, it is the coming to presence of man that is now being ordered forth to lend a hand to the coming to presence of technology' (QT: 37).

This reflects what was previously discussed in terms of total mobilisation and the transformation of humanity into the primary resource of technology. Precisely in inaugurating space programmes, developing new generations of computer technology or managing genetic engineering projects, humanity is absorbed into the service of technology itself, 'lending a hand' to the coming to presence of technology and forgetting the question as to its own essence and meaning. In this situation it follows that humanity's repeated attempts to control technology, to manage the pace of change and innovation, to retain a sense of direction in the whole, is inevitably futile, precisely because control, management and direction are themselves values inscribed in the basic project of enframing. The view that what we need to do in the face of environmental devastation is to manage our technology more effectively is itself a technological response to the crisis in which we stand.

So, three questions.

Firstly, if humanity itself is not the originator of enframing, what is? Secondly, if enframing is something that befalls humanity as a destiny, how can we hope to escape it? But, thirdly, why should we want to escape it? Why not just – 'enjoy!'?

Let us begin by asking, once more and quite simply, what it is that occurs in enframing. In enframing, as we have seen, the world is revealed in the aspect that enframing itself brings to appearance. Enframing is a mode of unconcealment, a way in which the world is made present to us, and we establish ourselves as a presence within the world. Enframing is not an illusion, the imposition of an a priori schematisation onto an indifferent or resistant reality. Science and mathematics are forms of world-disclosure, unconcealment, truth. What is revealed in enframing belongs to Being – even if, as Heidegger repeatedly insists, enframing only allows that aspect of Being to come into view that serves to define beings or entities, regarding Being solely in its aspect of the essence of objects. But to be in a partial or one-sided relation to Being is not to be in no relation to Being; therefore enframing, for all its limitations, is a mode of coming to presence of Being.

As Heidegger puts it in one of the key words of his later philosophy, technology is a 'destining' of Being. Recalling that 'destining' (*Geschick*) has the twofold connotation of destiny or fate and of fittingness, the essence of technology can be seen both as a destiny sent by being, but also as a way in which Being adapts or fits itself to the receptive capacities of those to whom it is sent as a destiny. As the bearer of this destiny, then, humanity is not merely the passive victim of an alien fate, a necessity imposed from outside. This destiny is one that uniquely belongs to humanity and expresses its own capacities for interpreting Being.

To see what is going on here we must follow Heidegger in his further development of this concept in terms of his conception of the 'History of Being'. Postmodernity has, famously, been defined in terms of the jettisoning of the grand narratives of modernity; it would seem that narratives don't come any grander than Heidegger's 'History of Being', and the narrative of this history stands in the background of much of the later Heidegger.

Briefly, Heidegger sees this history in terms of a succession of epochs of Being, in which Being is realised under a succession of different forms of consciousness that enable a corresponding succession of different aspects of Being to be actualised in the concreteness of historical becoming. Thus far we could be talking of Hegel. However, whereas Hegel sees the historical sequence of epochs of Being as interrelated in a progressive, hierarchical and unitary development, such that each new epoch grows almost organically (Hegel is very fond of vegetable metaphors) out of the inner contradictions of its predecessor, Heidegger conceptualises the overall shape of history and the transition from one epoch to the next very differently. As Heidegger sees it, each new epoch, though not unrelated to its predecessor is, in a sense scarcely acceptable to Hegel, a distinctive, novel and 'other' destining of Being. A new epoch does not so much emerge as the resolution of the conflicts of the old, but, in a more radical sense, is a new beginning, issuing from a movement within Being itself, initiated from and therefore only comprehensible in relation to a dimension of Being that is not revealed on the plane of concrete historical becoming itself. The history of the rise and fall of civilisations is a history that cannot be understood solely in terms of intra-historical development. In terms of our earlier reflections about humanity's capacity to surmount the crisis brought about by the totalising of the technological consciousness, this means that any new development, any new, post-technological, post-enframing epoch would also need to be initiated from or by supra-historical Being. As Heidegger puts it:

> If the essence, the coming to presence of technology, Enframing as the danger within Being, is Being itself, then technology will never allow itself to be mastered, either positively or negatively, by a human doing founded merely on itself. Technology, whose essence is Being itself, will never allow itself to be overcome by man. That would mean, after all, that man was the master of Being.
>
> (QT: 38)

Seeing it in these terms means that, for Heidegger, the question as to the essence of technology is, essentially, a metaphysical question, insofar as metaphysics is defined as a concern for the question of Being. However, for the later Heidegger at least, it is clear that the metaphysical understanding of Being that has prevailed in the West from the time of Plato and Aristotle has itself been conducted within the paradigm of enframing. The meaning of Western metaphysics is thus, for Heidegger, to be found in reflection on the essence of technology. Consequently – and of decisive importance for Heidegger's whole reading of the history of philosophy – science and technology are not opposed to metaphysics in the way that they are for philosophers such as A.J. Ayer. Metaphysics is not vacuous speculation that has been supplanted by science. Rather, science and technology are the effective carrying-out of the projection, the disclosure of that truth of being that occurred first in Greek metaphysics.

However, the kind of agency that Heidegger ascribes to Being not only sounds metaphysical. It almost begins to sound theological. For Being seems to behave not unlike the Judaeo-Christian God, raising up and casting down nations at will, irrespective of their intra-historical aims and objectives. We shall consider at greater length in Chapter 8 whether Heidegger, a one-time candidate for the Catholic priesthood, does reveal himself in his later thought to be a theologian *manqué*. For now, however, we note only the plausibility of such a 'theological' reading, together with Heidegger's repudiation of it.

But, theological or not, what follows from the way in which Heidegger prioritises Being as the source of fundamental epochal change is that the historical process itself can no longer be understood as a progressive, teleological movement, as for Hegel. There can be no 'final judgment' on the level of history itself, just a succession of diverse epochs, that might limit each other reciprocally but do not define each other in their inner essence. Thus – and again we have to defer discussion of this to a later point – we must be ready to countenance the possibility of radical and irresolvable discontinuity between different epochs, different cultures and different languages. So, whereas for Hegel the civilisations of the East could be seen as primitive stages of the same historical development that culminated in Northern European Protestantism, it is an open question for Heidegger as to whether, for example, Europeans and Japanese can finally understand each other without violating their respective worlds of thought and language. It is possible that they are simply discontinuous, incommensurable zones of unconcealment, with no mediating term other than Being itself.

It is here that we see what Heidegger means by the errancy of Being. Again, whereas for Hegel historical development is continuous and purposive, Heidegger's diverse epochs of Being, since they cannot be spoken of as steps in a single progressive line of development, can be regarded as 'erring', wandering through history without goal or purpose – a vision that reflects the motif of 'the wanderer' in Nietzsche's writings.

Yet Heidegger claims that human beings are not simply passive in all this, and, as we have seen, destining itself involves adaptation to the receptive capacities of human beings. In the face of the danger posed by enframing, we are not simply condemned to wait fatalistically until Being 'decides' to send forth a new epoch. If that were so, then all talk of surmounting or overcoming the danger of technology would be merely utopistic. If we may not conceive of man as the master of Being, we are assured that '[m]an is indeed needed and used for the restorative surmounting of the essence of technology'(QT: 39). Indeed, as we have seen, Heidegger has stated that the achievement of a free relationship between humanity and technology is one of his fundamental aims in setting out to think about technology.

In what way then can humanity be free in its relation to technology? What can we actually do about our situation?

The first element in Heidegger's answer to this is one with which we are already familiar: that we do not allow ourselves to be mesmerised by technology itself and its 'success', but rather keep our sights on the *essence* of technology. But this cannot occur without a second element that has also been already adumbrated: that we confront the essence of technology in the light of what is truly essential to humanity: 'in order that man in his essence may become attentive to the essence of technology, and in order that there may be founded an essential relationship between technology and man in respect to their essence, modern man must first and above all find his way back into the full breadth of the space proper to his essence' (QT: 39).

But what is it that is proper to the essence of humanity?

The answer, according to Heidegger, involves thinking and language.

Before being able to decide what to do about technology, before being able to enter into a free relation to the essence of technology, it is necessary for us to know what it is to think, and to think means to deliberate upon language as 'the primordial dimension within which man's essence is first able to correspond at all to Being and its claim, and, in corresponding, to belong to Being. *This primal corresponding*, expressly carried out, is *thinking*' (QT: 41). The key to the question of technology, then, is to think upon Being.

Put like that, it sounds simple, but for Heidegger it is almost definitionally true that the simplest thing is also the most difficult.

In *What is Called Thinking?* he sets out to discuss just this: what is called thinking. That means trying to think. But trying to think, questioning what thinking is, implies, as Heidegger repeatedly insists, that 'we are not yet thinking'. This reflection leads him on to a formulation that runs like a refrain throughout the lectures: '*Most thought-provoking is that we are not yet thinking*' (WCT: 4).

Of course, Heidegger is aware that there is a great deal of intellectual activity going on in our world, with innumerable research projects, scientific and technological undertakings taking place all about us. However, for the most part all such activity is carried out within the paradigm of enframing. It is no surprise, in the light of everything that Heidegger has said about enframing, science and technology, to learn that 'Science does not think' (WCT: 8), a statement that, Heidegger admits, sounds shocking – but, like the statement 'truth is untruth', makes perfect sense within the overall context of Heidegger's own thought. That, however, does not get us off the hook of having to explain what Heidegger means by thinking, still less does it justify the overall orientation of thought within which the statement belongs. What, then, is this thinking? And what is it for thinking to concern itself with Being? To ask such questions with any degree of seriousness is, however, already to entertain the possibility that there may be a kind of thinking that is different from that of science, that is not yet another application of enframing, but, equally, is not merely vacuous. But is there such a thing?

Here, although we have come by a very different route, we arrive at questions that have been of concern to philosophers in the Anglo-Saxon mould no less than to those working within the Heideggerian and post-Heideggerian tradition. Does the language of science, or do propositions whose truth value can be formalised in terms of symbolic logic, exhaust everything that is sayable about the world? Is everything else mere expressive huff and puff? Since the heady age of Wittgenstein's *Tractatus* and Ayer's *Language, Truth and Logic* philosophers have become more cautious and more generous: more cautious regarding claims that the language of science is as simple and as 'objective' as it is popularly represented, and more generous in considering language as a rich and multi-faceted system whose capacity to communicate meaningfully cannot be limited to merely one of its many aspects and functions. If we admit such possibilities, then we are at least not going to dismiss in advance a venture of thought that seeks to enter into and explore this area. Nevertheless, we are not thereby required casually to admit each and every claim or formulation that sets itself up as speaking for the domain of the non-scientific. The point is precisely that not everything outside science is to be brought under the rubric of meaningless gibberish. However, because the rules for speaking meaningfully, insightfully and truthfully in this domain are by definition different from those that hold good within science and that have been nurtured by philosophical logic for over two millennia, we can scarcely expect to do more than move ever so cautiously. We are unlikely to stun the world with discoveries, results or innovations.

All this, I suggest, Heidegger accepts, and as we progress we need to keep open the possibility that, perhaps despite appearances, the later Heidegger is not the visionary prophet of grandiose pseudo-philosophical meta-narratives, but one who aims, by a variety of means (including renarrating the history of ideas), to prepare the way for a return to the simplest, most original question of philosophy. However, if what initially concerned us was the fear that, as Heidegger (quoting Nietzsche) puts it in *What is Called Thinking?*, the wasteland is continually growing, why should we be attracted by Heidegger's path of thinking? In the face of environmental catastrophe, the pauperisation of millions and the impoverishment of our cultural inheritance, why should we want to follow a line of thinking that, even at the outset, promises so little? Would we not do better, for example, having heeded everything Heidegger says by way of warning about technology, to apply our minds to developing new kinds of technology, kinds that do not degrade the environment or require the exploitation of human beings, kinds that open up liberative possibilities of common and planetary life?

Nothing that Heidegger proposes, however, excludes this absolutely. His argument is simply that, if we do only that, we will leave aspects of the common life of the mind unexamined. His question, in other words, is not so much a question concerning what we should *do*, but a question as to how we understand ourselves in what we do. The danger, the wasteland, is not environmental degradation as such. The danger, for Heidegger, is that under the spell of enframing, dazzled by the success of technology, we simply forget to ask the question of Being. The paradox is that, in the mode of enframing, Being itself, by the self-concealment that is the necessary obverse of every movement of unconcealment, tempts us to forget Being. Although there may be a sense in which the devastation of the earth, world war and nuclear weaponry are the outcome of such forgetting, the connection is by no means direct or immediate. A more direct outcome is, simply, the impoverishment of thinking itself, and boredom as the nemesis of such impoverishment. The sheer difficulty of a way of thinking that seeks first what truly concerns it, Being, thus guarantees its own claim to be the best antidote to such thinking. But in the face of this difficulty, how are we ever to get started? Aren't we going to need something rather dramatic to get us going? We are indeed, and that is what Heidegger sets out to give us.

Chapter 4

Seeing things

The turn to art

A concern for art and, indeed, the privileging of the place of art in humanity's relation to Being, is often adduced as one of the defining characteristics of the later Heidegger. Is this 'turn to art' a matter of Heidegger, having conquered the heights of phenomenology and ontology, and having made important contributions to the history of philosophy, now expanding his repertoire and applying his methods and insights to the field of aesthetics? Or is it an integral part of his fundamental philosophical programme? In this chapter I shall argue that his interest in art is more of this latter kind. Indeed it is questionable whether it belongs to aesthetics in the narrow sense at all, for aesthetics, no less than metaphysics, is regarded by Heidegger as gripped by the spirit of enframing. Is it, nevertheless, a manifestation of Heidegger's fundamental romanticism that, faced with the typical post-Enlightenment choice between art and science, he chooses art? So how does this turn to art connect with his politics and the global confrontation with technology?

In order to attempt an answer to these questions, let us go back to 13 November 1935, when Heidegger delivered a lecture 'On the Origin of the Work of Art' to the Art-Historical Society of Freiburg-im-Breisgau. This lecture was subsequently repeated in Zürich (in January 1936) and in Frankfurt (in December 1936), being revised and expanded in the process. It was not published until 1950, when it was included in the collection *Holzwege*.[1]

The timing of the lectures is itself potentially significant for understanding Heidegger's engagement with questions of art. For the origin of the 1950 text goes back to the time when, on Heidegger's own account of things, he had come to realise that National Socialism was not going to fulfil the expectations he had attached to it.[2] Already in 1934 he had resigned from the rectorship. Can this text, then, be read as an early marker on his path of inner emigration? Suggestive here is the early adumbration of the critique of technology, a question that, as we have seen, is intimately connected with Heidegger's initial enthusiasm for and later disenchantment with Nazism. But if this is so, and taking into account the first series of lectures on the poet Hölderlin, dating from 1934–5, does it mean that we are to interpret the turn to art as an archetypal gesture of romantic thought, a retreat from the glare of public life and the rigours of a totally mobilised society into the inner sanctuary of a private aesthetic sphere?

Appearances, however, can be deceptive, and as we look further into the text it soon becomes clear that this is not a work of aesthetics in the narrow sense of a sub-discipline of philosophy, nor is it exclusively about art. Indeed, a closer look at the title might suggest that Heidegger did not himself claim that it was about art but about the *origin* of the work of art. And, just as we have learned that the origin of technology is nothing technological, so we should now be prepared to hear that the origin of the work of art is nothing 'artistic'. It is unsurprising, then, that as we follow Heidegger's account of this origin we are led into a domain that, as he understands it, is prior to art in the sense in which the term is generally used (i.e., in relation to what are called the fine arts). Indeed, this domain is prior to the split between art and science that is one of the characteristic features of our civilisation.

In the light of this comment, it can be claimed that, in terms of Heidegger's own intentions, we should not read *Origin* as a simple expression of romantic withdrawal, a retreat from the world in which technology and politics hold sway as the final outcome of the metaphysical world-view. Rather, in Heidegger's own terms, it is itself a thinking confrontation with the fundamental decision facing humanity in relation to the advent of planetary technology. Even more grandly, it becomes possible to read *Origin* as a key to the origin not only of art but also of history, and of humanity's historical existence and destiny. Thinking of *Origin* in this way also helps us to see how it can be taken as an early fruit of the 'later Heidegger'. For whereas historicity was conceived in *Being and Time* in terms of the individual subject (although, as the rectorial address showed, this could be interpreted in terms of the nation or *Volk*, regarded as a corporate individual), 'decision' is no longer a matter of will and resolution but involves a much higher level of receptivity to what comes, as it were, from beyond humanity.

How, then, does *Origin* itself arrive at this point?

Let us begin with the first work of art mentioned in the text, a painting of a pair of shoes by Van Gogh, and, before we come to the controversial question of the shoes themselves, it is worth considering why Heidegger should pick on a work by this particular artist, by Van Gogh.

Heidegger had been very taken with Van Gogh's *Letters* which he read when they were published during the First World War. Why? On the basis of Heidegger's own letters and comments made in the lectures on ontology, one element would seem to have been the way in which Van Gogh's decision to give up training for Christian ministry and devote himself to poverty and painting reflected just the kind of *existentiell* confrontation with existence that preoccupied Heidegger in the years leading up to *Being and Time*. When Heidegger cites Van Gogh's assertion that he would prefer to die in a natural way rather than learning to understand death academically, we can see how the painter could serve the philosopher as an *existentiell* paradigm of authenticity, grounded as his concept of authenticity was in the individual's resolute confrontation with death.[3] However, the kind of use to which Heidegger puts his comments on the painting of the shoes in *Origin* points away from this idea of the artist as lonely existentialist hero.

In fact, as the text proceeds it becomes ever clearer that one of Heidegger's aims in it is to break the spell of an understanding of art that focuses exclusively on the creative figure of the artist. This view that, in Heidegger's own words, 'the work arises out of and by means of the activity of the artist', is, he says, the 'usual view', and this 'usual view', he declares in the opening paragraph of the lecture, is what he is setting out to overthrow, or, minimally, to supplement, by focusing – as the title suggests – on the work rather than on the artist. For, as he asks, 'by what and whence is the artist what he is?' Answer: 'By the work ...' And, Heidegger adds, both artist and work are what they are only in relation to something else, to 'art' itself, which is 'prior to both' (PLT: 17).

It is extremely important that the 'usual view' that Heidegger here confronts is also the focus of discussion in the lectures on Nietzsche from the winter semester of 1936–7, lectures collectively entitled 'The Will to Power as Art'. Here Heidegger identifies the conviction that 'Art must be grasped in terms of the artist' (N 1: 71) as one of the defining statements of Nietzsche's whole approach to art. This is further complemented by Nietzsche's other basic principles of art, as expounded by Heidegger: that 'art is the most perspicuous and familiar configuration of will to power'; that 'art is the basic occurrence of all beings; to the extent that they are, beings are self-creating, created'; that 'art is the distinctive countermovement to nihilism'; and that 'art is worth more than "the truth"' (N 1: 75).

Set against the horizon sketched by these principles, and even without going into any further explanation of them, we can see how Heidegger's determination to challenge the 'usual view' of art will involve him in far-reaching decisions on a variety of issues. For if Nietzsche, far from being an 'untimely' or eccentric thinker (as he so often pictured himself), is in fact representative of the basic metaphysical outlook of modernity, then reconceptualising the relationship between artist and art-work will require giving consideration to the nature of will to power, how beings are, nihilism and truth.

Let us try to put this in less Heideggerian and less Nietzschean terms.

The most usual view of art in our culture, we might guess, is that art is primarily a way of representing things, an attempt to depict the world, and to show what the world is like. The person on the pavement doesn't like Picasso, because Picasso's paintings aren't life-like. Simple realism, it could plausibly be claimed, is the most commonly held aesthetic of our time. However, even everyday talk about art doesn't stop there. Let's think about a different medium: cinema. Three people come out of a movie, perhaps a new film by Scorsese. 'I didn't like it,' says one, 'there was too much swearing and violence. I like to be entertained when I go out.' 'But that's how the characters would behave in real life,' says the second (a simple realist), 'You wouldn't expect small-time New York gangsters to be otherwise. That's what I like about the film: it really shows you what that kind of life must be like.' 'Maybe,' says the third, 'But this is no documentary, this is about the themes of all great art down the ages: passion, betrayal, redemption. *The Last Temptation* or *Mean Streets* – these are the archetypal Scorsese themes!' 'But that's just my point,' retorts the first speaker, 'Why is he so obsessed with violence, why can't he show us something more cheerful, something more edifying?'

None of our characters are great aesthetic theorists, but the terms of their discussion reflect some of the knottiest debates in aesthetics. The second character has been portrayed as a simple realist: the success or failure of a work of art is in terms of its faithfulness to life. The third character more obviously embraces what Heidegger regards as 'the usual view', i.e., that art is primarily an expression of the vision of the artist and that, consequently, the meaning of art lies in the subjectivity of the artist. At this point, however, the first speaker reminds us that there are widely differing and often conflicting ways of evaluating such a vision, over and above the debate as to whether the work effectively communicates what the artist wants to show to the recipient. The artist's vision is itself an expression of values that the recipient may or may not find acceptable. The judgment on the work of art, then, becomes a judgment about values, in this case about whether Scorsese's view of the world is one that we should be ready to embrace. But this judgment itself hinges on how we judge the world to

79

be: is Scorsese's vision itself complicit in the violence it portrays, and do we too become complicit by enjoying it voyeuristically, or does he show us a truth we need to confront if we are to know the whole meaning of human life? Now this last question is no longer the question as to the simple representational accuracy of the film. It is about what matters most in human life.

This imaginary conversation has brought into focus three of Heidegger's five points: that the meaning of art is grounded in the activity of the artist; that art manifests will-to-power in the sense that it embodies the artist's will to communicate his vision to the audience; and that art represents the basic occurrence of beings, in that the kind of evaluative appraisal of the work of art hinges on fundamental decisions concerning what the world is like. But it also throws light on the remaining points (that art is the counter-movement to nihilism and that art is more important than truth). For it is precisely the outcome of the debate between the first and third interlocutors that decides what meaning the phenomenon itself – in this case the life of the gangsters portrayed in the film – is to have. Art provokes the question as to the meaning of what, in itself, is a bare concatenation of events: this is the life these people lead, no better, no worse, no different ontologically from any other kind of life, but what are we to make of it? Whatever we do make of it, we will need to make a judgment that involves an imaginative and evaluative envisioning of life that is essentially of the same kind as the judgment involved in appraising a work of art. So, finally, art is more important than truth, in the sense that art exemplifies the kind of evaluative vision that determines how we see and how we judge the values embodied in the world and it is this vision that decides what, for us, is to count as truth in human affairs.

For the purposes of this exegesis of Heidegger, it is not necessary to suppose that what Heidegger calls 'the usual view' is the universal view. Even in our imaginary conversation we have allowed another voice, that of the exponent of art-as-imitation, to be heard. All that matters, for now, is that Heidegger's point – and thus his subsequent argument – really does take its departure from how art is experienced and (if only by implication) understood in the everyday encounter with art – although it may be added that, in his own cultural context, where Nietzsche was such a massive influence both on artists and aestheticians, Heidegger's assumption that this is the usual view is perhaps more plausible than in some other contexts.

All of this, however, leaves open the question as to whether this 'usual' way of talking and thinking about art is adequate or justifiable. If not, what are we to do? Might we, for example, reconfigure the order of precedence between artist, work and object such that the object takes first place and the tyranny of the creator-artist is overthrown?

It might be supposed that this last move is the one Heidegger is about to make, but in fact he is going to argue for something much more far-reaching. For the production and reception of works of art is, as he sees it, not merely a matter of individual vision and cannot be improved merely by talking up the objective aspect of art. *For his examination of the work of art will call into question what it means to represent or to perceive anything at all, or, more precisely, to represent or to perceive anything as anything.* In other words, it leads to the question as to why we don't just see the world but, instead, see the world (and all the particular things within the world) in a certain way, as a world of such and such a kind, comfortless or welcoming as the case may be. In this way, then, Heidegger invites us to ponder how we can decide about the work of art without first deciding what we mean by 'representation', 'reality' and 'world'.

But if Heidegger's aim is to unsettle the 'usual view' and its one-sided privileging of the creator-artist, why does he begin with Van Gogh, a painter who, more than most, stood for the modernist ideal of the anguished creator-artist, the solitary genius compelled to overthrow all the prevailing rules of artistic representation so as to give shape to his own unique vision and who, in so doing, became incomprehensible to his contemporaries in order to bequeath to us a whole new way of looking at the world? Later on in the text Heidegger will look at works of art – works like a Greek temple – that are more obviously suited to his own purposes. Why begin with an artist who would seem to exemplify the view he wants to overturn?

The question itself suggests one possible answer: that, if Heidegger is to succeed, he must do so against the strongest of counter-examples. If his new approach provides a better way of looking at this (supposedly) supreme example of the individual creator-artist, then it will have little to fear from whatever other counter-examples are brought against him. In other words, he is not saying that works produced by creator-artists are dangerously subjective and should be brushed aside in favour of other, let's say more contemplative, works. The aim is not to introduce a way of deciding between good and bad or between acceptable and unacceptable works of art, but to find a better way of understanding art as such. And that, again, is why he must take the question back to the most basic questions of represen-tation.

Other explanations have, however, been offered in the secondary literature. One that has a certain currency is that Heidegger is not really concerned with Van Gogh's painting at all, except insofar as it provides a convenient, though specious, jumping-off point for his idyllic evocation of the world of the peasant woman whose shoes the painting supposedly represents. This is in turn seen as part of Heidegger's Nazistic and uncritically sentimental valorisation of Germanic peasant life. Worse still, as the art critic Meyer Schapiro famously pointed out, there is no reason to suppose that these shoes belonged to a peasant woman at all. More probably they were the painter's own shoes! Heidegger, then, is doubly reprehensible. Firstly, he is simply mistaken, and, secondly, his mistake reveals all too clearly the role of Nazi ideology in his whole intellectual project.[4]

Schapiro's point invites two initial comments. Firstly, as we have seen, one of Heidegger's aims is to undermine the 'usual view' of art. Primarily this meant toppling the creator-artist from the pedestal onto which late Romanticism had elevated him. But it doesn't stop there, since it also involves challenging the equally conventional form of the art-as-imitation view. Precisely with reference to the shoes, Heidegger asks rhetorically 'Is it our opinion that the painting draws a likeness from something actual and transposes it into a product of artistic – production? By no means. The work, therefore, is not the reproduction of some particular entity that happens to be present at any given time' (PLT: 37). This suggests that the historical identity of the actual shoes used as a 'model' by Van Gogh is not in itself impor-tant for understanding the work of art *qua* work of art. In this respect it is perhaps regrettable if Heidegger has made a factual error, but that does not of itself destroy his whole argument.

However, a careful reading of the text does not justify the assertion that Heidegger ever actually claims that Van Gogh's painting is a painting of a pair of peasant woman's shoes. To be sure he does use the painting to accompany his evocation of the world of the peasant woman, but nowhere does he say they are her shoes that Van Gogh painted. Indeed, he does not directly address the question of the 'ownership' of the shoes at all.

These comments may seem to have left the more serious charge unaffected: that, whoever's shoes these may have been, Heidegger uses Van Gogh's painting as an excuse for a piece of Nazi cultural propaganda.

In the preceding chapter, I argued that we cannot immediately conflate Heidegger's penchant for a pre-industrial agrarian way of life with the Nazi ideology of 'Blood and Soil'. A similar caution is called for with regard to the interpretation of the 'peasant' shoes, but the situation is, I believe, still more complicated. To see this, however, it is necessary to look again at the context of the *Origin*.

One of the most notorious cultural events of the whole Nazi era was the 1937 exhibition of degenerate art. The category of degenerate art was fairly ill-defined and perhaps, even, incoherent, but it included contemporary movements such as Expressionism – of which Van Gogh was generally taken to be a precursor. Andreas Hüneke has described as 'crucial' in determining whether a work of art was degenerate in the Nazis' sense of the term such factors as '"Distortion" of natural form, particularly of the human figure, and "unnatural" colors' (Hüneke 1991: 124). In the light of such 'criteria' it is not at all surprising that a number of paintings by Van Gogh were taken into the haul of 17,000 works impounded from museums and galleries, and five of them appeared in the 1937 exhibition in Munich (although with characteristic cynicism both Göring and Hitler were involved in selling on or attempting to sell on Van Gogh paintings to raise revenue[5]). Although the exhibition of degenerate art was not held till 1937, and therefore post-dated the lectures on which *Origin* is based, the ideological line on Van Gogh had been made public long before that (e.g., in Rosenberg's *The Myth of the Twentieth Century*, perhaps the most widely disseminated work of Nazi 'theory' after *Mein Kampf*).

A further aspect of this is that the very concept of degenerate art was, of course, linked to Nazi racial theory and the biologistic interpretation of Nietzsche's will-to-power, an interpretation which understood will-to-power as a kind of quasi-Darwinian life-force. In this connection it is not merely Van Gogh's works but his personality and madness that also 'prove' the degeneracy of his art. For Heidegger, however, it was axiomatic that will-to-power was not a biological concept, and that even in Nietzsche's own terms the concept of a biologically degenerate art made no sense.

What does this tell us about Heidegger's procedure in *Origin*? The mere fact that Heidegger is taking as his point of reference a painter held in ill repute by Nazi ideologists does not seem to throw much light on his philosophical intentions. Are we to draw the conclusion that this is some kind of intra-party squabble and that Heidegger is trying to persuade those who first heard his lectures that it's alright for Nazis to like Van Gogh, since the painter shares their own affinity with traditional peasant ways of life? However, we should remember that the period when Heidegger was giving these lectures was precisely the period in which he seems to have been beginning what I have called his inner emigration, a period of disillusionment that had especially to do with the Party's failure to break loose from the grip of technological thinking. The world of the peasant woman, in this context, is not so much a Nazi icon as a reminder of what Heidegger regards Nazism as turning away from. At the same time, and this is perhaps a crucial point in mapping Heidegger's complex stance towards modernity, Van Gogh was undoubtedly known as a modernist, avant-garde painter, and it is striking that the other painters to whom Heidegger was particularly attentive, Cézanne and Klee, were also distinctively modernist. The world of the peasant woman, as disclosed by Van Gogh's painting, then, is not simply a piece of the rural past, but, insofar as we only gain access to it through the work of art (and, quite particularly, this work of modernist art), it is a world to which we can relate only and exclusively on the basis of our own modern experience.[6]

There are, then, a number of elements in Heidegger's account of the shoes as a means of controverting the 'usual view' of art that, at least implicitly, undermine some of the bedrock principles of Nazi aesthetics. This is, as we shall see later, vitally important in assessing the way in which Heidegger construes the relationship between poet and nation (especially as exemplified in Hölderlin). If there is a 'true' or 'spiritual' Germany, it is not to be found along the path of racial purity but in the lived world of a way of life and, furthermore, it is most easily accessed by means of an artistic vision that, itself grounded in the experience of modernity, overreaches the accidental genius and anguish of the individual artist.

But this is already to pre-empt our discussion of what we actually see in this 'world' and how the work of art helps us to see it. Before addressing these questions directly, though, we have a further preliminary question to deal with, the question of the 'thing'.

What is a thing?

In declaring his intention to move beyond 'the usual view' of art, Heidegger seeks to shift the emphasis from the artist to the work. As he does so, he is struck by the contrast between the spiritual or rapturous state of mind typically ascribed to the creator-artist and the fact that the work of art is a thing. The Van Gogh painting gets its first mention as an example of this 'thingly' aspect of art, as an object that can be carted around like any other thingly object, such as coal, logs or a sack of potatoes. This thingly element, he says, is something that all works have, and the examples he chooses – the painting or, later, the Greek temple – seem well-chosen to illustrate this. But even an art-work of an apparently more spiritual or ethereal kind – Beethoven's string quartets, to use another of Heidegger's own examples – cannot escape the dimension of thingliness, for when not being realised as music the scores 'lie in the storerooms of the publishing house like potatoes in a cellar' (PLT: 19). Even the work in performance is inseparable from the thingly element of sound itself as vibrations in air. The same is *a fortiori* true of architecture, sculpture, painting and the other arts.

Naturally, Heidegger is very well aware that this is precisely the opposite of what much academic and popular talk about art has chosen to think about. Such talk usually emphasises the ways in which the art-work is not a 'mere' thing but a bearer of meaning, functioning as allegory or symbol to manifest 'something other' (PLT: 20). This 'other' dimension of meaningfulness is generally regarded as the authentic element in art, what makes it art, but once again Heidegger refuses to let this usual view pass unexamined. On the contrary, he suggests that we cannot have an adequate understanding of the work unless or until we have taken its thingliness into account.[7]

Heidegger therefore goes on to list the three conceptions of the thing that have dominated thinking about the subject in the West, and that have done so to such an extent that they are regarded as self-evident and enter into everyday use without being seen as problematic.

The first view is that of the thing as the bearer of properties. The block of granite is the bearer of such properties as hardness, heaviness, extension, bulk, lack of shape, roughness, colour, dullness, shininess, etc.[8] This everyday understanding of the thing is expressed in the Latin philosophical vocabulary of the West in terms of the relationship between the substance of a thing and its accidents. This conceptual schema has been widely assumed to be all-encompassing and has been applied to everything from God and His attributes to the block of granite. It is also reflected in (or is it, perhaps, a reflection of?) the basic sentence structure of our language, in which meaning is constructed by means of the relationship between subject and predicate.

But this conception of the thing, Heidegger tells us, 'does not build upon the thingly element of the thing, its independent and self-contained character' (PLT: 25). We sense, he says, that this construal of the thing is an inappropriate rationalisation that does violence to its object. Thus, to take an example Heidegger hints at and discusses elsewhere, religious believers spontaneously feel repelled by the God of the philosophers, the Absolute Being accompanied by such imposing attributes as being-his-own-cause, omniscience, omnipresence, infinity, etc. Such a God, they say, is not the God known in worship and prayer. At the other end of the scale, an understanding of the block of granite framed in terms of the relationship between substance and accidents will never let us see what a stone-carver sees in it.

In *What is Called Thinking?* Heidegger invites his audience to abandon for a moment the standpoints of scientific enquiry and, even, of philosophy, to step outside the lecture hall and just look at a tree in bloom. 'The tree faces us. The tree and we meet one another, as the tree stands there and we stand face to face with it. As we are in this relation of one to the other and before the other, the tree and we *Are*' (WCT: 41). This encounter, Heidegger insists, is no mere idea. It does not involve any conceptualisation of the tree as a being of such and such a kind, nor any thematic observation of its distinguishing properties. To say that it is a cherry tree of a particular species, at a particular stage of its reproductive cycle (in bloom), swaying in the April breeze – none of these technical or poetic observations is necessarily incorrect but they are not what strike us in our encounter with what Heidegger calls 'the undisguised presence of the thing' (PLT: 25). If we imagine that the standpoint of science and philosophy is 'normal', then this encounter will seem like a leap, Heidegger suggests – and indeed it is, for there is no chain of reasoning that links the scientific view with that of the immediate encounter. Yet this leap is not some kind of mystical experience; it is simply a leap 'onto the soil on which we really stand' (WCT: 41). Indeed, it is a leap onto the soil on which we really were standing all along.

However, to return to *Origin*, Heidegger recognises that this challenge to the normal view could itself be misconstrued as an example of a different but no less misleading concept of the thing. This is the concept of the thing as, in the strict sense, an *aesthetic* object, that which is given to us in and through the senses, as if our encounter with the tree were to be understood as a kind of surrender to the sheer sensory impact of the colour that dazzles the eye, the scent that tickles the nostril and the caressing wind.

Once again, however, Heidegger brushes this aside. It is not the case that we first receive a mass of sensations and then transform them into an experienced object, but we see the object simply as what it is: 'We hear the Mercedes in immediate distinction from the Volkswagen' (PLT: 26), he remarks. That is to say, we never just hear a bare sound or see a bare colour. These are not the primary data of perception but abstractions from what is given concretely in actual existence.

Although Heidegger spends less time in the text of *Origin* on this way of misconceiving the thing, his brief comments here are the merest tip of the iceberg and touch on some of the fundamental philosophical commitments of his approach to phenomenology. The clearest statement of what Heidegger understood by phenomenological method is, perhaps, to be found in lectures that formed the basis of *Being and Time*, although the introductory methodological sections did not appear in the published version.[9] These are now available in English as *History of the Concept of Time*.

Of immediate relevance to the discussion of the thing in *Origin* is the exposition given in these lectures of the principle of intentionality. Now, although the critique of technology is scarcely developed in such relatively early writings, part of the attraction of phenomenology to Heidegger was to find a way of breaking the grip of the scientific positivism that seemed tailor-made as an ideological underpinning for a technological society. Whatever the justification of such an approach in the natural sciences, it was, Heidegger believed, fundamentally injurious to the human sciences and, above all, to philosophy. For positivism systematically ignored the question of intentionality, a concept that lay at the heart of phenomenological method.

What does Heidegger understand by intentionality?

At its simplest, intentionality is 'a structure of lived experience as such' (HCT: 29). It is, of course, a structure of a particular kind, one that enables us to bridge the gap between subject and object that has long puzzled philosophers.

> *Intentio* literally means directing-itself-toward. Every lived experience, every psychic comportment, directs itself toward something. Representing is a representing of something, recalling is a recalling of something, judging is judging about something, presuming, expecting, hoping, loving, hating – of something.
>
> (HCT: 29)

Consciousness, in other words, is never self-contained but, even in its simplest forms and functions, reaches out beyond itself 'toward something', as Heidegger puts it. However, in order to escape solipsism it is not of itself sufficient merely to observe that when I think I think 'of' something, since this gives no guarantee that what I think of really exists outside consciousness. How, then, can the doctrine of intentionality, thus defined, do more than articulate the aspiration to transcend a subjectivistic or solipsistic view of consciousness?

The first step in Heidegger's response to this implied charge is that the customary way of posing the question already involves a misrepresentation of the fundamental issue. We should not begin with the classical scenario of an inner psychic event on one side and a physical object out there on the other. No matter how hallowed by convention this picture may be, the question it suggests is only a derivative, or secondary, issue. More basic than the question of perception, couched in such terms, is that of what Heidegger calls comportment (*Verhalten*). What does this mean? Let us take Heidegger's own example. I come into a room and see a chair. Now, the chair that I thus see is not in the first instance the object of detached empirical perception. It is simply the chair I have to push out of the way, or walk round, or sit on, or on which the cat is already sitting. In such ways I live out an intentional comportment toward the chair long before I ever isolate it as a distinct object of perception. Clearly, the comportment in which I encounter the chair doesn't just involve what I subsequently isolate as 'the chair', but embraces the whole complex of lived experience in which I encounter the chair itself: everything that has to do with my going into this particular room.

Intentional comportment is not, however, introduced by Heidegger as a step in an argument that would culminate in my being able to say with confidence that the chair 'really' exists as a physical object in three-dimensional space. The concern that is revealed in intentional comportment is not the perceived entity, but the perceivedness of the entity, the entity 'as it is perceived, *as* it shows itself in concrete perception' (HCT: 40), '*the way and manner of its being-perceived*' (HCT: 40), 'the how of its being-perceived ... the how of its being-intended' (HCT: 45).

This may still fall short of providing an adequate response to the charge of subjectivism. Nevertheless it does show us what Heidegger thinks is being aimed at in phenomenological investigation, namely, the uncovering of this 'as', 'way and manner', or 'how' of the perceivedness of the object. To go back to our example, the chair is disclosed to me in the first instance 'as' the chair I want to sit on, or from which I have to shoo off the cat.

However, there are two further refinements to the theory of intentionality we must take into account if we are to understand the philosophical significance that Heidegger ascribes to it.

The first concerns the distinction between intentional presuming and intentional fulfilment. Presuming, in this context, means simply alluding to what is perceived in a general, empty, merely formal way, as when I report to a friend in the corridor outside the room 'There's a chair in that room'. The friend will perfectly well understand what I say, but this will say nothing to him of how he will encounter the chair for himself when he goes in, whether he sees it as a tasteful antique chair, a shabby old thing, an obstruction or a convenience. The intention has become detached from its object, and the object itself, the chair, is correctly identified but not thought in its concrete specificity. Intentionality is said to be fulfilled in concrete intuition such that I have 'the entity present in its intuitive content so that what is at first only emptily presumed in it demonstrates itself as grounded in the matter' (HCT: 49).

However, no more than in *Origin* does Heidegger understand intuition here in terms of the immediacy of sense experience. My grasp of the chair as that from which I have to shoo off the cat is in some sense prior to its impact on me as a congeries of sense data. In this connection Heidegger claims that there is a categorial structure given in intuition. Now, clearly, in the light of his comments about substance and accidents (and of what he will go on to say about matter and form) Heidegger is not wanting to endorse either a Kantian or an Aristotelian theory of categories, and certainly against Kant, if not Aristotle, he is not suggesting that we have at our disposal a table of categories that we simply 'apply' in intuition. Instead, the 'how' of our intuition always involves a certain structuring of experience that is embedded in the most fundamental dimension of experience itself. I see a row of trees, a flock of wild ducks, Heidegger says, and that I see them *as* a row or a flock 'is not based upon a prior act of counting. It is an intuitive unity which gives the whole simply. It is figural' (HCT: 66).[10]

Against this background, we can see that Heidegger's apparently buccaneer brushing-aside of the second view of the thing, the thing as what is given to us as the object of sense-experience – a view which 'makes it press too hard upon us' (PLT: 26) – presupposes an extensive philosophical preparation, the outcome of which is that, for Heidegger, sense experience is never 'raw' but always already interpreted, experienced 'as' this or that object of intentional comportment.

This discussion will provide a reference point for further elements in Heidegger's treatment of both things and works of art, but what of the third view of the thing that he regards as characteristic of the popular view?

This is the view that the thing is to be understood in terms of the distinction between matter and form, such that 'the thing is formed matter' (PLT: 26). More precisely, the thingly element in, e.g., the work of art is 'the matter of which it consists' (PLT: 27). Perhaps this is the most common-sense way of understanding the thing. Certainly, Heidegger comments, it is '*the conceptual schema which is used in the greatest variety of ways, quite generally for all art and aesthetics*' (PLT: 27). And not only in art and aesthetics: 'Form and content are the most hackneyed concepts under which anything and everything may be subsumed' (PLT: 27). Add to this the refinement that form is correlated with rationality, logic and subjectivity, whilst matter is linked to the irrational, the illogical and the object, then, Heidegger says, 'representation has at its command a conceptual machinery that nothing is capable of withstanding' (PLT: 27).

Heidegger is particularly interested in the fact that the matter–form distinction makes clear that whatever is analysed in such terms is being looked at, more or less explicitly, in terms of its usefulness, as 'equipment' to be used for such and such a function. Form is not regarded as something that, as it were, grows out of the matter or co-originates with it. Form is what is imposed or impressed upon matter for a specific end or purpose. When we are confronted with a thing (Heidegger's examples are a jug, an axe and a shoe) the material element is subordinated to the form, which, in turn, is subordinated to the use to which the thing is to be put, so that what we want to know about the jug is whether it is capacious enough or whether it leaks, and about the axe whether it is sharp enough or heavy enough, and about the shoe whether it fits and is water-proof (or, it may be, fashionable). 'Usefulness is the basic feature from which this entity regards us' (PLT: 28), Heidegger comments.

These remarks suggest to Heidegger a further, interesting observation: that what exists in this manner – i.e., what exists as 'useful' – is, or appears to us as, 'the product of a process of making. It is made as a piece of equipment for something' (PLT: 28).

Turning from jugs and shoes to the big picture, Heidegger then adds that the dominion exercised by the matter–form distinction was, historically, significantly enhanced by the way in which it was taken over from Aristotle by medieval Christian theology and applied to the total relation between God and the world, such that the world becomes what God has made for the fulfilment of His purposes, however these are conceived. But this effectively reduces the world to the status of mere instrumentality, a useful means to an end, rather than something of value in itself.

Inevitably we hear in such comments anticipations of Heidegger's later critique of technology, and this is borne out by further developments in the text. For a subsequent historical transformation of the conceptualisation of the thing, a transformation that was to prove decisive for the modern understanding of the world and of the things within it, occurred in the early scientific revolution and the incorporation of that revolution into the presuppositions of modern philosophy. In lectures given in the winter semester 1935–6 (and therefore concurrent with his reworking of the first version of *Origin*) Heidegger discusses this with particular reference to Newton and Kant. Stating that Newton is the founding figure of modern science, Heidegger draws attention to the title of Newton's magnum opus: the *Mathematical Principles of Natural Philosophy*. In this title we can immediately see that science, for Newton, is regarded as fundamentally mathematical. Now mathematics, as Heidegger understands it, is a way of knowing that draws upon or that brings to expression what we know, or presume we know, of things 'in advance' (WT: 73).

Think again of the example of the row of trees or the flock of ducks. Here we seem to be in the situation that our grasp of one-ness precedes our perception of any particular instance of a unitary phenomenon, such as 'a' row or 'a' flock. 'The mathematical,' Heidegger says, 'is this fundamental position we take toward things by which we take up things as already given to us, and as they should be given' (WT: 75). Mathematics is projective, in that it runs on ahead of actual experience, determining in advance and entirely in terms of its own self-determining laws what can and cannot count as knowable.

However, Newton's significance is not just that he made mathematics foundational for natural philosophy. It is also to do with the way in which this foundational role is further shaped by his first law of motion, the law of inertia: that, 'Every body continues in its state of rest, or uniform motion in a straight line, unless it is compelled to change that state by force impressed upon it' (WT: 78). Already in Newton's own time this was spoken of as 'a law of nature universally received by all philosophers' and today (that is, in Heidegger's day) it seems entirely uncontroversial. Heidegger, however, draws attention to the scale of the revolution in thought that the formulation of this law involved. Previously the dominant view of motion had been that of Aristotle. This differed from the Newtonian view in two key respects. Firstly, whereas on the Newtonian view the basic form of motion was linear, and objects only divert from linear motion under external pressure (e.g., gravity), Aristotle had given the highest dignity to circular motion, such that it was the circular motion of the heavenly bodies that held the universe together in a coherent whole. Thus, whereas on Newton's theory the moon would fly off into space if it were not constrained by the gravitational pull of the earth, for Aristotle the circular motion of the moon belongs to the moon's nature. Secondly, Newton's law applied to all bodies without exception, whilst Aristotle had held to the view that each body had a different kind of motion according to its specific nature.

When Newton's law of motion is developed on the basis of mathematical method a significantly novel view of nature and of the thing emerges. Nature 'is now the realm of the uniform space-time context of motion' (WT: 92), 'Bodies [now] have no concealed qualities, powers and capacities' but 'are only what they show themselves *as*' (WT: 93) and are thus available without remainder as objects of observation and experimentation. The uniformity of bodies requires uniformity of measure, and this is precisely numerical measurement (WT: 93–4). But, given the understanding of mathematics as projective, i.e., as determining what can or cannot be known of things in advance of actual experience, 'the basic blueprint of the structure of everything and its relation to every other thing is sketched in advance' (WT: 92). Nor is it simply the case that mathematics predetermines what can be known of each individual entity or of any particular local ensemble of entities that become the object of scientific scrutiny – i.e., it is not just a 'method'. Because of the interconnectedness of all bodies, the mathematical projection 'first opens a domain where things – i.e. facts – show themselves' (WT: 92). Mathematics, in other words, does not merely give us a method, a means by which to know better things with which we are already familiar in a rough-and-ready way, it determines the whole field of possible experience, the kind of world in which it is possible for anything that is knowable to be. Its laws provide the model for laws of nature.

This, Heidegger continues, is fundamental to Kant's concept of *pure* reason. For Kant's pure reason is something very different from the rationality of man 'the rational animal' of previous centuries. Pure reason bespeaks the mathematical predetermination of the realm of knowable beings. A doctrine of pure reason is a doctrine that 'What is a thing must be decided in advance from the highest principle of all principles and propositions, i.e. from pure reason, before one can reasonably deal with the divine, worldly, and human' (WT: 110–11). On this basis, Heidegger concludes that Kant is not concerned with 'the question of the thingness of the things that surround us' but with 'the thing as an object of mathematical-physical science' (WT: 128).

This, then, is where we are led by the view of the thing that bases itself upon the form–matter distinction: mathematics, pure reason, is the form that, determined in advance, projects itself upon and impresses itself upon the matter of the world. And what follows from that? What follows, according to Heidegger, is not only that the world is laid open without remainder, without any hidden corners, to the omniscient eye of modern science, it also means that the world in its entirety is made available to us as a resource for technological manipulation. Indeed, as we have seen, it is virtually axiomatic for Heidegger that technology does not follow upon science as a chance outcome or fortuitous application of scientific 'results', but that the determining of the world as what is mathematically knowable is, from the very outset, geared to the purposes of technological manipulation and management. What Newton and Kant provide is thus the blueprint for transforming the world into sheer resource, mere equipmentality.

Having exposed the 'boundless presumption'[11] and 'semblance of self-evidence' of these customary ways of regarding the thing, Heidegger has to consider whether there is in fact any alternative. Does the way of science exhaust the possible ways of looking at things?

Looking at things

The prospects would not seem hopeful. However, the lectures on the history of the concept of time are once more instructive. Having expounded the phenomenological concept of intentionality in terms of its fulfilment in categorial intuition (the seeing-how or the seeing-as that, Heidegger claims, is already present in the simplest and most primitive acts of consciousness and is not merely something added on), he then goes on to explore how phenomenology tries to get at and show this seeing-as.

Phenomenological method is, he says, fundamentally descriptive, but not 'merely' descriptive. It does not simply reproduce the object in the medium of a prose commentary. It is rather an 'accentuating articulation' of what is given in the intuition and, as such, is analytical. In describing an object phenomenologically, I don't just record my first impressions but aim at laying bare the categorial structure that is given in and with experience, even though I may not immediately notice it in the moment of experience itself. Thus, I don't usually notice that in saying 'Look at that flock of ducks' I am presupposing the categorial intuition of the one-ness of the flock as a concrete phenomenon. But this one-ness is not an a priori structure that I lay upon the phenomenon. The flock really is a flock, the row of trees really is a row of trees. In this way, Heidegger says, phenomenological description is also ontological. For the focus of phenomenological enquiry is indicated by the word itself, as Heidegger famously interprets it. For the *phainomenon* is that which shines forth from itself. It is no 'mere appearance'. The phenomenono-logist, therefore, is one who allows the theoretic gaze to rest upon the phenomenon and makes manifest in discourse, *legein*, the categorial structure of the phenomenon.

What is needed, then, is not to come up with an alternative definition or concept of the thing that could be put into play against the prevailing views, but to return to the thing itself, to redescribe it in the manner of an 'accentuating articulation' so as to allow what is given in the phenomenon, the categorial intuition, the seeing-as, to come to expression in its own terms.

And this is just what Heidegger proceeds to do in *Origin* with the shoes – but which shoes?

We have seen that Heidegger's treatment of Van Gogh's painting of shoes is controversial because his supposed identification of these shoes with the shoes of a peasant woman – who, in turn, is made to exemplify the peasant virtues of blood-and-soil ideology – brings his discussion into the orbit of his Nazism. It has also been claimed that this is an example of Heidegger's own ideological commitments running on in advance of the phenomena, because he has quite simply misidentified the painting, relying on nothing more than a fading memory of a painting seen in an exhibition in Amsterdam, and the shoes are in fact Van Gogh's own. On this reading the whole thing is nothing but an embarrassing mistake that does no more than illustrate Heidegger's contempt for facts, his art-historical amateurism and his political prejudices.

However, as we have seen, Heidegger nowhere claims that the shoes Van Gogh painted were 'actually' those of a peasant woman. All he says is that they are *like* those of a peasant, and then, later, he contrasts what the painting enables us to see with what such shoes would mean to a peasant woman. If the artist shows us the world of the shoes, the woman just wears them as a piece of equipment, without regard to their 'meaning'.

Yet, even if we clear Heidegger of crassly confusing the real identity and ownership of the shoes depicted in Van Gogh's painting, it can scarcely be denied that the section of the lecture where he leads up to a phenomenological description of the peasant woman's shoes is extremely confusing. As he switches back and forth between the shoes in the painting and the 'actual' shoes worn by an imaginary peasant woman, it is easy for the reader to become disoriented. Nevertheless, the production of this disorientation may itself be deliberate on Heidegger's part, and his procedure of oscillating between the painted and the actual shoes may be rhetorically intended to break the grip of the usual view in which we know in advance what is required for the thing to be accepted into the realm of knowable objects. It is, in other words, a deliberate exercise in defamiliarisation. But Heidegger's longer-term aims are not simply negative, since he breaks the spell of the usual view in order to make possible a different approach, one which would not determine in advance what it is for a thing to be a thing but would allow the thing itself to present itself to us as it is in its intuited figure.

If we were to concern ourselves exclusively with the painting, then we would find ourselves trapped within the prevailing canons of art criticism and aesthetics. If we were to concern ourselves solely with the shoes of the peasant woman we would never break out of a purely instrumental understanding of them as useful objects. Simply of itself the painting does not instruct us in how to regard the actual shoes, any more than Homer instructs us in the art of war or *Moby Dick* in the art of whaling. If we 'simply look at the empty, unused shoes as they merely stand there in the picture, we shall never discover what the equipmental being of the equipment in truth is' (PLT: 33).

'And yet –' Heidegger concludes baldly, offering no immediate explanation as to what this 'And yet –' might mean. Indeed, to be consistent, he cannot. As with the confrontation with the tree in blossom, we can only proceed by means of a leap, albeit a leap into what is most familiar, most everyday. And where does this leap take us? Into one of Heidegger's most celebrated pieces of phenomenological description.

Since Heidegger claims that phenomenological description answers in every detail to what is disclosed by the phenomenon, it follows that, like poetry, it cannot easily be précised. However, a couple of sentences illustrate both how Heidegger used the method and what he saw in the shoes.

> On the leather lie the dampness and richness of the soil. Under the shoes slides the loneliness of the field-path as evening falls. In the shoes vibrates the silent call of the earth, its quiet gift of the

ripening grain and its unexplained self-refusal in the fallow deso-
lation of the wintry field ... This equipment belongs to the *earth*,
and it is protected in the *world* of the peasant woman.

(PLT: 34)

Previously we heard Heidegger arguing that phenomenological
description, understood as 'accentuating articulation', arises out of
the categorial structure that is given in intuition itself. At first glance
there is nothing here that recalls anything like what we find in either
Aristotle's or Kant's list of categories. However, given Heidegger's
positioning of his own task in relation to that of the history of philosophy, this should not surprise us. For what we see here are in fact the
beginnings of a whole new schema of fundamental ontological categories, the first of which are *earth* and *world*.

In wearing the shoes, in living her life, the peasant woman is sure of
and inhabits her world without anything being missing from it. She
does not need either artists or philosophers to put her right about any
aspect of her world, to make it fuller or more spiritual. It is complete
in itself. But what the art-work does is to 'let us know what shoes are
in truth' (PLT: 35), i.e., it reveals them in their world. The painting,
then, is not to be evaluated in terms of its faithful imitation of any
particular pair of actual shoes, but rather by allowing us to see the
'equipmentality of equipment', the world of work figured in the
particular instance of the shoes.

What does Heidegger mean by this opaque formulation?

This does not become entirely clear in the first section of *Origin*,
where the discussion of the shoes takes place. It is, however, clarified
retrospectively, in the light of what Heidegger goes on to say about the
second work of art to which he devotes an extended discussion: the
Greek temple.

Again the thick, analytically accentuating articulation cannot
easily be paraphrased, and again what comes into view in terms of
categorial structures are those already encountered in the case of the
shoes: earth and world.

The temple, Heidegger says, 'first gives to things their look and to
men their outlook on themselves. This view remains open as long as
the work is a work, as long as the god has not fled from it' (PLT: 43).

In giving things their 'look' and men their 'outlook on themselves' the work 'sets up' a world (PLT: 44) or 'makes space for' a world (PLT: 45) by bringing it into the Open, revealing, laying bare, disclosing its structure.

Although it remains hard and perhaps even futile, to attempt any binding definition of what Heidegger means by 'world', several things are clear. The first, which follows from everything that has been said so far, is that the art-work does not predetermine the world in the way that, according to Heidegger, mathematics does. In 'setting-up' a world, the art-work is not imposing a projective enframing. Rather, it allows the world to come to appearance – not, of course, as 'mere' appearance but as the shining-forth, the phenomenalisation of what, in truth, it is. The second is that the cumulative metaphors (or more than metaphors?) of light, vision, shining forth and openness suggest that Heidegger does not want us to be thinking of a private, imaginary world, a fantasy world that might serve as a retreat for dreamers and romantics. It is, on the contrary, open and public, the world of a people, the Hellenes, or the Germans. Thirdly, and in close relation to the preceding two points, although 'world' in Heidegger's sense is something different from the world that science takes as its object it is not a world that is separable from materiality. On the contrary, materiality is even more necessary, even more present, than when we approach the world with regard to its equipmentality. I shall shortly return to this point, but before that one further comment about the relationship between work and world is in place.

The work does not bring the world into being. Van Gogh's painting did not create the life of peasants. But by showing us the *truth* of peasant shoes, Van Gogh enables us to see the world of the peasant, to have a sense for the meaning of peasant life, that is not revealed in the daily grind of living a peasant-like life. In this regard it could be said that there is both an analogy and a dis-analogy between the function of the work of art and the process of psychoanalysis. Both are concerned with bringing hidden truths out into the open. However, the truth revealed in analysis, even if – perhaps especially when – it is indeed the truth, is likely to be experienced by the patient as challenging or contradicting his own everyday understanding of himself and his world. If psychoanalysis is to save, it must first destroy. So too, perhaps, philosophy. But the way in which the work of art works is, according to Heidegger, very different: it is not hostile to that which it discloses, nor does it set itself up as offering an alternative explanation or interpretation to that which already prevails. It simply (but Heidegger is, of course, always insistent that the simple is always the most difficult) lets the world appear as it is, in its being.

But, perhaps once more in contrast to psychoanalysis and certainly in contrast to Newtonian science, the revelation of the world in the work of art does not and does not intend to bring *everything* out into the open. Integral to its revelation of the world is its acceptance that the life-world of the human subject is what it is only in relation to what is not luminous, what does not appear, what is preserved in darkness and is not available as a resource for use or as an object of knowledge. But, precisely because what is thus concealed is integral to the world and to the revelation of the world as world, this too is involved in the art-work. What we are talking about here is, in fact, nothing other than what Heidegger calls 'earth', the dark, ever unillumined ground on which the open space of world is set.

Thus, for example, earth is present in the stone out of which the temple is built.

> A stone presses downward and manifests its heaviness. But while this heaviness exerts an opposing pressure upon us it denies us any penetration into it. If we attempt such a penetration by breaking open the rock, it still does not display in its fragments anything inward that has not been disclosed. The stone has instantly withdrawn again into the same dull pressure and bulk of its fragments. If we try to lay hold of the stone's heaviness in another way, by placing the stone on a balance, we merely bring the heaviness into the form of a calculated weight. This perhaps very precise determination of the stone remains a number, but the weight's burden has escaped us ... The earth appears openly cleared as itself only when it is perceived and preserved as that which is by nature undisclosable ... The earth is essentially self-secluding.
>
> (PLT: 46–7)

The relationship between world and earth is, in human experience at least (and perhaps none of this makes any sense purely 'objectively', i.e., apart from the existential interest of human beings – no matter what Heidegger's reservations about humanism), both reciprocal but also conflictual. World struggles to free itself from earth, light from darkness – but earth absorbs world, drawing it back into the pre-conscious darkness from which it emerged. The precise state of balance between these conflicting forces determines the exact form of the world in any particular epoch. Perhaps in the 24-hour-a-day illumination of the contemporary city 'earth' may seem to have been finally vanquished. Perhaps – or perhaps we are simply unable to recognise the form that earth is taking for us today, excluded as it is from what is framed by the enframing gaze of technological rationality.

Earth and world, then, emerge as two of the fundamental terms of Heidegger's new categorial schema. As his thought develops they will be added to and further clarified, until he arrives at what he will call 'the fourfold' of earth, sky, gods and mortals. This fourfold offers Heidegger a way of envisaging beings that, he believes, is radically distinct from, though not absolutely unrelated to, the 'nature' of natural science whose laws are conformable to those of mathematics in such a way as to be altogether and entirely available for technological manipulation.

Strikingly, both art and the thing remain crucial to Heidegger's attempts to articulate the fourfold. Thus, in the 1950 lecture on 'the thing' he takes an everyday earthenware jug and embarks upon a phenomenological description that aims precisely to bring into view what 'never comes to light … never gets a hearing' (PLT: 170) in the scientific view: the thing in its thingness. Again, the following extracts aim to do no more than give a flavour of Heidegger's way of carrying out such a description. The jug, he says, is a hollow vessel, that takes what is poured into it and preserves it. However, the truth of the jug is only fully revealed when it is used for pouring.

> The twofold holding of the void rests on the outpouring. In the outpouring, the holding is authentically how it is. To pour from the jug is to give … The jug's jug-character consists in the poured

gift of the pouring out ... The giving of the outpouring can be a drink. The outpouring gives water, it gives wine to drink. The spring stays on in the water of the gift. In the spring the rock dwells, and in the rock dwells the dark slumber of the earth, which receives the rain and dew of the sky. In the water of the spring dwells the marriage of sky and earth. It stays in the wine given by the fruit of the vine, the fruit in which the earth's nourishment and the sky's sun are betrothed to one another ... In the jugness of the jug, sky and earth dwell. The gift of the pouring out is drink for mortals. It quenches their thirst. It refreshes their leisure. It enlivens their conviviality. But the jug's gift is also at times for consecration ... The outpouring is the libation poured out for the immortal gods. The gift of the outpouring as libation is the authentic gift. In giving the consecrated libation, the pouring jug occurs as the giving gift ... In the gift of the outpouring that is drink, mortals stay in their own way. In the gift of the outpouring that is a libation, the divinities stay in their own way ... In the gift of the outpouring earth and sky, divinities and mortals dwell *together all at once*. These four, at one because of what they themselves are, belong together. Preceding everything that is present, they are enfolded into a single fourfold.

(PLT: 172–3)

Are such passages, for all their extraordinary originality and force, testimony to the fact that Heidegger's concern with art and with the thingliness of things (and his desire to find a way of thinking that escapes the net of mathematical calculation) is, despite his protestations, mere poetic embellishment, a retreat into a private fantasy world after the failure of 1933? Or dare we assert that Heidegger is tentatively and provisionally adumbrating the first outlines of what might yet open a new path of thinking along which we might, collectively and not just singly, escape the wastelands of modernity and technology?

We are not yet in a position to answer such questions, since the work of art and the thing are not the only bases on which Heidegger attempts to think his way forward. For Heidegger's strategy is not simply the well-worn Romantic tactic of opposing art to science and tellurian values to the technological exploitation of the earth. Crucial here is the expansion of the initial insight into the thing that occurs when this insight is transposed into the medium of language that makes possible a history of thinking, and it is only in relation to this history and its present crisis that the full meaning of the thing comes into view.

We shall, as we must, return to the question of the status of the kind of invocations of the fourfold we hear in the meditation on the jugness of the jug. But we shall do so with the additional buttressing provided by a larger understanding of Heidegger's critical reading of the philosophical tradition, and, coming out of that, of the way in which he judges the most fundamental question facing humanity to be the question of Being: that is, the question as to what beings-as-a-whole, in their Being, i.e., the whole life-world of humanity, can mean for us today.

Chapter 5

Nietzsche

Heidegger's interpretation of Nietzsche was the most extensive of any of his rereadings of the history of philosophy. He gave a number of lectures and lecture series from the 1930s onwards on Nietzsche's thought as well as devoting much of the first part of *What is Called Thinking?* to him.

However, the importance of Heidegger's interpretation of Nietzsche is not simply a matter of quantity but has to do with the role that Heidegger ascribes to Nietzsche in the history of metaphysics. Arguably, the Nietzsche lectures were amongst the first fruits of Heidegger's 'turning', a view to which several aspects of the lectures give support. It is, for example, typical of the later Heidegger that his own thought is worked out in a very public dialogue with the tradition, whereas in *Being and Time* he wrote almost as if he was writing from scratch, reinventing philosophy on the basis of a pure phenomenological analysis of Dasein as we encounter it in the world. Of course, this is, at one level, a deception, since *Being and Time* involves a constant debate with Heidegger's sources. Nevertheless, the willingness to position his own thought by means of a critique of the tradition is, if not new, carried to new levels in the Nietzsche lectures. It is also striking that the lectures mirror another aspect of the turning, namely Heidegger's shift away from the supposedly subjectivist approach of *Being and Time* to an emphasis on the priority of Being. It is the core of Heidegger's criticism of Nietzsche that Nietzsche, above all other philosophers, constructed a metaphysics of pure subjectivity. And these lectures are also important in terms of Heidegger's relation to Nazism. In the famous interview 'Only a God Can Save Us' in *Der Spiegel*, given in 1966 but published on his death in 1976, Heidegger asserted that 'In 1936 I began the Nietzsche lectures. Anyone with ears to hear heard in these lectures a confrontation with National Socialism' (Wolin 1993: 101). He also claimed that the lectures were kept under surveillance by Party agents. In this connection it is important to remember that Nietzsche had very high prestige amongst Nazi ideologists. In his 1931 book *Nietzsche the Philosopher and Politician*, Alfred Baeumler, a leading Nazi philosopher, had offered an interpretation of Nietzsche that placed almost exclusive emphasis on Nietzsche's category of 'will to power' and had interpreted this in a biological sense. Both of these emphases, however, were to be contested in Heidegger's own lectures. Whereas Nazi Nietzscheans took Nietzsche at his word when he claimed to have 'overcome' the metaphysics and the morals of Judaeo-Christian tradition, Heidegger's own judgment on Nietzsche was that he was the last metaphysical thinker of the West and that (although this is no mean position) Nietzsche's thought is strictly a penultimate step in the history of ideas, since what is now required is to step, or rather to leap, out of the history of metaphysics into a new way of thinking. Nietzsche is not the paradigm we should seek to emulate, but the end of the line. In these respects we can see how Heidegger's critical view of Nietzsche does support his claim regarding the political significance of the lectures.

The various lectures and discussions of Nietzsche's work found over many years in Heidegger's work cover many different themes. They include often quite detailed readings of Nietzsche's own texts, but also involve bold rereadings of Plato, Descartes and other texts.

Now, although it would be perfectly feasible simply to set out what it was Heidegger found in Nietzsche, that is not how I aim to proceed in the present chapter. Rather, I want to look at these texts as throwing light on Heidegger's hermeneutical approach. Precisely because Nietzsche is the figure on whom he writes most extensively, his Nietzsche-related works provide perhaps the clearest exemplification of how Heidegger thought we should go about reading a philosophical text. In other words I shall be asking about the interpretative principles and directives that govern Heidegger's approach. Although some of these are peculiar to his reading of Nietzsche, the broad picture that they collectively offer is generally speaking paradigmatic for Heideggerian hermeneutics. However, the way in which Heidegger reads Nietzsche is inseparable from what he thinks he finds in him. The 'how' reveals the 'what' in such a way that an examination of Heidegger's method of reading Nietzsche will also take us a long way towards understanding his view of Nietzsche the thinker.

The hermeneutical principles and directives I have mentioned include both general principles and particular directives, and they also include both positive instructions as to how we should read Nietzsche and also negative instructions as to how not to read him. Taken together, these amount to a coherent if provocative hermeneutical strategy, and as we proceed we shall do well to take note of its strengths and weaknesses.

I shall begin, perhaps perversely, with the negative instructions: how not to read Nietzsche. Some of these can be understood fully only in the light of the overall picture, but they nevertheless give a preliminary taste of what is to come.

In accordance with what we have already seen of Heidegger's rhetoric of superiority and his commitment to challenging the usual, metaphysically dominated view, it is unsurprising that a number of these instructions concern the requirement that a genuinely philosophical approach should break loose from everyday ways of understanding great thinkers.

Thus, firstly, we must put behind us any desire to base our understanding on what we know of Nietzsche the man, or Nietzsche's personality (N 3: 4). That is particularly important in this case because of the way in which the early reception of Nietzsche's work took its lead from the critical perspective of George Brandes, a perspective which laid particular emphasis on the personality of the author, understood in its biographical, psychological and social dimensions, as determinative for the meaning of the work.

But, then, secondly, we must be sure that we are not seeing Nietzsche as a cause. We must neither celebrate, nor imitate, nor revile, nor exploit him (N 1: 4). Nor should we be motivated by the desire to refute him (WCT: 54). Precisely because of Nietzsche's closeness in time (to Heidegger's generation but also to us, at least relative to, e.g., Descartes and Plato), we must be beware of confusing Nietzsche's ideas with our own. On the other hand, if it is necessary to avoid a certain way of having Nietzsche as a contemporary, we must also be wary of the traps in certain kinds of historicising approaches. Historical correctness is not decisive in philosophy. For example, Kant's treatment of Plato and Aristotle rates pretty poorly as historical research, although, Heidegger says, Kant is one of the few thinkers to have really grasped and carried forward some of the problems at the heart of their work (N 3: 8).

Next comes a whole cluster of warnings against talking about Nietzsche in the manner of the 'idle talk' castigated in *Being and Time*. So, we will not find Nietzsche (Heidegger is, more precisely, talking about the superman at this point) 'in the places of remote-controlled public opinion and on the stock exchanges of the culture business' (WCT: 72). We must put aside 'common ideas and views' and desist from 'shouting'. We should not 'busy' ourselves with Nietzsche or approach him in a merely haphazard way. Nor should we succumb to what Nietzsche himself calls 'blinking', i.e., an approach in which we allow ourselves to be dazzled by the sheer glitter and sparkle of the surface of Nietzsche's text (WCT: 82–4).

Even if we are progressing beyond the truly vulgar, merely external approaches, however, there are further cautions we need to observe. These relate to 'versions' of Nietzsche, or of what is believed to be philosophical method, current in our time. Thus we must not categorise Nietzsche as a poet or 'poet-philosopher', or a philosopher of life (Heidegger is referring specifically to the movement in ideas known as *Lebensphilosophie*), nor yet as a psychological thinker (WCT: 89). These ways of categorising him may be proposed as ways of enhancing Nietzsche's reputation by opposing him to merely academic philosophy, but they are in fact ways of pre-emptively fore-closing the possibility of reading him as a philosopher. If such tactics inappropriately inflate Nietzsche's reputation, it is no less misleading to regard him as someone whose 'teaching' can be extracted from his work and summarised in an 'overall exposition' of his philosophy, and then commended or refuted (WCT: 52).

How, then, are we to read Nietzsche positively?

We could, perhaps, begin by considering a number of general points that may have a special resonance in the case of Nietzsche but that are also generally applicable across the field of philosophical hermeneutics.

The first is what is Heidegger's most fundamental hermeneutical principle, first laid down in *Being and Time* and never subsequently revoked. This is the principle of the hermeneutical circle. To understand what this means, we must first take note of the situation that Dasein, the human being as being-in-the-world exists understand-ingly, 'as understanding'. That is to say, we are never in the world in such a way that we have no understanding at all of where we are, what we are doing, what is happening to us or who we are. No matter how inchoate or primitive it may be – 'Me Tarzan, you Jane!' – our comportment is always guided by a certain understanding of ourselves and our situation. Most people most of the time don't reflect on this but simply take it for granted. However, interpretation does not involve the introduction of any new content into our lives. Interpretation does not begin with the discovery of some new fact about ourselves. Interpretation is essentially the unfolding of our tacit, lived self-understanding (Heidegger's term, *Auslegung*, literally means 'laying out'). Thus, 'In [interpretation] the understanding appropriates understandingly that which is understood by it. In inter-pretation, understanding does not become something different. It becomes itself' (BT: 188/148). In other words, and as Heidegger goes on to say, 'interpretation is grounded in *something we have in advance – in a fore-having*. As the appropriation of understanding, the inter-pretation operates in Being towards a totality of involvements which is already understood' (BT: 32/150), and this pre-understanding – also defined in terms of '*something we have in advance …a fore-sight*' and '*something we grasp in advance* … a *fore-conception*' (BT: 32/150) – always guides interpretation. The 'meaning' of a situation, an event, or a text is the articulation, the clarification, the laying-bare of that which we project upon it, i.e., what we see in it.

We can already see how this hermeneutical principle corresponds to central elements in Heidegger's account of phenomenology. The claim that the phenomenologist looks at what is given in perception with an eye to what shows itself as the matter of an accentuating articulation could be translated into the realm of interpretation virtually without further qualification. Indeed, already in *Being and Time* and increasingly in his middle and later work Heidegger is less and less concerned with the kind of questions concerning perception that occupied his earlier phenomenological endeavours and more concerned with what gives itself in language and, above all, in texts.

This account of interpretation as the unfolding of what is given in the pre-understanding may seem extraordinarily subjective, since there seems to be no reason for the pre-understanding of the interpreter to be challenged or constrained by anything external. This objection, however, overlooks the way in which Heidegger here presupposes the view of Dasein as being-in-the-world, i.e., Dasein is not the thinking Cartesian ego but the concrete being existing in the world and always already involved with its human and non-human environment. In terms of Heidegger's understanding of phenomenology, intuition is not conceived as a subjective mental event but as a datum in which self and world are linked in a particular and concrete manner. What matters is to understand what is given in, with and under the occurrence of intuition, not how to think past it to things-in-themselves. The aim is not to get beyond what is given, but to get really into it.

Similarly, against the charge that he has locked himself into a vicious circle such that he makes interpretation incapable of ever learning anything really new, Heidegger ripostes that '[A] definite ideal of knowledge … is itself only a subspecies of understanding … What is decisive is not to get out of the circle but to come into it in the right way' (BT: 32/153). Nevertheless, we should not simply take Heidegger at his word. Thus, although he often speaks of his interpretative engagement with the thinkers of the past as a dialogue (e.g.,

WCT: 51, 55), it has seemed to many readers to be more like a mono-logue in which Heidegger talks to Heidegger, whilst the text itself is reduced to the status of a mere occasion or pretext.[1] In the light of this it might prove a useful hermeneutical rule for Heidegger readers that they should stay alert to the question as to whether or how far in any particular case Heidegger is really engaging with what is given by his chosen text, as against projecting his own 'pre-understanding' onto it. (This remark is, I should emphasise, intended as a genuine question, and not as a conclusive mark 'against' Heidegger.)

Nietzsche, then (or any text, understanding 'text' here in the widest sense as any cultural product) will only speak to us if our questioning of his work is appropriately shaped by our own genuinely *existentiell*, pre-philosophical possibilities and questions, by what we bring to the text from our time and our context.

The second point, and one that is absolutely central to Heidegger's reading of Nietzsche, is that a genuine, or what Heidegger calls an 'essential', thinker is one of 'those exceptional human beings who are destined to think one single thought, a thought that is always "about" *beings as a whole*. Each thinker thinks only one *single* thought' (N3: 4).[2] In this regard the essential thinker operates very differently from the scientific or academic researcher. 'The researcher needs constantly new discoveries and inspirations, else science will bog down and fall into error' (WCT: 50). The thinker does not need to convert his ideas into 'much-prized "reality"' (N 3: 4) and aspires neither to 'renown' nor 'impact'. Great thinkers are often known to history simply on the basis of a single saying – a comment that illuminates Heidegger's own penchant for speaking of 'the word of Nietzsche' or 'the word of Heraclitus', etc. The interpreter's aim, then, is to identify this single thought, this 'word'.

It is important to realise that the hermeneutical principles being expounded here are not linked like mere beads on a string but have an accumulative force. Thus, the claim that each essential thinker thinks only a single thought, put together with the principle of the hermeneutical circle, issues in the recognition that if we are to be capable of understanding the essential thinker our own thought must stand in the power of a single thought. Indeed, we might even infer that, insofar as the essential thinkers belong in a single history of mutual interpretation, the whole history of philosophy is the history of a single thought. This may seem like a bold, perhaps even a bizarre idea. However, there is a sense in which this is just what Heidegger does claim, and that the single thought of the thinker Nietzsche is precisely the thought in which this whole history is gathered into a single, decisive point. This is obviously not a claim that can be left unchallenged. Nor can we do away with the problem by noting (as is correct) that an analogous assumption pervades German philosophy from Hegel onwards (including Nietzsche). For if it is already somewhat daring to define an essential thinker as someone who has but one essential thought (and after all, Heidegger himself listed *four* fundamental doctrines in relation to Nietzsche: will to power, nihilism, eternal recurrence and the superman), how much more rash to ascribe unity to something as large and complex as the Western philosophical tradition. Isn't Heidegger's procedure here arbitrary, a case of corner-cutting on a colossal scale?

Perhaps it would be difficult to disprove the charge entirely, but we might borrow a reflection from Kant in support of Heidegger's claim. In his *Critique of Pure Reason* Kant argued that one of the a priori synthetic ideas which it is necessary for us to assume in all thinking, but which can never be demonstrated to be true, is the idea of the unity of the world. Just imagine what it would be like if we did not make this assumption. If we did not presuppose that what presented itself to us in experience was part of a single, coherent system, then we would continually have to negotiate the possibility that at any moment anything might happen, that the prevailing laws of nature might suddenly be suspended and new laws come into operation. Life would be like sliding from one of an infinite number of possible universes into another. Heidegger's scale is somewhat smaller, but something analogous applies here too. For even if the history of philosophy contains many diverse elements, elements that are not simply reducible to each other, if we regard that history as constituting a unified field of enquiry, then we have to assume that it does hang together in some kind of unity. If it did not, how could we be so confident in knowing that, for example, Plato belongs to the history of philosophy but Charles Dickens does not? Even if we are unable to define that unity in advance, and even if we are prepared to leave the precise boundaries undefined, the assumption that there is a unity is, I suggest, one that any account of the history of philosophy must make. Otherwise what we are dealing with will simply fragment ceaselessly in our hands. Enquiry *is* guided by the projection of a unified field, although, of course, it doesn't follow that Heidegger's own understanding of this unity is correct.

At a more individual level, the assertion that each essential thinker thinks only a single thought might seem to open the door to any and every philosophical Quixote. Does it mean that to become a philosopher all we need do is go off and think up a novel thought?

Heidegger, at least, would not allow this, for not any thought qualifies as 'essential' in his sense. How, then, are we to recognise an 'essential' thought? Genuine thinking, according to Heidegger, '*takes its way* already *within* the total relation of Being and man's nature, or else it is not thinking at all' (WCT: 80). In other words, the crank whose single thought is, say, that Kierkegaard has been unjustly marginalised by the community of Anglo-American philosophers, and whose life work is devoted to making them realise that Kierkegaard is, after all, a genuine philosopher in their terms, or the enthusiast who wants to demonstrate to philosophers that their supposed freedom from prejudice is nothing but an unexamined prejudice against the theological sources of philosophy – neither of these could count as an essential thinker in Heidegger's sense. Their arguments may well merit consideration at the bar of scientific, historical, psychological, social, epistemological or logical reason. But the single thought of an essential thinker does not concern any such arbitrary or isolated point. For essential thinking is oriented towards beings-as-a-whole. Beings-as-a-whole are the fundamental and exclusive concern of the essential thinker. And this gives us a third hermeneutical principle: that interpretation, too, must seek to elucidate the meaning of beings-as-a-whole.

Fourthly, and as a further refinement of the preceding points, Heidegger also claims that the essential thinker is not concerned with beings-as-a-whole simply as the object of disinterested, theoretical speculation, as if it were a matter of assigning beings-as-a-whole to their appropriate place in some already assured conceptual or categorial schema. Beings-as-a-whole are not just lying there waiting to be

discovered, but our comportment towards them is a matter of decision. The essential thinker, therefore, is one 'whose whole thought
thinks in the direction of a single, supreme decision' (N 3: 5). With
specific regard to Nietzsche, Heidegger formulates this decision in the
following terms: 'Is the man of today in his metaphysical nature
prepared to assume dominion over the earth as a whole?' (WCT: 65).

This leads, fifthly, to a further distinction between the thinker and
the researcher. For the thinker is not concerned with the correct definition of beings-as-a-whole or with the best theoretical model by
which to think them, but, on the contrary, with bringing to the fore
'the *questionableness* of beings as a whole' (N 3: 6). This is not simply
a by-product of the thinker's task, but is the very point of his enquiry,
so that by disclosing the questionableness of beings-as-a-whole he
opens a space within which genuine decision can occur. In other
words, if beings-as-a-whole are thought of under the rubric 'nature'
and nature is conceived as governed according to predetermined laws,
whether they are the laws of God or of science, no final significance
can be attached to human decisions, since the scope of our decisions is
constrained on all sides by law. If, on the other hand, the essential
nature of beings-as-a-whole is itself brought into question, then our
relation to that nature is itself open to question and our own way of
deciding the question becomes possible, relevant, urgent and important. To discover this questionableness for ourselves, through
dialogue with the essential thinkers, is, then, a further aim of
hermeneutical philosophy.

Sixthly, a further aspect of this questionableness is that the
meaning of beings-as-a-whole at which the thinker and his interpreter
aim is never going to be reducible to a single general principle, something that can be clearly defined and delimited. On the contrary it will
be 'inexhaustible' (WCT: 77). The 'multiplicity of possible meanings
is the element in which all thought must move in order to be strict
thought' (WCT: 51). This might at first glance seem to go against the
requirement that what we are after is a single thought. However, the
contradiction would itself arise from misconceiving what Heidegger
means by 'thought' as the content of single, simple proposition, i.e.,
'the thought that x'. Thought, here, is rather being thought of as an
active, questioning process of unconcealing.

Again, we can see a clear interconnection between this 'multiplicity of possible meanings' and the claim that the thinker's task is not that of mere theoretical, scientific knowledge but takes the form of a decision, since in face of this multiplicity we cannot avoid deciding which should be given priority.

Seventhly, Heidegger, in this respect not unlike Hegel, criticises the limitations of representational thinking. Such thinking, he says, is condemned to 'freeze in the finality of ... *rigor mortis*' (WCT: 103). Why? Because in binding my thought to a specific representation, whether to a sensuously determined 'image' or (and here Heidegger would depart from Hegel) to the kind of abstract representation encountered in philosophical concepts, I am giving it a fixity that necessarily belies the temporality that utterly permeates the human way of being-in-the-world and from which thinking itself cannot be excepted.

Putting this another way, we might say that it is a requirement of essential thinking (and interpretation) that it do justice to time. This is crucial, and I shall return to the issue of Nietzsche and temporality below.

A further, eighth, point arising from this concerns a particular and, in the history of philosophy, a particularly important mode of representation: writing. In an image that, admittedly, broaches issues that go beyond those we are considering here, Heidegger explains how Socrates is to be regarded as 'the purest thinker of the West' (WCT: 17). What does this mean, and how does it relate to the task of interpretation?

Thinking, Heidegger is arguing, is called for or provoked by the situation that that about which we most need to think is constantly withdrawing itself from us. This withdrawal leaves a vacuum that, like the sudden loss of atmospheric pressure, creates a draught, a wind blowing through and shaking the presumed solidity of the over-familiar everyday world. 'All through his life,' writes Heidegger,

> Socrates did nothing else than place himself in this draft, this current, and maintain himself in it. This is why he is the purest thinker of the West. This is why he wrote nothing. For anyone who begins to write out of thoughtfulness must inevitably be like

those people who run to seek refuge from any draft too strong for them. An as yet hidden history still keeps the secret why all great Western thinkers after Socrates, with all their greatness, had to be such fugitives.

(WCT: 17)

Thinking, then, has an inherently problematic relation to written texts, something that must inevitably colour our interpretative approach to the written texts in which the thinker's thought is recorded. The letter killeth – or at least renders the path of thought enigmatic. This comment also relates back to the strictures Heidegger places on a purely historical or summarising approach to philosophy.

All that has been written here about the characteristics of the thinker and his thought has been with a view to considering Heidegger's understanding of the task of interpretation. We have learned that interpretation will only deserve to be taken seriously when it brings us into the orbit of the single thought of the essential thinker and enables us to encounter that thought in such a way as to become open to the decision it demands of us concerning our comportment towards beings-as-a-whole. But in setting out Heidegger's prescriptions for going about this, it has become clear that he is not offering anything like a method in any conventional sense. On the contrary – and this is a further, ninth principle of Heideggerian hermeneutics – we can only arrive at the point of understanding the thought of an essential thinker on the basis of a leap: 'the leap alone takes us into the neighbourhood where thinking resides' (WCT: 12). We may recall the leap that brought us into the encounter with the tree in blossom, a face-to-face encounter in which each is present to the other as what it is. This encounter is no mere 'idea' but an event. 'Let us stop here for a moment, as we would to catch our breath before and after a leap. For that is what we *are* now, men who have leapt, out of the familiar realm of science and even … out of the realm of philosophy' (WCT: 41). But, it will be recalled, this leap does not hurl us into some weird existentialist abyss, it simply returns us to 'the soil on which we really stand'.

Applying this to the question of interpretation, we may say that the leap of interpretative understanding is not the outcome of some new information about, e.g., the tree. It is not the result of finding the missing piece of the jigsaw, the clue that led us to the conclusion of our research. Rather it is a leap out of the scientific, academic approach into a direct encounter with the meaning of the text. Yet, this is not the discovery of some occult meaning – Nietzsche's 'secret note' – but, in accordance with the principle of the hermeneutical circle, the disclosure of what has really guided our questioning all along, the soil on which we already stood. Consequently, under-standing Nietzsche does not depend on the exhaustiveness of our knowledge of Nietzsche's texts or Nietzsche's sources or the history of the reception of Nietzsche's ideas. Perhaps we must read *some* Nietzsche before we can claim to understand him (though Heidegger is never exactly clear on this!), but, however limited or extensive our knowledge, we have to be ready to leap into the thought that is both given by the text and yet (remembering the problematisation of writing) concealed by it.

Grammar, context, connotation, denotation, signification and reference, singly and collectively, fall short of what is decisive in the written text of an essential thinker. Everything depends, says Heidegger (in what we may take as a tenth hermeneutical principle), on the note or tone of the saying. It is not *what* is asserted, not the propositional content of the text that counts, but what is *said* in it (WCT: 37). And if we are to hear what is said in it, then we must learn not just to read but to listen, to hear how the thinker thinks what is expressed, but also distorted, in the oral or written media of represen-tation.

With this we come to what is perhaps the most demanding – and, at first glance, most peculiar – of all of Heidegger's principles of inter-pretation. This is that we not only seek to attend to the how, the tone or note of essential thought, concealed as that is by representation, but also endeavour to hear 'what is unthought' in it, since it is in this *unthought* that the true depth and uniqueness of a thinker is to be found. 'The more original the thinking, the richer will be what is unthought in it. The unthought is the greatest gift that thinking can bestow' (WCT: 76).

We might begin to understand what Heidegger is saying here by referring back to his description of Socrates as the purest thinker of the West because of the way in which Socrates stood constantly in the current of thinking, a current produced by the withdrawal of what Socrates sought to think. Thought is, in other words, always led or lured on by what it has not been able to pin down. The knowledge that a train-spotter craves, a sighting, numbered and dated in a book, can indeed be exhaustively 'known', since it is no more than the accumulation of information. Real thinking, however, is always concerned with what resists easy representation, articulation and expression. Nor do we need to see anything intrinsically mystifying in this. Even the kind of academic research that Heidegger continually sniffs at is typically directed towards what is not yet known, proven or shown. Indeed, despite the provocative way in which he puts it, can we not hear Heidegger as simply restating the Aristotelian principle that philosophy begins in *thaumazein*: wonder, astonishment, puzzlement?

This is not to belittle his claim, to reduce it to the 'mere' regurgitation of an entirely conventional and somewhat empty truism. It is simply to warn against dismissing it out of hand. But having accepted the possibility that Heidegger is not being entirely vacuous, we must then face the challenge of this 'unthought', for, above all with regard to the interpretation of an essential thinker, it has all the gravity of any essential thought concerned with our relation to beings-as-a-whole, the utter questionableness of that concern and the unique way in which this concern is figured by the thinker.

The twelfth and final general principle of interpretation builds on but goes one step beyond stipulating the unthought as the matter to be interpreted. Since it has not itself been expressly thought by the thinker (Nietzsche) we are seeking to interpret, what is to be thought is not in the power of the thinker himself. What we are really pursuing, then, is not him, not this thinker, not his articulated thought, but what he didn't think, what, in withdrawing from him, called upon him to think. Thought is not the possession of even the most essential thinker, but is the gift of Being itself, i.e., it is possible only on the basis of a self-imparting of Being in its withdrawal from our immediate apprehension.

Perhaps it is no wonder, therefore, that in *What is Called Thinking?* Heidegger continually repeats the refrain that we are still not thinking. Indeed, if thinking can occur only as the gift of Being, is thinking a human possibility at all? Is the understanding of an essential thinker an achievable task?

In case this seems too discouraging, however, we may once more have recourse to the hermeneutical circle. For applying this principle in the present case would mean that we can indeed experience thinking as the gift of Being *if* we are already, in our pre-understanding, attentive to the call of Being (or, to put it less anthropomorphically, *if* the question of Being already belongs within the circle of our pre-philosophical, pre-ontological concerns). Guided by that pre-understanding, we may be led to a final understanding of the essential thinker as a witness to the destining of Being, its self-withholding and self-bestowing, coming from beyond him yet echoing within the written record of his thought.

We now turn to those hermeneutical principles that are specific to Heidegger's reading of Nietzsche. Some of these may be regarded as particular applications of the more general principles, whilst others relate to issues that are unique to Nietzsche's work or to the reception of that work (although even the former inevitably acquire a distinctive colour or tone when applied to Nietzsche). We have also to remember that, in the spirit of true hermeneutical circularity, the general principles are only clarified in the course of the labour of interpretation itself.

Bearing in mind the spirit of the cautionary remarks issued by Heidegger in relation to, e.g., a merely biographical or psychological approach to the subject, we may note the following comment found in Heidegger's 1961 preface to the published version of the Nietzsche lectures.

'Nietzsche' – the name of the thinker stands as the title for the *matter* of his thinking. The matter, the point in question, is in itself a confrontation. To let our thinking enter into the matter, to prepare our thinking for it – these goals determined the contents of the present publication.

(N 1: xxxix)

Can we, in a preliminary way, state how our reading should be directed in order to uncover this matter? What is it we are looking for in reading Nietzsche?

The general trajectory of Heidegger's own Nietzsche-interpretation – remembering that with Nietzsche, as with any essential thinker, the long-term aim is to hear that which is unsaid and even unthought in Nietzsche's sole decisive thought – is determined by his repeated claim that, over against those readings that would reduce Nietzsche to a poet, a philosopher of life or a Social Darwinist, Nietzsche is fundamentally a metaphysical thinker. He is this first and foremost by virtue of the fact that it is Nietzsche who decisively puts the question as to whether humanity as we know it is morally prepared to assume dominion of the planet. In asking this question in the way that he does, Nietzsche speaks the language of a two-thousand-year tradition (WCT: 75),[3] but he does not simply continue that tradition. 'Nietzsche' is not one more name in an open-ended, ongoing history but the name for a matter to be thought in which 'all the themes of Western thought ... fatefully gather together' (WCT: 51). Nietzsche is 'the *last metaphysician* of the West. The age whose consummation unfolds in his thought, the modern age, is a final age' (N 3: 8, cf. N 1: 4).

Here, then, we have the explanation for Heidegger's extensive engagement with Nietzsche: that, perhaps in the spirit of Hegel's invocation of the Owl of Minerva (goddess of wisdom), who flies only at dusk, Nietzsche provides a final standpoint from which we can look back over the whole preceding history of Western metaphysics and, for the first time, understand what has really been going on.

However, it is not as if the great tradition of philosophy simply came to a shuddering halt in Nietzsche's thought. Nietzsche is not simply 'the end of the line'. His thinking marks the end of philosophy in such a way as also, if understood aright, to open up the prospect of something radically new. Nietzsche is not just the last metaphysician of the West, he is also a transitional figure, a duality prophesied by Zarathustra himself, who speaks of his descent into the world and into the clamorous throng of the market-place as a going-down (*Untergang*, also meaning 'downfall' or 'decline' as in Spengler's *Decline of the West*) and a transition (*Übergang*, literally a going-across). Nietzsche himself (i.e., his thought), Heidegger says, is the 'transition from the preparatory phase of the modern age ... to the beginning of its consummation' (N 3: 6).

If Nietzsche is in this way a transitional thinker, and if in our attempt to understand him we are aiming beyond Nietzsche's own thought to that unthought aporia that stimulated and provoked Nietzsche himself into thinking, then we will not want to stop at the point at which Nietzsche himself arrived, i.e., the end-point of metaphysics. Having come to see the way in which Nietzsche brought about the end of metaphysics, we will also need to find in or through him that which points towards the advent of something new. Having found Nietzsche, says Heidegger, quoting Nietzsche's last letter to Brandes, the task will be to lose him – though this, he adds will prove no easy task. In any case, we have to be assured in our finding, before we can set about losing. We must first encounter Nietzsche's thought if we are to lose it (WCT: 51–3).

'Nietzsche', i.e., the matter of his thought, is, of course, only available to us through his books. Of these books it is above all the notes published posthumously under the title *The Will to Power* that are the chief object of Heidegger's interest. The history of the transmission of these notes and their subsequent publication in a selection and an order that was not Nietzsche's own, raises major critical issues. Heidegger, however, does not enter into the details of philological or text-critical debate, although he is aware that at many points his interpretation does raise philological questions. Heidegger is, after all, in pursuit of Nietzsche's sole thought, and, ultimately, of that which Nietzsche himself neither said nor thought in this sole thought. Interpretation, thus conceived, takes precedence over any narrowly philological considerations. With specific reference to *The Will to Power* Heidegger wrote that the 'lack of completion could only mean that the inner form of [Nietzsche's] unique thought was denied the thinker – yet perhaps it was not denied at all; perhaps the failure lies only with those who blocked the path with hasty and altogether timely interpretations, with the all-too-easy and all-too-corrupting superciliousness of all epigones' (N 3: 12).

As in the case of the encounter with the tree in blossom, interpretation does not wait upon scientific results, but leaps into the midst of what is already familiar, something that the fragmentary and incomplete nature of the text does not prohibit but maybe even facilitates:

'these paths and trains and leaps of thought' (N 3: 13) are more than sufficient to provoke us to think again what was thought in them, and, of course, to think beyond them.

Can we then say what Nietzsche's sole thought was?

It is in the first instance, Heidegger says, will to power, but he immediately adds that will to power cannot be separated from the doctrine of eternal recurrence – 'eternal recurrence is of necessity included in the thought of will to power', both doctrines 'say *the same* and think the *same* fundamental characteristic of beings as a whole' (N 3: 10). The conjunction of these two doctrines constitutes the centre of gravity of Nietzsche's thought, and their unity is to be found in the fact that, for Nietzsche, they are both thought in the spirit of and from the standpoint of his project of a revaluation of all values. If we do not grasp this 'then we will never grasp Nietzsche's philosophy. And we will comprehend nothing of the twentieth century and of the centuries to come, nothing of our own metaphysical task' (N1: 17). For all the apparent arbitrariness and, in the case of eternal recurrence, their superficially mythological form, what Nietzsche expresses in them is the same as what is expressed in, for example, Descartes' scientific humanism: the ambition of the human subject to stamp Becoming, a world in flux, with the character of Being, or permanence (N 2: 201–2). To objectify the world in such a way that it is reliably knowable and manipulable, and that what is known will always recur in the same predictable form. It may sound poetic or mythical, but 'eternal recurrence' expresses precisely the requirement of predictability that Cartesian science places upon the world, enframing it as material for technological management.[4]

It is perhaps almost superfluous to point out that such a strong and forceful reading is inevitably controversial, within and beyond the community of Nietzsche scholars. Many philosophers (and, for that matter, many who would like to advance Nietzsche's cause by seeing him as primarily a kind of poet) would take issue with Heidegger's claim that Nietzsche is first and foremost a metaphysical thinker. Even if that designation is, in some sense, accepted, it remains to be decided whether Heidegger's specific characterisation of Nietzsche's metaphysics is fitting, or whether the particular doctrines he makes the focus of his interpretation have the kind of centrality or the meaning that he claims for them. Instead of entering into these debates, I shall focus on an issue that goes right to the heart of what Heidegger regards as the core of Nietzsche's revaluative project, the critique of the spirit of revenge (*ressentiment*). I do so because, in the way that Heidegger deals with it, it is especially fruitful for understanding what, according to Heidegger, it means to read Nietzsche and, by implication, what it takes to be a good reader of philosophical texts.

Heidegger discusses the issue in *What is Called Thinking?* in the light of *Thus Spoke Zarathustra*, Part Two, Section Three: 'On Deliverance (or Redemption)'. Here the spirit of revenge is said by Zarathustra to have been 'the subject of man's best reflection', i.e., the hitherto prevailing characteristic of philosophical thought. To be delivered from this spirit of revenge, Zarathustra says elsewhere, would consequently be 'the bridge to the highest hope ... a rainbow after long storms' (WT: 85). It would, in terms of earlier comments, be a way of transition, of moving over from the end of metaphysics to the beginning of whatever lies beyond the metaphysical.

But what is revenge? It is, in Zarathustra's most succinct formulation, 'the will's revulsion against time and its "It was"' (WCT: 93).

Remembering Heidegger's warnings against biographical or psychologising readings, this is not a therapeutic hint as to how to become kinder, more generous, more magnanimous human beings, but a metaphysical issue, an issue for thought, concerning thought and, as such, concerning an essential decision regarding beings-as-a-whole. Will, the will that experiences revulsion against 'time and its "It was"', is not my arbitrary individual will, what I wish for myself. '"Will" and "willing" are the name of the Being of beings as a whole' (WCT: 95).

Putting it very broadly, Heidegger's point is that it is a fundamental assumption of the metaphysical tradition that beings-as-a-whole, and therefore each being in particular when it is thought with regard to its Being, to its place and state within the whole ensemble of beings, is thought in such a way as to detemporalise it, to cut out its thoroughgoing transiency. More precisely, 'The revulsion of revenge is not against the mere passing of time, but against the time that makes the passing pass away in the past, against the " It was"' (WCT: 103). What this means is that in the experience of revulsion humanity experiences itself as subject to determination by the past, as constrained by a frozen 'fixed rigidity', a past in which temporality has congealed in such a way that, to borrow a formulation of Kierkegaard, it has become 'more necessary than the future' (WCT: 104). What I am – my essence, the kind of being I am, we are – is determined by my history, by what I have been, or by the way in which I became what I am. This history in turn determines the range of future possibilities now available to me.

Continuing to bear in mind that this is not conceived here by Heidegger (nor, according to Heidegger, by Nietzsche) as a merely psychological or moral issue (as it is for Christian thinkers like Kierkegaard or Heidegger's one-time colleague Bultmann[5]), what is at issue is a defining characteristic of the prevailing metaphysical way of forming ideas (WCT: 55), namely, 'ideational or representative thinking' (WCT: 64).

Thus far, we may say, Heidegger is aiming to think *with* Nietzsche, but we are rapidly reaching the point at which we will need to think beyond Nietzsche, to hear what is unsaid or unthought in Nietzsche's words and, in the light of that, to understand how Nietzsche's explicit, written thought distorts or falls short of its own intention to surpass metaphysics.

Nietzsche's procedure at this point is to invoke eternal recurrence. For eternal recurrence gives the assurance that the past is not simply frozen past-ness. If all things recur, then 'It was' is also an 'It will be', and, as futural, can be the object of a volitional act, the future that I choose for myself, so that, turning once more to the past and envisaging the 'It will be' as an 'It was', I can say 'I willed it thus'. In such a way the doctrine of eternal recurrence gives the will – humanity in its decision concerning the meaning of beings-as-a-whole – the possibility to understand itself as free and thus as the ground of its own being: 'the will which wills itself eternally as the eternal recurrence of the same' (WCT: 107).

But at this point Heidegger breaks off. Nietzsche's thought does not, after all, provide final illumination, neither for us as Nietzsche's readers, nor for Nietzsche himself. This 'high point' of Nietzsche's thought 'remains wrapped in thick clouds', 'in a darkness from which even Nietzsche had to shrink back into error', or, less dramatically, '[Nietzsche's] various attempts to demonstrate that the eternal recurrence of the same was the Being of all becoming led him curiously astray' (WCT: 108; cf. N 4: 199).

Nietzsche is the last thinker of metaphysics, but he does not think the thought that is needed if we are to discover a way forward, a new beginning for philosophy. That his theory of eternal recurrence led him into a cul-de-sac and entangled him in confusing cosmological speculations does not so much demonstrate our superiority, however, as underline the extreme difficulty of finding or making that new beginning. Thus 'Nietzsche's attempt to think the Being of beings makes it … clear … that all thinking, that is relatedness to being, is still difficult' (WCT: 109–10).

We may appear to have lost sight of our intention to keep to the exposition of Heidegger's hermeneutical principles and to have wandered into the field of substantive questions in Heidegger's Nietzsche interpretation. Yet in the last resort this is an artificial distinction, for interpretation itself means trying to think the matter to be interpreted. In any case, Heidegger's reflections on the spirit of revenge have a directly hermeneutical application. For to read Nietzsche himself (or any major figure of the tradition) without ourselves being subjected to the spirit of revenge would, as Heidegger understands it, be to read him as a contemporary. Liberated from the spirit of revenge, the thinker is no longer a mere figure of history, trapped in the *rigor mortis* of the past, the object of antiquarian curiosity. His 'It was' has the potential to become our 'It will be', to open up possibilities for our own thinking. Accordingly, the community of essential thinkers converses in a time that is not that of everyday, historical time.[6] Heidegger's aspiration as an interpreter of Nietzsche is not simply to be able to say who Nietzsche was in his own lifetime, or who he is for us today, but who he will be (N 3: 3). Who he is for us today is already saturated by the everyday popular and academic talk about Nietzsche the man and the historical figure. Who he will be remains to be decided, and that decision is itself the business of interpretation.

Consequently, interpretation is not a matter of making (in this case) Nietzsche 'relevant' to us by coming up with a reading that answers to the questions of our age. It is precisely in order to liberate Nietzsche from the requirement to be timely, the prophet whose time has come, that we allow him to think and to speak in and out of his own time, for, freed from the spirit of revenge and its implicit fear of time, letting Nietzsche be in his own time no longer means losing him for ours: the difference between his time and ours is no longer experienced as injuring our freedom, nor yet as excluding Nietzsche from our future. In this regard, and given the status of Nietzsche amongst Nazi ideologists (i.e., as the most 'timely' of philosophers), we can see a further element of how these lectures involve an implicit critique of Nazi thought and develop the framework of Heidegger's critique of technology.

We have heard Heidegger say that this is difficult. No wonder that he concurs with Nietzsche in the judgment that the philosopher is and should be 'a rare plant' (N 3: 3). Nevertheless, philosophers, genuine thinkers, are needed in 'times of great danger', times when time itself accelerates, and philosophers, together with artists, may 'assume the place of the dwindling *mythos*' (N 1: 3). For when time itself accelerates we are more than usually likely to succumb to anguish concerning time and to fall under the spirit of revenge, to seek fixity and order. By taking upon itself the slow, difficult burden of interpretation, thinking frees itself from the tyranny of time, and opens up the trans-historical time of authentic thinking.

Throughout this consideration of Heidegger's Nietzsche we have been accompanied by Heidegger's mantra that the essential thinker thinks only one thought and that, consequently, the dialogue of essential thinkers (including the dialogue of Heidegger with Nietzsche) is in truth a monologue, and the history of philosophy the unfolding of a single thought. But what, then, does it mean to say that this history is coming to an end? That we must reach beyond what Nietzsche, the thinker who thought the one single thought of metaphysics most decisively, thought into what neither he nor the tradition itself thought or could think? Is such a venture a complete leap in the dark?

Heidegger thinks not, for if the dawn and subsequent history of metaphysics represents the unconcealment of a single thought, a single truth, history has recorded, in an appropriately enigmatic and fragmentary way, the original occurrence of that unconcealment. In the history of the earliest thinking of Greek philosophy we may look for hints as to how to think otherwise than metaphysically, and, as we aspire to freedom from the spirit of revenge, find in that interpretative engagement with the past the possibility of a new future for thinking.

Chapter 6

The first and second beginnings of philosophy

The return to the first beginning

We have encountered several hints as to what led Heidegger to the study of the Presocratics. Let us now try to pull together the various threads of the complex network of philosophical motivations that generated this, one of the most characteristic features of the later Heidegger. This will, inevitably, mean recapitulating some points we have already considered, but locating them specifically in relation to what Heidegger understood as a return to the first beginnings of philosophy.

As Heidegger tells the tale, the history of metaphysics finds its consummate philosophical expression in Nietzsche and its consummate practical expression in planetary technology. Leaving to one side the question as to whether this situation is sustainable in environmental terms, we have seen that it constitutes a danger to thinking, insofar as an unholy alliance of scientific-technological discourse, the levelling jargon of the media and the technicisation of philosophy itself obliterates the original task of thinking, namely, the thinking of Being. So complete is this obliteration that we have to face the most uncomfortable and thought-provoking fact that we are not yet even thinking about it. But if we are not thinking, and do not even know what it might mean to think, how can we ever begin to do so – or begin to do so again, assuming that thinking was something that happened once, before it was obliterated by the shadow of metaphysics? Perhaps the encounter with the work of art or with the thing can jolt us into an awareness of possibilities of thinking other than those to which metaphysics-technology has accustomed us. Perhaps the reading of the works of essential thinkers can point us towards what needs to be thought. Perhaps, if we had the courage for it, we could just leap out of our conceptualising habits onto the soil where, in truth, we already are. Indeed, unless we are prepared to leap, it seems that neither art nor things nor philosophers can help us.

But what determines whether such leaps occur? Is it just a matter of chance if an individual realises the possibility of breaking out of the metaphysical mind-set and reinaugurating a time of thought? Certainly, the task of thinking cannot happen without the individual, yet, as we have seen at many points, the contemporary planetary hege-mony of technology is not the result of a haphazard sequence of brilliant individual inventions and discoveries but the outcome of an original destining of Being. The task of thinking individualises, since we can each of us only ever think for ourselves. Perhaps it individu-alises even more than the confrontation with mortality. And perhaps these two are inextricably bound together. But thinking individualises only on the basis of and in relation to the history in which we partici-pate. From Plato to Nietzsche the history of Western thought has been the development and clarification of one single way of conceiving the Being of beings, and if we are in any sense to 'over-come' this history, we can do so only in the light of another destining on the part of Being, a self-disclosure of Being that calls upon thought to re-shape itself from the ground up. We cannot simply drop out of the world of metaphysics, and even if we try to do so we will probably find that our so-called 'overcoming' of metaphysics is but one more twist in the metaphysical tale. So it was for Nietzsche; why should we expect to do better? But if the overcoming of metaphysics is not a task for any individual genius, Heidegger does not anticipate some kind of public, global revelation of post-metaphysical truth, some new 'Law' of thinking flashed around the earth and unifying humanity in a new paradigm. In this regard he takes issue with his friend Ernst Jünger's image of nihilism as approaching a 'zero point' or 'meridian', a line beyond which the negativity of nihilism will, as it were, become the baseline of a new era. For Heidegger, the question of the line is not a historical question in this sense (see Heidegger 1974).

If, then, what is called for does not lie in our own power as individuals, nor is to be conceived as some kind of global revolution, is there anything we can do as individuals?

Surely we can at least do this: we can begin to work towards a view of metaphysics that takes in the whole sweep of its history, from Plato to Nietzsche. This means that we must both gain insight into the fundamental nature of metaphysical thinking, something for which the study of the essential thinkers in their individual works can prepare us, and understand metaphysics in its historical unfolding. Indeed, for Heidegger these are inseparable, and his own work shows a continual counterpoint between the search for the basic principles of metaphysics and the demonstration of how these principles become operative in history – a dual approach that has some analogy to Hegel's counterpoint of logic and phenomenology, idea and manifestation, despite all the differences between their understanding of the nature of historical change. In engaging with the tradition in this way we gain a preliminary view of metaphysics as a whole, something that is itself a necessary preliminary to leaving it behind.

But if the attainment of such an overview is a key to understanding our present crisis, its nature and its genealogy, does that of itself solve anything? Doesn't it still leave us waiting upon a new destining of Being (and, given Heidegger's view that the era of technology's consummation is only just beginning, it would seem that we must be prepared for a long wait)?

Undoubtedly the theme of waiting is important for Heidegger. And maybe 'only a God can save us'. Nevertheless, for all its massive and imposing unity, the history of metaphysics is neither as complete nor as self-contained as it may at first appear. Quite apart from the opportunities offered by art and by such things as our everyday encounters with, e.g., trees in blossom, we might find matter for thought in the reflection that the metaphysical epoch of Being is a very particular historical event. It is, for Heidegger, coterminous with the history of the West, the 'Abendland' ('land of evening'). It is not even a possibility for the East, and if, today, the East too is falling under the sway of technology, then this inevitably coincides with the process of Westernisation. But the point in insisting on the identity of metaphysics and the West is not only to draw a line between Western and non-Western cultures. It is also to locate metaphysics in a very particular history whose origin has a very particular place and time. The place was Greece, the time, very approximately, that of Socrates.[1]

As we saw previously (see Chapter 1 above), there is no ultimate explanation for such destinings other than the self-giving, the generosity of Being itself. At the same time, the historical situatedness of the beginning of metaphysics does provide an opportunity for us to look behind metaphysics and thereby to see its distinctiveness, its *difference* from what had gone before.

Perhaps we cannot escape, still less overcome, metaphysics by our individual mental efforts. Nevertheless, by entering into dialogue with those original thinkers who preceded metaphysics we might begin, through them, to learn what non-metaphysical thinking might be like.

Here, then, we see Heidegger's motivation for the preoccupation, so characteristic of his later thought, with the Presocratics – above all (though not exclusively) with Parmenides and Heraclitus, since it was precisely in the conscious and deliberate debate with just these two thinkers that the history of Western thought began. Between them they created a body of topics that were to be central to Plato's dialogues and that were to remain central to the subsequent philosophical tradition, topics such as Being, Non-being, Becoming, the One, Alterity, Time, Motion, Permanence and Logos. Parmenides' insistence that only Being is, and that Non-being is not, contrasted with Heraclitus' picture of a world in constant and ceaseless flux, set up a tension that has run through the history of philosophy, as thinkers from Plato to Hegel have attempted to balance or mediate what have been perceived as the two extreme positions. They therefore stand at the very boundary of that history – of it, yet not in it. They are its founders, and yet they stand outside it. As Heidegger sees it, we have no reason to suppose that they thought such matters as Being, Time or Logos conceptually, in the manner of later philosophy, and what Plato's mediating interpretation of their work achieved was precisely to cover up and conceal their distinctive way of addressing such questions. If, then, it were possible to understand them in their own terms, then we might have a uniquely significant insight into what it might be like to think non-metaphysically. Bearing in mind these reasons for returning to the Presocratics and recalling Heidegger's comments about writing, it is, for Heidegger, fortuitous that, whereas Plato bequeathed to posterity a body of writings covering the whole spectrum of the philosophical curriculum, the Presocratics left only fragments, often preserved only in quotations given by later writers ranging from Aristotle to early Christian apologists such as Clement of Alexandria. For Heidegger, of course, the conviction that an essential thinker thinks only one single thought means that these fragments are enough, and more than enough, for us to enter into a thinking dialogue with their authors. However, because his aim is precisely to understand them non-metaphysically, and because they have been read for millennia through the prism of metaphysical presuppositions, Heidegger's first task is always to retranslate them, to rescue their words from the metaphysical reading that existing translations impose upon them. In the second half of this chapter we shall see how he does just this with one of the fragments of Parmenides, a fragment that is conventionally translated 'One should both say and think that Being is' and which Heidegger renders 'Useful is the letting-lie-before-us in (the) taking-to-heart, too: being present'.

This forewarns us that we are likely to encounter much that is startling in Heidegger's return to the Presocratics. Nevertheless, at another level this return fits into a well-established pattern in German thought. Most obviously relevant to Heidegger is the example of Nietzsche, for whom the phenomenon of Socrates represented the decay of the early Greek ideal, and the subjugation of the freer spirit of the Homeric heroes to the constraints of Athenian rationality. In those heroes we see how humanity could be, if it were not shackled by the illusions of idealism and morality. Hegel, too, especially in his earliest writings and the *Phenomenology* looks back to this (admittedly somewhat ill-defined) era as a time when religion, the community and the individual co-existed in a harmonious inter-action: 'The nation that approaches its god in the cult of the religion of art [Hegel's appellation for the religion of early Greek society] is the ethical nation that knows its state and the actions of the state to be the will and the achievement of its own self' (Hegel 1977: 435–6). For Hegel as for Nietzsche this was an age when the expression of life in cultural and political forms was spontaneous and uncoerced. In this respect, their interest in it was not just a matter of antiquarian curiosity, since it also offered a model or analogue of how things could be again: for Nietzsche in terms of releasing the blonde beast from the cage of Platonic virtue and Christian conscience, for Hegel the recreation of a unitary politico-religious culture, in which religion was no longer a repressive tool in the hands of an authoritarian State but the living, festive and imaginative medium that bound the indi-vidual to the life of the community.

We can detect elements of both of these earlier ways of revisiting Presocratic Greece in Heidegger.[2] But if this helps to rescue Heidegger from the charge of mere eccentricity or antiquarianism, it may also expose this aspect of his thought to the charge that it is symptomatic of his 'archaic politics', another manifestation of his repudiation of modernity and its Enlightenment values and the desire to recreate a unitary society on the basis of non-democratic, non-rational values.

Such charges cannot be easily or straightforwardly answered. However, I should like to make three comments that give a rather different spin to the question. The first is that Heidegger's expositions of the Presocratic thinkers are often amongst his most tentative, ques-tioning and allusive texts. Heidegger does not regard it as obvious that we can 'know' what the Presocratics really meant, precisely because it is an open question whether they thought at all in terms of the cate-gories that we simply assume to be the 'normal' categories of thinking and knowing. In this connection Heidegger offers a caution against being misled by the term 'the Presocratics' itself. Referring to this designation, and to Nietzsche's variant 'the Preplatonic philoso-phers', he comments that 'The two designations are alike. The unexpressed standard for considering and judging the early thinkers is the philosophy of Plato and Aristotle. These are taken as the Greek philosophers who set the standard both before and after themselves. Traversing Christian theology, this view became firmly entrenched as a universal conviction, one which to this day has not been shaken' (EGT: 14).[3] In other words, we are not to approach these thinkers with the assumption that they represent only a primitive, poetic or mythological adumbration of what was to find definitive expression in Plato and Aristotle. They are not simply forerunners, but may represent the possibility of another way of thinking. If we are to read them in such a way as to uncover this possibility, however, we will need to approach them with all the caution we can muster. For, as Heidegger insists, we cannot even assume that where their vocabulary coincides with that of later philosophy it means the same. His co-participant in the Heraclitus seminar of 1966–7, Eugen Fink, remarked in reply to a leading question from Heidegger as to whether one can 'speak of a philosophical sense at all' in Heraclitus' words that 'we may not speak of a conceptual meaning of Heraclitus' sayings. Since we have the language of metaphysics behind us, we must attempt to avoid being misled by the developed thought path of metaphysics' (Heidegger and Fink 1979: 50–1). Later in the same session Heidegger comments that the language of the archaic Greeks is fundamentally determined by its rhythm, in what he regards as the original Greek sense of the word as measure or imprint. This, Heidegger says, 'is the substrate of language' in that era. And he adds, in dialogue with Fink, that 'this language knows no sentences ... [FINK:] ... that have a specific meaning. HEIDEGGER: In the sentences of the archaic language, the state of affairs speaks, not the conceptual meaning (Heidegger and Fink 1979: 55, cf. WCT: 212).

We shall shortly be seeing how the second part of *What is Called Thinking?* offers an interpretation of Parmenides that depends precisely on reading a particular one of his sayings without the conventional assumptions concerning grammar and conceptuality. For the present, however, I wish only to emphasise how Heidegger is not approaching the Presocratics as if they had the 'answer' to the intellectual crisis of our time, for that would mean regarding them as essentially speaking our language. Instead, they assist us in revealing possibilities of thinking that have been occluded by the dominant tradition, not so as simply to controvert or overthrow that tradition but rather, precisely by challenging its claims to universality and normativity, to deepen and to sharpen it and to disclose its fundamental assumptions. In entering with the Presocratics into this fundamental questionableness of the tradition, we do not immediately get the basis for a new beginning of philosophy or the beginning of an 'other' thinking, but, in questioning (and remembering all that was said in the previous chapter about the aim of interpretation as being to give insight into the questionableness of beings rather than to explain them), we open ourselves to such a possibility.

The second caution regarding Heidegger's return to the Presocratics is that, as has been hinted at, it is never separable from his concern for the contemporary planetary crisis. His is very much a two-horizons hermeneutic, whereby the ancient text is made to speak in relation to a guiding question generated by the contemporary situation of thought and, in turn, to illuminate that situation. This does not, of course, mean that we are licensed simply to appropriate the text to our horizon or read our concerns into it, but that our own concern with what it is to think the Being of beings opens our way of approach. Heidegger does not want to engage in the kind of direct encounter between ancient text and modern questions that happens when Christian theologians ransack the Bible for its teaching on homosexuality or the environment. He does not want simply to apply the teaching of the Presocratics to the question of technology, but it is essential that this latter is indeed the context in which the return to the first beginning of philosophy occurs (cf. GA 15: 389ff.).

We can take the point still further. For the return to the so-called Presocratics is not simply the attempt to read ancient texts in the light of modern questions and thus bring about an exchange between past and present. For our contemporary questions are not just about what it means to exist or to be now, they also concern the future of thought itself. Therefore the return to the 'former dawn' of philosophy is undertaken in the expectation of a 'dawn to come' (EGT: 18) and with the expectation that, although we seem to be 'latecomers' in the history of 'the land of the evening', we may yet prove to be the 'precursors of an altogether different age' (EGT: 17, cf. WCT: 185).

The third cautionary note has particular reference to the suspicion of a link between Heidegger's return to the Presocratics and his 'archaising politics'. Heidegger's readings of Presocratic texts questioningly adumbrate a possibility of thinking that is excluded by the conceptual systems of Western thought and that, if it is to be realised at all, belongs to a dawn that has not yet arrived. It is therefore not surprising if, at the conceptual level, the actual yield of these readings seems extremely meagre. If these readings were to be appropriated by a political philosophy of any kind, they would require considerably more concrete development than Heidegger himself ever provides. At this point, then, I will only repeat what I have previously claimed in relation to Heidegger's Nazism and his later philosophy: that the philosophy is not so much a spiritualised archaic politics as an attempt to accomplish an inner emigration from the catastrophe of 1933. Certainly, apart from the trope of returning to the Presocratic era, there is nothing coming out of Heidegger's readings of these texts that parallels Nietzsche's praise of the guiltless self-assertion of the warrior hero.

It almost goes without saying that Heidegger's approach to the Presocratics is striking and highly original. To a considerable extent, although qualified by their ambiguous relation to the history of metaphysics, he reads them in the light of the same hermeneutical principles we uncovered in dealing with his Nietzsche interpretation. Here too the ultimate aim of interpretation is not mere scholarly or historiographical reconstruction but to think the matter of their thought and, in doing so, to seek out what was unthought within it. We cannot, however, achieve this by inference and deduction (although 'long, slow preparation' (WCT: 233) is necessary), but only 'by a leap, the leap of a single vision' (WCT: 232).

However, in the case of the Greeks this is complicated by a number of factors, including several of those we have been considering in connection with Heidegger's general approach to ancient texts. For, even if his proximity to Heidegger's own time posed particular problems for the interpretation of Nietzsche, Nietzsche did write a German that was essentially the German of Heidegger himself and his audience. The early Greeks, however, to state the obvious, thought and wrote in Greek and, as we have seen, a Greek that Heidegger believed to be significantly different from the Greek of Plato and

Aristotle. Theirs (the Presocratics') was a Greek in which neither the sentence structure nor the manner of conceptualising meaning can be assumed to be familiar. The work of interpreting these fragments, then, is unavoidably interconnected with the labour of translating them. Properly to translate them, we must understand them – yet we cannot understand them, it seems, unless we translate them, for, as we shall see in the following chapter, we are ourselves 'bound to our mother tongue' (EGT: 19).

Here, then, is a more than usually challenging case of the hermeneutical circle. Now, given that Heidegger refuses to call on historical or philological evidence in any decisive way to support his readings, how does he go about establishing a position within the circle, getting into it in the right way, as he put it? He does so principally by summoning the metaphor, and perhaps more than a metaphor, of *hearing*. Truly, understandingly to translate the texts of Anaximander, Parmenides and Heraclitus it is not enough to 'merely transpose' the Greek terms into German terms. 'Instead,' Heidegger says, 'what is needed is that we let the Greek words tell us directly what *they* designate. We must transplant our hearing to where the telling statement of the Greek language has its domain' (WCT: 238). 'The leap of a single vision' that constitutes the moment of understanding occurs, in this case, when Parmenides' words are 'heard with Greek ears' (WCT: 232). But how do we manage to give ourselves Greek ears? Not by familiarising ourselves with early Greek literature, since that would, once again, be to land in the domain of historiography and philology. Such hearing occurs when we are led by 'that which calls on us to think in the words' (WCT: 232). But that, as we might have expected, means to hear that 'which speaks in thinking, and perhaps speaks in such a way that its own deepest core is left unspoken' (WCT: 232).

Such reflections will not provide an argument sufficient to persuade those who do not already stand within Heidegger's own hermeneutical circle to enter it. Indeed, they may well seem to a sceptical bystander to represent the endless spiral of ever-diminishing, ever more self-absorbed circles. They do not *justify* the standpoint from which the circle is drawn, except insofar as, along with the whole work of exposition itself, they show that Heidegger is operating in a consistent and coherent manner.

Heidegger's critics, then, will predictably charge him with arbitrary and forced translations, and he himself anticipates just this kind of criticism. In response he adduces the inevitability of the hermeneutical circle not only in his own case but also in that of his critics. Essentially, he says, there is no alternative. Even when the conventional scholar claims to be working 'in an objective manner and without presuppositions' (WCT: 176) the very appeal to objectivity and to the lack of presuppositions is itself 'an interpretation as charged with presuppositions and prejudices as is possible in this case'. Provocatively, he adds that 'It rests on the stubborn and widespread prior assumption that one can enter into dialogue with a thinker by addressing him out of thoughtlessness' (WCT: 176). Even more irritable is his comment in the lecture on the fragment of Anaximander that 'we will refrain from the futile practice of heaping up references to serve as evidence; this kind of annotation usually proves only that none of the references has been thought through. With the aid of this commonly adopted method one usually expects that by shoving together one unclarified reference with another every bit as unclear clarity will suddenly result' (EGT: 22).

Yet if this seems to be no more than an impatient outburst against the time-consuming sifting and comparison of sources that occupies the philologist, it contains a warning that one does not need to go all the way with Heidegger to take to heart. To take an example that will occupy us at some length: simply to translate Parmenides as saying 'One should both say and think that Being is' does not really tell us anything unless or until we know what Parmenides meant by Being – and the same applies to every other ancient instance of the term: i.e., we cannot illuminate Parmenides' saying from what Plato says about Being unless we know what Plato himself meant, etc. Heidegger does not throw up his hands in despair at this point, but simply reminds us that presuppositions are unavoidable, and that a positive way of looking at this situation is to acknowledge it and to seek maximum clarity as to our own pre-understanding, our own guiding question. This will, minimally, put us on our guard against uncritically assimilating the prejudices of others, such as Hegel's recommendation that it is Aristotle who provides the 'richest source' and most dependable guide for understanding the Presocratic thinkers (EGT: 15).

Heidegger, as I have said, anticipates criticism and is well aware that in setting out to re-envision the Presocratics his will, initially, be a minority voice. Acknowledging this he accepts that he can only make haste slowly. In this spirit fifty pages of *What is Called Thinking?* are taken up with the translation of a single line by Parmenides. Neither the translation nor the understanding revealed in the translation can, however, be regarded as anything like an objective 'result'. Only in the struggle to understand is understanding vindicated. The readiness to commit oneself to the struggle is the precondition of understanding and thinking.

The word of Parmenides

Precisely because of the importance Heidegger attaches to the *process* of interpreting, I shall focus this account of Heidegger's interpretation of the Presocratics on just this attempt to translate and to interpret this Parmenides text in the second part of *What is Called Thinking?*, the text listed as Fragment 6, *chrē to legein te noein t' eon emmenai*, which, as Heidegger notes, is usually translated as 'One should both say and think that Being is'. In making this our focus, it has to be acknowledged that other important elements of his return to early Greek thinking will be lost to view. Nevertheless, it well exemplifies both his manner of approaching these thinkers and the kind of thinking he arrives at by engaging them in dialogue.

We can, fairly easily, see three of the key themes of the later Heidegger in this brief 'word': saying (and, with that the whole question of language), thinking and Being. However, the topics suggested by these three words do not exhaust Heidegger's analysis and, as we shall see, the *chrē* (translated 'One should') occupies a prominent place in his interpretation of the fragment as a whole. Indeed, Heidegger says that it is 'the key word' in Parmenides' saying.

Recalling what was said previously about sentence structure and conceptuality in early Greek thinking and language, it is perhaps no surprise that Heidegger begins his assault on the conventional interpretation by repunctuating Parmenides' saying and writing it on four separate lines, thus:

Chrē:
to legein te noein t':
eon:
emmenai

which, still for the time being keeping within the rules of conventional translation, Heidegger renders 'Needful: the saying also thinking too: being: to be'.

In other words, whereas the conventional translation conceives the sentence as unified syntactically, Heidegger sees it paratactically. What is going on here?

Syntax, Heidegger says, 'is the study of sentence structure in the widest sense' (WCT: 183). A sentence conceived syntactically is a sense unit of which the various parts are drawn together into a relation that, at its simplest, synthesises two elements, subject and predicate, in the form 'x is y' ('The grass is green', or, less obviously, 'I'm going running', or 'John hits out'). As in Heidegger's discussion of the conventional ways of understanding the thing, this sentence structure reflects (and perhaps determines) a way of conceiving objects themselves as subjects or substances that are the bearers of their predicates, attributes or properties. Greenness is a property of grass itself. If, for Heidegger, that falls short of the truly decisive duality of matter and form, it is enough to show one of the most characteristic tendencies of Western metaphysical history. To understand something, to have a concept of something, is to be able to specify the attributes of which it is the bearer. To know the meaning of the term God would be to know that God is that being whose properties are (amongst others) self-causation, omnipotence, omniscience, 'always to have mercy', etc.

In a paratactic sentence, however, the elements are not synthesised into a formal unity. There is no obvious ordering of the relationship between the words, no clear subject and therefore no predicate, and therefore, we might conclude, no meaning. If moreover, in the manner of metaphysics, we conceive of the world itself as a conglomerate of entities each of which is a distinctive substance that is defined in terms of its attributes, paratactic sentences will necessarily be incapable of saying anything meaningful about how the world itself is. In this perspective we would have to translate a paratactic into a syntactic sentence before we could do anything with it.

The view that parataxis represents a deficient mode of speech is illustrated by the fact that we tend to regard it as the hallmark of primitive language or of children's first forays into sentence formation (as in the sentence given by Heidegger, 'Bow-wow, bad, bite', which, if we were to 'translate' it into a 'proper' sentence, might run 'The dog is barking angrily and is threatening to bite me'). In this respect, Heidegger acknowledges, some commentators might be only too happy to think of Parmenides as a writer of paratactic sentences, since this would confirm the view of him as a primitive 'pre-'philosopher.

This, of course, is not Heidegger's own intention. However, he does not offer any initial justification for this procedure of reducing the sentence paratactically other than by commenting that 'We call the word order of the saying paratactic in the widest sense simply because we do not know what else to do. For the saying *speaks* where there are no words, in the field between the words which the colons indicate' (WCT: 186).

For now, we will have to leave it at that, and look to the exposition of the saying that will retrospectively make clear the rationale behind Heidegger's procedure.

In presenting the exposition of the saying, I shall slightly adapt Heidegger's own division of the topic and look in turn at his account of (1) what is needful; (2) saying and thinking; and (3) Being. In the light of Heidegger's decision to read the saying paratactically, it should, however, be emphasised that no single one of these topics can be taken as the foundation on which the others rest, but – not forgetting his remark concerning the role of the colons – each is to be seen in its reciprocity with all the rest.

Having offered the translation 'needful' in his introductory analysis of the fragment, Heidegger's interpretation begins by amending this to 'it is useful'. This may at first glance seem to bring Parmenides into the orbit of instrumental, calculative thinking, as if the saying and thinking of Being was useful 'for' something, but this, as Heidegger explains, is not how he wants us to hear it. '"Using",' he says, 'does not mean mere utilizing, using up, exploiting. Utilization is only the degenerate and debased form of use' (WCT: 187). What he has in mind is instead a way of using things that respects their integrity and allows them to be what and as they are. 'When we handle a thing, for example, our hand must fit itself to the thing. Use implies fitting response' (WCT: 187). We might, for example, think of the way a master musician, a classical guitarist perhaps, handles the instrument, seemingly allowing the instrument itself to deliver up the harmonic, melodic and tonal possibilities of which it is capable, so that, as we watch and listen, performer and instrument seem almost inseparable, as if a current is flowing between them, and it is from this current, not from performer or instrument in isolation, that the music itself sounds forth. The instrument in its thingly aspect is no mere mechanism onto which a predetermined concept of the piece of music is stamped, but the instrument itself 'plays'. As Heidegger puts it, 'So understood, use itself is the summons which demands that a thing be admitted to its own essence and nature, and that the use keep to it' (WCT: 187). However, the scope of the expression, as Heidegger understands it, goes beyond individual and exceptional cases of appropriate use (like that of the guitarist). It points to the whole realm of 'usage and custom', to ways of doing things, of living and being, that are not simply made up, but that predate the efforts and innovations of individual practice.

In his lecture on the Anaximander fragment, Heidegger conducts an analogous exegesis of the participial form (*chrēon*) of the verb from which *chrē* is derived. Here he makes two points that usefully supplement the discussion in *What is Called Thinking?*. Firstly, he asserts that the verb *chrēon* is suggestive of the noun *ho cheir*, the hand. The verb itself thus concerns what happens when I extend my hand to something or place my hand upon it. But this should not be heard in the sense of constraining the object or exerting force upon it in such a way as to justify the translation of *chrēon* by 'necessity'. As Heidegger puts it '*chrhao* means to place in someone's hand or hand over, to deliver, to let something belong to someone' (EGT: 52). As he goes on to add, this does not mean 'handing-over' in such a way that the giver then has nothing more to do with what has been given. On the contrary, the continual involvement of the giver remains a condition of the gift being handed over. Perhaps, to take a trivial example (again, not Heidegger's own), we might think of parents giving their child a pet, knowing that their guidance and instructions will continue to be necessary if the pet is to be well looked after. They cannot just say, 'over to you' and wash their hands of it.

Heidegger is not, of course, concerned about children and pets, but with something fundamental to thinking. Thus he formulates the meaning of *chrēon* in the most general terms as 'The handing over of presence which presencing delivers to what is present, and which thus keeps in hand, i.e. preserves in presencing, what is present as such' (EGT: 52). For all its initial obscurity, the structure of this definition follows the pattern set out in the example of the gift of a pet quite closely. However, really to see what is going on here we need to know more about the terms presence and presencing, crucial terms in Heidegger's philosophical vocabulary to which we shall return later.

The second useful comment in the Anaximander lecture concerns the way in which *chrēon* can be translated as 'usage'. Usage is linked by Heidegger to the Latin 'frui' and the German 'fruchten, Frucht' (to fruit, fruit) which is translated by Heidegger as 'to enjoy'. Enjoyment, though, is not to be understood as the simple consumption of what is enjoyed. Rather, the point is (once again) that what is to be enjoyed is preserved as a condition of the enjoyment, as when I enjoy being in my garden or enjoy my friends. Of course, Heidegger is not wanting to psychologise here, and his point is not to draw attention to an aspect of human behaviour but to say something about Being. Thus 'usage is thought as essential presencing in being itself' (EGT: 53). In this ontological sense, usage is the occurrence that allows entities, 'beings', to be present in the space between what Heidegger calls the 'twofold absence' of their arrival and departure, their coming into being, into presence, into the world, and their ceasing to be.

These comments enable us to restate the relationship between presence, presencing and truth (understood in the sense of *alētheia* or uncovering): presencing is that which occurs in uncovering as the manifestation or shining forth of things as present in the (temporal) present in which they are. Usage is what allows this occurring and this uncovering to take place in the way that it does.

At the same time 'usage' also suggests a way of giving things their due in such a way as both to let them flourish (giving them space, as it were) and to limit and bind them. We human beings, together with all things that are, are in being only for a while, and it is usage that sets the boundaries of this 'while', allowing beings to become present but also requiring them to step back, to return to obscurity when their allotted time is up: 'usage delivers to each present being the while into which it is released ... Usage is the enjoining and preserving gathering of what is present in its presencing, a presencing which lingers awhile according to each particular case' (EGT: 54). Nevertheless, it is also important to remember that, precisely in thus enabling the occurrence of presencing (understood as the uncovering of beings) usage also sets boundaries in such a way that presencing may not 'petrify into mere persistence' (EGT: 54). Usage is not simply to be understood conservatively, in the sense of being a principle of presence or of the becoming-present of entities, since it is also what gives to beings their temporal character, their way of being transient.

Returning to *What is Called Thinking?* we find Heidegger addressing a question that has haunted this account of usage, namely, who or what is the subject of usage? Who or what brings beings into the radiance of presence? Who or what sets bounds to their continuance in being?

Heidegger has translated *chrē* as 'It is useful', but now states that he does not understand this as impersonal or subjectless in a negative sense. Nor is 'It' simply a neuter form, in contrast to masculine and feminine. The grammar and logic of 'it' sentences, such as 'it is windy' or 'it is snowing', have, Heidegger suggests, been less than adequately explained by scholarship. Certainly, he says, it would be very inappropriate to even try to answer the question as to who or what 'it' is that 'is windy' or 'is snowing'.

Such sentences have an irreducibility that has a certain fascination for Heidegger, most famously in connection with the expression 'there is' ('es gibt': literally 'it gives'). This suggests to Heidegger an ultimate givenness, a simple thereness that characterises the world as such, meaning by 'world' the world that, as being-in-the-world, Dasein is always already 'in', not the world that is the object of science, an ensemble of objects set over against the epistemological subject.

One especially important aspect of this 'there is' is that what is given in it, the world that we simply find being there with us in it, is inseparable from temporality. And it is no accident that the phrase occurs in the expression 'there is time' ('Es gibt Zeit'). The allotting to beings of their time is inseparable from allotting to them the possibility of presencing, although this, as we have seen, also means consigning them to transiency by setting limits to the time they have. This too belongs to their 'being given'.

In this connection, it is worth noting that here, in *What is Called Thinking?*, Heidegger muses that it might only be when 'It is useful' is 'thought through generously and adequately' that we would be able to 'define more closely what "there is" says' (WCT: 189). This suggests that the aim of reflecting upon a phrase such as 'there is' is not to strip the world down to some fundamental principle, 'thereness', but to see its irreducibility in an essential connection with usage in such a way as to hint at that endless occurrence in which the whole realm of beings is allotted its times and seasons, the places and occasions of their appearance and disappearance, their coming in and their going out. In other words it speaks of the way in which beings become, the way in which beings are in time and as temporal, and, in the same breath, of the way in which this becoming is subject to measure and order, albeit a measure and an order that is not reducible to any anthropocentric principle.

For theological commentators Heidegger's discussion of 'there is'/'es gibt' seems to resonate with theological themes such as creation, providence and grace. Their interest is understandable. 'Usage' seems to be behaving like a personal God, giving, disposing, taking away. Once more postponing the question as to the extent to which Heidegger can legitimately be read theologically, it is sufficient for now simply to note his own refusal to be appropriated in that way. For, as Heidegger sees it, the theological tradition in its entirety is entangled in metaphysical thinking. How then can it provide a perspective from which to understand the premetaphysical *chrē* of Parmenides?

Remembering the non-syntactic interrelationship of the elements of Parmenides' saying, we turn now to the second element in it, saying and thinking.

Heidegger once more begins with the conventional, dictionary meanings of these terms in order to thrust them aside in favour of his own formulations. Usually, then, *legein* is taken to mean 'stating' and *noein* 'thinking'. These terms, according to the received wisdom of philosophy and according to logic are interdependent. Logic as 'the theory of *logos* and its *legein*, is the theory of thinking ... Both *legein* and *noein* are seen as the definitive character of thinking' (WCT: 197). Here, then, is another assumption for Heidegger to question, and he does so by pointing out that this identification of *logos* and *noein* with thinking and of thinking with logic belongs to the time of Plato and Aristotle, whereas the question now is precisely how to step back to what thinking might have meant before they 'founded' the Western tradition of metaphysics. And, in terms of the guiding question of *What is Called Thinking?*, Heidegger reminds us that this question concerns what calls for thinking – that is, what calls upon thinking to think – so that simply to say that *logos* and *noein* mean 'to think' says nothing to those who have not yet discovered what thinking itself means.

Legein is said to mean 'stating', but what does that mean, heard in Greek? Heidegger says that it does not mean simply 'to speak'. 'The meaning of *legein* does not necessarily refer to language and what happens in language' (WCT: 198). *Legein* is, etymologically, related to the Germanic word 'lay'. If, then, we take *legein* to mean 'to lay' (that means laying something out) this does not preclude 'saying', for, as Heidegger observes, 'when someone tells us of an event, he lays it out before us' (WCT: 198). Citing another Parmenidean fragment, Heidegger contrasts the 'nimble tongue chattering away' with *logos*, the discriminatory laying out of an issue so as to enable it to be seen for what it is. In this connection we might also recall what was said in the preceding chapter about Heidegger's concept of interpretation as 'Aus-legung', the laying out of what is given in the question.

To understand what is involved in this laying-out, Heidegger pre-empts what he regards as an implied contrast between *logos* and *thesis*.

Guided by etymology alone, we might conclude that *logos* as laying-out means laying something out flat, whereas *thesis* means setting something up and making it stand before us. But this contrast is overdrawn. The *logos* and the *thesis* are interdependent, since 'what has been set up [*thesis*] always means to the Greeks that which has come to lie, and so does lie, before us' (WCT: 201). The Greek *thesis* is not yet the 'Ge-stell', the construct or enframing carried out by technological thinking. What is 'set up' in the sense Heidegger is considering here is not set up as resource, as the object of technological manipulation, but – bearing in mind everything that was said above about usage – 'is released into the freedom of its station and is not the effect of our doing and thus dependent on us' (WCT: 201). *Logos*, then, is what lays out before us what is set up for our consideration.

But if Heidegger's emphasis thus far seems somewhat passive, there is another side to it. This is brought out by his discussion of *noein*. It is usually translated as 'to perceive', but, he says, we should not think of perception as simple receptivity. '*Noein* as perceiving included also the active trait of undertaking something. In *noein*, what is perceived concerns us in such a way that we take it up specifically, and do something with it' (WCT: 203). How we take it up, what we do with it, he further describes as taking something to heart.

At this point he refers back to an earlier discussion of the root meaning of the German word 'denken', 'to think'. There, in the light of Old English usage, he claimed – in a word-play that works equally well in English or in German – that thinking and thanking are not merely interconnected but are interconnected in such a way and at such a level as also to bring memory into the picture.

> The originary word 'thanc' is imbued with the original nature of memory: the gathering of the constant intention of everything that the heart holds in present being ... In giving thanks, the heart gives thought to what it has and what it is. The heart, thus giving thought and thus being memory, gives itself in thought to that to which it is held. It thinks of itself as beholden, not in the sense of mere submission, but beholden because its devotion is held in listening. Original thinking is the thanks owed for being.
>
> (WCT: 141)

Although Heidegger insists that this is not within our own subjective control, and is not something that we 'do' in any conventional sense, it is not a matter of mere passivity either, and we must be active in it.

A striking point in this account is that memory, in thankful thinking, actively taking to heart its being beholden to being, is understood with regard to the fundamental phenomenological concept of 'intention'. We can therefore see how memory, as a 'constant intention' to what is held 'in present being', remains related to Heidegger's much earlier yet consistently fundamental sense of phenomenological intuition as arising on the basis of an intentional comportment that allows the presencing/uncovering of beings.

Heidegger goes on from these considerations to try to think *legein* and *noein* together. Their conjunction, he says, is 'the fundamental characteristic of thinking which here moves into its essential nature' (WCT: 211).

Noein 'unfolds out of *legein*' and is therefore 'not grasping but letting come what lies before us' (WCT: 215), while the heart actively holds to and safeguards what has been gathered out of that which lies before us. Such thinking is not the 'Begriff', the grasping concept favoured by Hegel. Thinking is not primarily determined by conceptuality, but by its appropriateness to what lies before it, and whether it 'befits the matter' (WCT: 212).

But if thinking is in this way directed by what lies before it, by what calls on it to think, what *is* given to thinking to think?

With this question we follow Heidegger to the last two words of the fragment: *eon; emmenai* – conventionally translated as 'Being is'.

Heidegger begins by noting that these are in fact different forms, the participle and the infinitive respectively, of the same verb. But the participle itself can have two meanings. It can be the 'x' itself that is, e.g., 'blossoming' (Heidegger's example), 'the rosebush or apple tree' perhaps (WCT: 220).[4] Or it can mean the act of blossoming. In the first case it effectively functions as a noun, a substantive, whilst in the latter it functions verbally, as indicative of a process.

Is this just a quirk of grammar, one of those curious rules we learn at school? Of course not. In Heidegger's eyes this twofold meaning reveals that the subject matter itself is twofold. A tree in blossom is not pure process: although it has no existence other than its existence as this tree that is blossoming in this particular moment as I look at it here and now; yet it is also that which blossoms, and the process of blossoming itself can have no meaning unless there is something that blossoms. The twofold form of the participle, then, catches something of the fundamental interdependence of being and becoming, that things are what and as they are only as they come into and pass out of being, in the space and time of presence that is allotted to them.

However, the example of a flowering tree is just an example, and Heidegger's real concern is with a very specific and perhaps unique participle, *eon*, taken from that very specific and perhaps unique verb 'to be'. Upon this verb depends the basic possibility of saying anything meaningful at all, since it is implicit in the very structure of assertion, as the copula in the formula 'x is y' (although the verb does not itself need to appear in any actual sentence, i.e., it is implied in but not stated in 'She looks good', etc.). Yet, foundational and universal as it is, it is also strangely elusive, since there seems to be no obvious shared meaning uniting all the various ways in which the copula is used in everyday language. What links the various meanings of being in such disparate sentences as 'The cat is orange', 'John is angry', 'God is merciful', 'That idea is interesting' and 'Bach is sublime'?

Confronted with what may appear to be a virtually undefinable array of usage, Heidegger is not discouraged, and affirms his view that, in this particular case, the twofoldness of the participial form gives us an important clue. For, he says, ' a being has its being in Being, and Being persists as the Being of a being' (WCT: 221). In other words, the duality of the nominal and verbal forms shows us something essential about the meaning of Being. Being is never otherwise than the Being (substantive) of beings (verbal: i.e., beings in the process of be-ing). It is this interdependence, Heidegger goes on to say, that is at the heart of Plato's concept of *methexis* or participation: i.e., the way in which a particular being or entity, existing as a being, a temporal process, is what it is by virtue of its participation in a form, an idea, and thus in Being, in what 'is' and does not pass away.

We can now appreciate the force of the two words conventionally translated 'Being is', *eon emmenai*. For the second of these, *emmenai*, does not simply duplicate the first but emphasises the sense implicit within it. Rather than 'Being is', then, Heidegger translates them as 'beings in Being'.

However, he is still not quite convinced that we have heard these terms in the Greek way. As long as we believe that the task is to translate them into our language, we will miss what is perhaps even more important, namely, to 'transpose ourselves into what speaks from these words', a transposition that can only occur in and as a visionary leap (WCT: 232).

And so Heidegger himself makes a bit of a leap. Abandoning the caution of his fifty-page attempt to translate the 'word' of Parmenides, he declares that the time has come to 'state directly' what is seen in the leap. 'Whatever has been seen can be demonstrated only by being seen and seen again' (WCT: 233). He is well aware of just how high the stakes are in this visionary leap, since *eon* is 'the decisive rubric of Western European thinking' and the way in which we understand it is decisive for humanity's global encounter with technology.

What, then, do we see in and as a result of this final, decisive leap of interpretation?

We see, says Heidegger, that the Greek 'to be' means 'to be present'. Being is what is present to us, or, remembering the inescapable verbal dimension of *eon emmenai*, Being is what presences: *eon* is 'the presence of what presences' (WCT: 235).

So the outcome of Heidegger's immense labour of interpretation is as follows: 'Useful is the letting-lie-before-us, in (the) taking-to-heart, too: being present.'

Now this may seem to be a somewhat paltry yield in proportion to the energy expended in reaching it, and it may seem hard to understand how or why it is decisive for our encounter with technology! However, before we get too cynical we must remind ourselves that Heidegger is not interested in the kind of quantifying, calculative thinking that issues in measurable 'results', so the 'result' of his translation may not be the most important thing. Even so, it is hard to resist the conclusion that all he offers is, finally, a bare tautology that amounts to no more than 'Being is beings in being' or 'Being is being present'. Can something as empty as this really be the ultimate goal of thinking?

The tone of such a question may be hostile, but Heidegger would almost certainly listen to it with equanimity, since he seems happy to accept that fundamental thinking is indeed tautologous. Thus, in the Zähringen seminar of 1973, and again with reference to Parmenides, Heidegger translates the Greek *esti gar einai* (Fragment 6,1 – again 'conventionally' translated 'Being is') as 'Presence, that is to say, presences'. Heidegger expressly refers to this as tautological thinking, and, interestingly, explicitly links it to the basic thrust of phenomenological thinking: 'it is,' he says, 'the original meaning of phenomenology' (GA 15: 399).

In order to see Heidegger's point, let us once again recall what was said previously about categorial intuition as the fulfilled intuition in which I see, for example, the row of trees *as* 'a' row, or the flock of ducks *as* 'a' flock – in which, that is, the structure of the phenomenon is immediately present to the intuition itself. Heidegger's early phenomenological research had arrived at this account of categorial fulfilled intuition as a way of undercutting the split between subject and object that he had encountered in the dominant positivism and neo-Kantianism of the late nineteenth and early twentieth centuries. Here, however, Heidegger is not directly concerned with particular issues in the problem of knowledge, but with Being itself, beings in Being, the presencing of what is present. The categorial intuition of fundamental ontology thus becomes in *What is Called Thinking?* a leap into vision, a letting-lie-before and taking-to-heart of the twofoldness of Being. In thinking we see what it is for Being to be, for presence to be present. As Heidegger put it in the Zähringen seminar with reference to the categorial intuition, the 'is' is seen, though not as sensuous. (GA 15: 375–6)

If these comments start to help us to see how the apparent vacuity of Heidegger's 'tautological thinking' may actually make a contribution to one of the fundamental questions of modern philosophy, the closing pages of *What is Called Thinking?* contain a number of references to Kant that further underline the point. Parmenides' saying, Heidegger now says, has its equivalent in Kant, namely, in the doctrine of synthetic judgments a priori and in Kant's assertion that 'The conditions of the possibility of experience in general are at the same time conditions of the possibility of the objects of experience'

(WCT: 243). Both the saying of Parmenides and that of Kant point to the unity of what, since Kant, has been called the subjective structure of thinking and the world that is represented in it. However, Heidegger claims, there is something in Parmenides which is lost in the Kantian formulation. For, as translated by Heidegger, thinking and saying, letting-lie-before-us and taking-to-heart, are called into life by the summons of Being as the being present of beings, that is to say, by a leaping vision, a categorial intuition of what is present in its presencing. Now, although Kant holds that the objectivity of what is given to consciousness in presentation presupposes some kind of intuition, that intuition only becomes objective and is only allowed to count as 'real' as a result of applying the synthesising structures of the mind. In the Kantian perspective, we do not see Being in beings, but we construct beings as beings according to the laws of logic and a priori judgments. For Kant and for Hegel alike, says Heidegger, this results in 'the ontology of absolute subjectivity' (WCT: 238). From there it is only one small step to Nietzsche, and to the unashamed proclamation of the absolute subjectivity of the metaphysical tradition as a whole (even though, of course, Nietzsche himself believed he was overturning that tradition, and not, as Heidegger believed, consummating it).

Does this then mean that Heidegger is to all effects and purposes retreading the path of German idealist philosophers such as Fichte and Schelling who sought to 'overcome' what they experienced as the unacceptable dualism of Kant by claiming that we are capable of an intellectual or aesthetic intuition in which thought becomes transparent to its own ground? It would be hard to deny some echo of this in Heidegger's own philosophical project, and, very broadly, there is some justice in assimilating him to the line of Romantic philosophy they inaugurated. Yet there are differences, and Heidegger is not simply a philosopher of identity, a comment that is relevant not only to his relation to the German idealists, but also to those who from the side of deconstruction see him as promoting a monolithic foundationalism based on the intuition of Being as presence.

What is it, then, that makes Heidegger's tautological thinking different from the philosophy of identity of the idealists, with their deduction of the whole system of knowledge from the one basic principle: A = A?

To answer this we must go back once again to the way in which Heidegger understands presence. It is not hard to see how presence, in its twofoldness of verbal and nominal dimensions, as the coming to presence of what is present, might be seen as converging with truth, understood as *alētheia* or unconcealment. For presence is the presentation to consciousness of present, unconcealed beings. Becoming unconcealed is coming into presence. We see a mountain: the mountain is present to us: the mountain stands before us as unconcealed. Yet *that* we see the mountain at all, *that* the mountain is unconcealed, is possible only within a larger context of unconcealment – e.g., the landscape within which or as a part of which the mountain appears. The presence of specific things as 'objects' of consciousness, standing forth in unconcealment, can occur only against the background, or (to use a more Heideggerian term) in the open space of a more original unconcealedness of beings-as-a-whole.

In part this larger context refers us back to the discussion of the *chrē*: for there we saw how beings come to be present only within the context of a disposing of the times and places of their appearing by the occurrence that Heidegger called simply 'useful'. This 'useful', that gives time and place to phenomena in their appearing as fugally articulated, is, however, never itself the object of an intuition, nor does it act as a foundation. In other words, the immediacy in which thinking confronts the presence of beings is not at all the same as the intellectual intuition of Fichte. It is also relevant at this point to recall the interdependence of unconcealment and concealment, of truth and error. As a coming out into the luminosity of appearance, unconcealment is itself inseparable from its penumbra, its tacit dimension. Every revelation is also a veiling. The relation to the presence of beings is not envisaged by Heidegger in terms of a perspicuous consciousness's transparency to its own ontological foundations, but as finding ourselves in an open, illuminated space amongst beings. We can never get behind the fugal disposing of 'it gives', 'there is'. In this we find also the roots of the difference that, whereas the idealists promoted a view of will or practical reason as virtually limitless or as setting its own limits, Heidegger allows for a note of acceptance or passivity, such that the will can only operate within the boundaries set by the 'useful' disposing of beings.

Elsewhere, Heidegger makes his point concerning the impossibility of a philosophy of identity by exploiting the ambiguity of the German term 'Riss', which can mean either 'outline' or 'rift'. In beholding something as present I see it as this specific thing against an unthematised background, a flock of ducks against the evening sky, the mountain within the landscape. However, by the very act of distinguishing it, by seeing this movement within the process of becoming *as* a flock, or this stillness within a sea of shapes *as* a mountain, I detach the flock or the mountain from its background and, as it were, tear it (the verb 'reissen' also means 'to tear') from its context. By taking to heart and holding in thought the presence of the mountain *as* mountain, I bring about a rift or fissure between the mountain as present, as unconcealed, and that which falls back into the penumbra of concealment. Bearing in mind that Heidegger is not so much concerned with questions of perception but with the question of Being, we can see that even Being itself in its nominal/verbal twofoldness is not to be understood as a simple 'given', the ultimate object of categorial intuition, the foundation on which all other intuitions rest. For Being itself can only come to presence, can only be as being, on the basis of another twofoldness, namely, its relation to non-being, to what is not. Being never emerges into the simplicity of indubitable and infinitely transparent presence. Being, too, stands under the law of 'useful' disposing or measure, and is present only in relation to the double absence of 'no longer' and 'not yet', standing out in unconcealment only on the basis of a rift or fissure in Being itself. For all his conservatism in the face of what he experienced as the nihilism of modernity, Heidegger shows himself here to be not so far from Sartre's insistence on the impossibility of a Being that is both in-and-for-itself, or Derrida's assertion that every representation is also a depresentation.

Such reflections are connected with Heidegger's extreme caution with regard to the extent to which the early Greeks are able to guide contemporary thinking. By returning to these thinkers we can rediscover the meaning of truth as *alētheia* and of being as the presencing of presence. Unlike the philosophical tradition that began with the translation of Greek into Latin, the Greeks themselves kept their thinking within the limits of what was present to them, and, consequently, their thinking is uniquely revelatory of the dynamics of presence. Nevertheless, Heidegger says, 'presence did *not* become problematised, questionable to them as the presence of *what* is present' (WCT: 235). Precisely because they thought within the openness of unconcealment, *that* there was unconcealment at all did not become problematic for them. They did not know the question 'Why something rather than nothing?'

For us, however, this side of the wasteland of modernity, the question of nothing is ineluctable. We do not experience ourselves as living within the encompassing luminosity of truth. Our experience is that of exile, of subjects sundered from their world. Perhaps, then, we may summarise Heidegger's view of the lure, yet also of the limitation, of the earliest Greek thinkers by saying that they reveal to us the possibility of thinking otherwise than in the mode projected in logic and consummated in global technology, but that possibility is just that, a possibility: it cannot *be* our way. For our need was unknown to them.

Is that it? Are we, after all, alone, abandoned to the sheer flux of historicity in which our final nothingness is all too plainly revealed?

To go further we would require a guide who had shared our modern experience yet, from within it, had found another path of thinking. Such a guide would, of course, be all the more persuasive if he, too, spoke from a certain familiarity with the Greeks and if he knew of the possibilities for an alternative way of thinking offered by art. Can we think of such a guide? Heidegger could: the poet Hölderlin. 'Hölderlin,' he said in introducing a reading of Hölderlin's poetry, 'is for us a destining'.

As we now turn to the role of Hölderlin in Heidegger's thought and, in and through Hölderlin, his construal of the relationship between poetry and philosophy, it is absolutely vital to see that this is not merely a literary sideline for Heidegger, as if Heidegger was a professional philosopher who also took an interest in poetry. Rather, the encounter with Hölderlin lies on the same path of thinking that had led Heidegger to the work of art, to the thing, to Nietzsche and to the

Presocratics, the path of seeking what it is, in this technological waste-land, to say and to think Being in beings, what, ceaselessly, calls on us to think.

Chapter 7

Hölderlin

The approach to Hölderlin

In addition to his many expositions of the 'great thinkers' of the philosophical tradition, Heidegger was also a keen reader and interpreter of literature, especially poetry. Some of his literary interests found little obvious expression in his published works (thus, despite anecdotal evidence as to the large influence on him of Dostoevsky there is little mention of the Russian novelist in any of Heidegger's own lectures or writings). Others, however, became the focus of important philosophical reflections. This is especially true of German poets such as Georg Trakl, R. M. Rilke, Stefan George, Gottfried Benn, the dialect poet Johann Peter Hebel and, most importantly, Friedrich Hölderlin – to whose work Heidegger devoted several series of lectures, as well as occasional addresses, and many passing references and discussions, totalling four volumes in the collected works (even recording a reading of Hölderlin's poems). Indeed, after Nietzsche,

Heidegger devotes more space to Hölderlin than to any other writer or thinker.

We have already seen how Heidegger experienced the work of art as offering a way to break the grip of technologically oriented thinking, a way to a more originary encounter with things, and, in that encounter, to a disclosure of the world constituted as and by the fourfold of earth, sky, mortals and the gods. A painting, a temple and a jug are variously adduced as occasioning such disclosures. These works, whether they are 'high' or 'low' art, are each of them dumb things, and whilst this may make them effective in countering the mind-set of enframing by helping us to break free from habits of thought dominated by the technicised language of science, the media and everyday idle talk, it also limits them. Such works, Heidegger says, indeed '*All art*, as the letting happen of the advent of what is, is as such *essentially poetry*' (PLT: 72). Does this, then, mean that all the arts – architecture, painting, sculpture and music – must somehow be hierarchically subordinated to poetry in the narrow sense? This had, famously, been the strategy pursued by Hegel in his *Aesthetics*. There the hierarchy of the arts was ordered along a scale that marked the progressive diminishment of the role of spatiality and externality in favour of temporality, interiority and spiritual truth. In this scheme painting comes to rank 'higher' than sculpture, because it is only two-dimensional and therefore less external and also because it is more expressive of feeling by virtue of colour, music is 'higher' than painting, because it is essentially temporal and expresses inner feelings more directly than does painting, whilst poetry is 'higher' than all, because it is both temporal and inward. Such a classification of the arts, typical of idealist aesthetics, was, however, alien to Heidegger's intentions. For undergirding Hegel's entire schematisation of the arts was the privileging of reason and logic over the whole realm of art. Putting it at its simplest, art was but a moment in the unfolding of Spirit which was most truthfully and appropriately to be grasped by dialectical reason.

For Heidegger, by way of contrast, the peculiar importance of art is precisely connected to its power to break the stranglehold of a philosophy of consciousness. Poetry in the narrow sense is, in this light, 'only one mode of the lighting projection of truth' (PLT: 73) that occurs in all art. 'Nevertheless,' Heidegger continues – and this 'nevertheless' (perhaps, after all, predictable) is a crucial moment in the whole structure of Heidegger's thinking – 'the linguistic work, the poem in the narrow sense, has a privileged position in the domain of the arts' (PLT: 73). This step is crucial, because, having used his meditation on the thingly character of the work of art to undermine the domination of enframing (and thereby, apparently, dislodged language, logos, from its role as the defining characteristic of humanity), Heidegger is now about to reinstate language – but language experienced and understood quite otherwise than when propositional assertion is seen as the most proper form of language use. This becomes clear in Heidegger's subsequent comments, as he continues by saying that

> To see this only the right concept of language is needed … [Language] not only puts forth in words and statements what is overtly or covertly intended to be communicated; language alone brings what is, as something that is, into the Open for the first time. Where there is no language, as in the being of a stone, plant and animal, there is also no openness of what is … Language, by naming beings for the first time, first brings beings to word and to appearance. Only this naming nominates beings *to* their being *from out* of their being. Such saying is a projecting of the clearing, in which announcement is made of what it is that beings come into the Open *as*.
>
> (PLT: 73)

Language, and poetry as the art of language, is, then, privileged by Heidegger after all – but not, as for Hegel, because it subordinates the thingly element of its object, its matter, or because it expresses a higher (in the sense of more interior, more rational) mode of consciousness. Poetry, no less than the temple or the jug, is what it is by virtue of its power to let rock become hard, metals to shimmer and colours to glow: i.e., to let the world be made present in its worldly character. Poetry is not a means of transcending or spiritualising experience, but a mode of unconcealment, of letting beings appear in their being, *as* what they *are*. It is, very precisely, 'the saying of world and earth, the saying of the arena of their conflict and thus of the place of nearness and remoteness of the gods' (PLT: 74). As such it is inherently and intimately connected with truth: not so much the pinnacle of the hierarchy of the arts as the deepest revelation of what is. As such – and this will become particularly important in connection with Hölderlin – it is also inherently and intimately connected with the life of the people, the *Volk*.

Because of the connection of poetry to truth, it is inevitable that philosophy will be guided into a certain proximity to poetry. But this is not in order to subject poetry to 'the cold presumption of the concept' (GA 39: 5) or to penetrate behind poetry's pictorial language to 'what' is being expressed in it. On the contrary, the philosopher is concerned with the word of the poet in order the better to learn thinking itself. 'Thinking is almost a co-poetising ('Mitdichten')' (GA 52: 55).

The philosopher is no literary critic; he approaches poetry as a cadaver on a dissecting table, subordinating it to his narrowly philosophical interests. He is not concerned with poetry as a work of literature but with the *essence* of poetry: namely, that which makes it possible for poetry to be revelatory of truth. If the poet produces a poetic word, the thinker thinks Being, although, equally, poetry is not naive, since the poet no less than the thinker is engaged in a questioning of existence (GA 52: 134).

Rather than attempting to spell out the relationship between philosopher and poet in general terms, however, it will be more fruitful to follow Heidegger in his exposition of that poet in whom the essence of poetry is most clearly revealed: Friedrich Hölderlin.

Poetry is notoriously untranslatable, and even well-translated poetry does not always travel. In the early twentieth century Hölderlin achieved considerable posthumous popularity in Germany itself and, as Heidegger himself comments, Hölderlin's poetry vied with the writings of Nietzsche and Goethe for the honour of being the most popular reading of German soldiers in the First World War. Yet he remains little read in English, a fact which has to do both with the intrinsic difficulty of his work, its Classical formality, and its strongly national concerns. Before coming to Heidegger's own Hölderlin interpretation, then, it may be useful to sketch a brief outline of

Hölderlin's life and work. In doing so I am not aiming at anything like an adequate portrait of either the man or his work, but simply to introduce the reader who is entirely unfamiliar with him to some basic points for orientation.[1]

Friedrich Hölderlin lived from 1770 to 1843, spending most of his life in his native Swabia in Southern Germany. At Tübingen University he was a close friend of both Hegel and Schelling. Like them, he was a student in the famous college known as the Stift, where, officially at least, he studied theology, despite not having any distinct vocation to the priesthood. Following a well-established pattern, and with the benefit of patronage from Schiller, he spent some years as a private tutor, in the course of which (again following a well-established pattern) he fell in love with the woman whose children he had been employed to teach. This was Susette Gontard, who was to be the great love of Hölderlin's life. After a brief period in Bordeaux, and following Susette's early death, he experienced an intense schizophrenic episode in 1802. Despite the care of friends and the prospect of secure appointment as Court Librarian in Homburg, the illness recurred four years later, and from 1807 until his death in 1843 Hölderlin lived in the charge of a carpenter in Tübingen, in a tower (still known as Hölderlin's tower) overlooking the river Neckar.

The Germany of Hölderlin's formative years was, like the rest of Europe at that time, caught up in the ferment of the French Revolution and the series of wars set in train by that event. It was a period when the whole question of German identity was highlighted, as the French invasion exposed the fragmentation of Germany into a multiplicity of principalities and small states that, separately, were unable to defend themselves effectively. At the same time, the authoritarian and often reactionary nature of the small states, as in Hölderlin's home state of Baden-Württemberg, pushed many of Hölderlin's generation into taking up a critical stance toward their rulers – as students, Hegel, Schelling and Hölderlin had all been disciplined for planting a 'liberty tree' and singing revolutionary songs. Culturally and intellectually there was a sequence of criss-crossing battle-lines to engage the attention and define the agenda of young intellectuals. So, for example, there were the conflicts between established Christianity, thoroughly integrated into the structure of the

State (as in the Lutheranism of Hölderlin's background and university education) and the un- or even anti-dogmatic pursuit of intellectual and moral autonomy inspired, most recently, by Kant and Fichte; or between a Classicism that looked to Greece as the model of enlightened, rational order in art and society alike (as in Schiller) and a Romanticism that valorised the world of the Middle Ages, its chivalry and its mysticism, and that was inspired by the beauty and sublimity of Germany's rivers, mountains and forests. Such tensions could easily be interpreted in terms of the empty formality of reason on the one hand and deep, substantial passion on the other. Whether these could somehow be united – as Schiller envisaged in his *Letters on Aesthetic Education* – or whether they set the scene for the agonies and despairs of Romantic nihilism was a question that received various answers in the lives and works of many writers, artists and philosophers in the early nineteenth century. Indeed, as has been seen, they lived on to influence the cultural and political horizons of Heidegger's own time.

These polarities are, not surprisingly, echoed in Hölderlin's poetry – although they appear there in a startlingly original form. Whereas Hegel resolved the threatened bifurcation of consciousness by means of a dialectically phased sequence of syntheses between the conflicting elements, Hölderlin never achieved any settled outcome of his poetic pursuit of a harmony that he envisaged as a return to the luminous presence of the Greek gods on German soil, a union of Christ and Dionysos, or the synthesis of a romantic view of nature with the striving for political freedom. Hölderlin's work thus becomes shot through with a lost past that is, nevertheless, recognised as irretrievable in its own terms, fating the poet to seek a destiny commensurate with his modern European reality. This pervasive sense of loss, though not without parallel in Schiller's own work, separates Hölderlin from the optimism of his patron, whilst his commitment to the redemption of the national *polis* marks him out from the more individualistic, anarchic Romanticism of a Friedrich Schlegel, and his passionate Hellenising also distinguishes him from the more gothic world of, e.g., Tieck, Wackenroder, Hoffmann and Novalis.

Heidegger's treatment of Hölderlin bears comparison with his

Nietzsche-interpretation. As previously indicated, Hölderlin receives almost as much attention in quantitative terms as does Nietzsche himself. Heidegger held three series of university lectures on Hölderlin's poems 'The Rhine' and 'Germania', 'Remembrance', and 'The Ister' in the academic sessions 1934–5, 1941–2 and 1942 respectively, together with a number of other addresses spanning the years 1936–8. In addition there are many important references to the poet scattered throughout Heidegger's late work, as is the case with the texts that are the main reference points of this study, *On the Origin of the Work of Art* and *What is Called Thinking?*. But although this alone should alert us to the importance of Hölderlin for the later Heidegger, bulk is not the only factor inviting a comparison with the Nietzsche-interpretation. It is significant that Heidegger himself bracketed his lectures on Hölderlin with those on Nietzsche as evidence of his intellectual resistance to Nazism, a comment that suggests that, here too, we may also expect to find material relating to the confrontation between contemporary humanity and planetary technology.

However, although there are undoubtedly many affinities between the lectures on Nietzsche and those on Hölderlin, there are some extremely important differences. Whereas Nietzsche is seen by Heidegger as the last great thinker of the West – the one in whom the error and the danger of metaphysics comes to its supreme expression – Hölderlin serves a more positive role, for in him we are invited to see the harbinger of a new beginning. In this regard Hölderlin's own constant dialogue with the Greeks is very significant and is seen by Heidegger as anticipating, mirroring and clarifying his own attempt to 'hear' the matter of early Greek thought. The contrast with Nietzsche is explicitly drawn in the 1941–2 lectures on 'Remembrance'. Heidegger remarks on what he sees as a fashionable tendency to assimilate the two, but states that, in his view, they are divided by an 'abyss', even though both of them are seen as determinative for both the immediate and the distant future of Germany and the West (GA 52: 78). Nietzsche is the voice of modern metaphysics, whilst Hölderlin presages the overcoming of metaphysics (GA 52: 143). Another contrast – not unconnected with this – is that, whereas Nietzsche conceived of Dionysos as a kind of trans-historical dimension of life, the Dionysian element in life, as it were, the absence of the old Greek gods is a decisive moment in Hölderlin's vision (GA 52: 143). In this respect Hölderlin is both more genuinely Greek and more open to the future. Another contrast emerges in relation to one of the highest compliments that Heidegger pays to Nietzsche, when he describes his thinking as a 'feast'. Remembering that the interpreter's aim is always to think what is unthought in the thought of the great thinker, we might infer that the 'feast' offered by Nietzsche's thought was not necessarily thought or understood by Nietzsche himself. This, however, contrasts with the role of the feast-day in Heidegger's inter-pretation of Hölderlin's poetry, especially in the lectures on 'Remembrance', and invites the reflection that, if Nietzsche the thinker is finally unable to deliver the feast promised by his thought, then we might turn to Hölderlin the poet for a more direct access to that which is given to thought to feast upon. The poet speaks what the philosopher is to think.

The place of Heidegger's Hölderlin-interpretation in his later thought is, however, not only determined by the way in which the poet is promoted as a decisive alternative to Nietzsche. It is, as previously suggested, also connected to the interplay between the experience of 'we moderns' and the Greeks. Despite the influence of Schiller, Hölderlin's own invocation of the Greeks does not so much emphasise their Classicism, i.e., what Nietzsche would later call the Apollonian aspect of Greek culture, but their openness to the intoxicating, ravishing presence of the gods, their immediate experience of the powers of nature in demi-gods such as Herakles and Dionysos. The bonding of the nation in the ecstatic experience of the festival is no less significant than the discovery of reason and the delight in dialec-tics. Yet, as stated above, Heidegger does not regard Hölderlin as proposing any kind of 'Dionysian-in-itself'. The whole tenor of Hölderlin's relation to the Greeks is determined by the sense, the conviction even, that the gods have fled. Paradoxically, however, their absence is a condition of their being the essential subject of poetry such as that of Hölderlin which adopts the elegiac mood. For the absence of the gods, says Heidegger, is their presence as having-been. This remark carries further implications, in that it is from the past participle of 'to be' (*gewesen*), that the German philosophical term for essence (also sometimes translated Being), *Wesen*, is derived. Thus, for Heidegger, essence, *Wesen*, is what has-been, *das Gewesene*. Not everything that is past partakes of this transformation into true essentiality. There is a past that is simply past, that is over and done with, 'unalterable, closed' (GA 52: 108), but there is also a past that, precisely by being past, is transformed into true essentiality. Moreover, what abides essentially in this way relates not only to the past but also to the future, since what concerns us essentially cannot but be of significance for our future. The encounter with the Greek world is, of course, an encounter of this essential kind.

We shall return to the question as to what exactly is involved in essential abiding in remembrance when we come to consider Heidegger's view of Hölderlin's poetic language and the significance of that for understanding language as such. At present we note only the role it plays for Heidegger in distinguishing Hölderlin's relation to the Greeks from that of Nietzsche. It also, of course, illuminates Heidegger's own concern to hear Greek thought with Greek ears – not for the sake of Classical revivalism, but in order to gain insight into what is essential in our present situation and in the decisions that face us concerning our future.

Another important element in Heidegger's approach to Hölderlin that once more touches on issues with which we are already familiar is the issue of German nationhood. Although Heidegger's interest in Hölderlin clearly predated his Nazi period, it is scarcely coincidental that his most intensive engagement with Hölderlin came in the time following the failure of the rectorship. In terms of the reading of Heidegger's disengagement from Nazism offered in Chapter 2, this is the time when Heidegger is seeking to redefine the meaning of nationhood (or homeland or fatherland) in such a way as to find in it a counter-movement to planetary technology, something he now saw Nazism as incapable of doing. Each of the poems he selects for comment in the three lecture series raises the question of national identity and the meaning of the *polis* for human life. Both in the 1934–5 lectures on 'Germania' and 'The Rhine' and in the 1936 lecture on 'Hölderlin and the Essence of Poetry' Heidegger insists on the relation to the people (*Volk*) as integral to the poet's vocation. Because poetry concerns 'the basic happening of man's historical

Dasein' (GA 39: 40), it also by definition concerns humanity's relation to beings-as-a-whole and the primordial temporality in which that relationship is stamped with the characteristics of a particular historical epoch. Such primordial time 'is the time of poets, thinkers and the founders of states, i.e., of those who essentially found the historical Dasein of a people and give them their fundamental character. These are the authentic creators' (GA 39: 51). This comment is much discussed in the literature on Heidegger's Nazism, but whether it is read as a grouping of Hölderlin, Heidegger and Hitler as the authentic creators of the new Germany, or whether it serves as a reminder that politics is fundamentally limited in its ability to define the authentic character of a nation, it minimally helps to underline the point that, in concerning himself with Hölderlin, Heidegger is not simply giving up on the issue of German identity, and his turning to Hölderlin is not simply an abandonment of the concerns that led him into the political arena in favour of poetry. Rather, it is an attempt to rethink from another angle the issues that had motivated his political misadventure. Irrespective of whether this is seen in terms of inner emigration or resistance, the spiritualising of Nazi ideology or of escapism, it points to the way in which 1933 was not a mere episode in Heidegger's life but connects in manifold ways with the fundamental elements of his later thought.

We might now be beginning to see why Hölderlin could become so important to Heidegger, but it remains to be seen how he understood his philosophical approach to the poet. We therefore turn now to look more closely at Heidegger's hermeneutical strategy, at how he read Hölderlin, at what he found in him and at the light his Hölderlin-interpretation throws on his later thought, especially his understanding of language. As was the case with Nietzsche, an examination of Heidegger's method of reading Hölderlin will take us a long way towards uncovering the yield of that reading.

Poetry and language

Heidegger is quite clear that, although he approaches Hölderlin from the viewpoint of a philosopher and thinker, Hölderlin himself is first and foremost a poet. Heidegger draws a sharp distinction, familiar to the Romantic era itself, between poetry in the sense of mere versifying and poetry (*Dichtung*; cf. *Dichter*: poet), in the strong sense. It is always this latter sense that applies to Hölderlin, and so the first aim in reading Hölderlin's poems is to read the poetry in them. For it is one thing to read a poem and become acquainted with it as a piece of literature, but it is something else again 'to stand in the domain of poetry' (GA 39: 19). Poetry in this strong sense is not the 'expression of experiences (*Erlebnissen*)' (GA 39: 26), nor, against Spenglerian and racist views, is poetry an expression of a certain form of culture or 'a biologically necessary function of a people' (GA 39: 27). The aim in reading poetry is not, as in the hermeneutics of the Schleiermacher-Dilthey tradition, to reconstruct the original intuition of the poet, since the word of a true poet transcends his own private opinions and experiences (GA 52: 6–7). Thus, the 'I' we encounter in Hölderlin's poetry is not that of the man who is the subject of a historical biography of Friedrich Hölderlin (1770–1843) but, precisely and solely, that of Hölderlin the poet, and, therefore, understandable only in the light of the poetic work itself. Hölderlin matters to us only 'insofar as the author brings the whole poem as a linguistic production into language', but 'the poem as a whole is language and speaks' (GA 39: 42) – i.e., it is language itself and not the arbitrary individuality of the poet that really speaks in the poem. Consequently, the word of the poet 'overreaches itself and the poet in its poetic achievement' (GA 52: 12).

We must therefore resist being seduced into merely marvelling at the beauty of a poem as a product of culture (GA 52: 21); nor is a poem to be 'explained' by reference to its historical context, nor even by comparison with parallel citations from the author's own work, since this is in each case to presuppose that we understand what the poem itself is about. However, only the poem itself can teach us what it is about (GA 52: 2f.).

Poetry, as a work of art, is a mode of truth as unconcealment, a naming of beings that calls them into being the beings that they are. It is this that requires us to recognise its proximity to thinking. Nevertheless, poetry is not philosophy, a point that is particularly important in the case of Hölderlin, who is known to have been so close to Hegel, and who was himself philosophically literate and who produced some prose works that could be categorised as philosophical. There is a deep affinity between Hölderlin and Hegel, says Heidegger, but in order to grasp this it is also necessary to grasp the division and the boundary that separates poet and thinker (GA 39: 129ff.).

Poetic language is not the language of philosophy. Since the time of Plato philosophy has placed itself in the service of univocity, a service standardised in formal logic. This has had the result of instrumentalising language and reducing it to a tool, a means of self-expression and communication (GA 52: 14ff.). At its most banal, this philosophically driven reduction of language manifests itself in the kind of 'Americanism' encountered in the spread of acronyms (GA 52: 10). As with Heidegger's critique of science and technology, so here the superficially 'high' standards of logical rigour are placed on a par with the most trivial, most levelled aspects of everyday modern life.

None of this should be taken as implying that poetry itself is inexact, for it has its own kind of rigour (GA 52: 26). Nor is the imagery of poetic diction a mere form concealing the 'true' content of the poem (GA 52: 29). In reading or listening to a poem, we can only attend to the poem itself, to the word that is unique to this singular linguistic construct, that overreaches the self-understanding of the poet, that is irreducible to the personal and communal circumstances of its production and inexplicable in terms of psychology, logic or philology.

As was the case with the essential thought of any great thinker, we must also remember that the truth of poetry is not only in what is said, but also in what is left in silence (GA 39: 41; GA 52: 39). Moreover, to understand this truth we must be genuinely concerned about who we are, in our own time. This is not simply a matter of chronological time, and whether we live in 1801 or 1934 is not ultimately important. What matters is that we are concerned about what it is to be, to exist, in time. (GA 39: 48f.)[2]

In an especially forceful passage that resonates with his many references to the role of the leap in thinking, Heidegger states that

> The poem is now no longer an even text, endowed with an equally flat 'meaning', but this linguistic construct is in itself a vortex that

snatches us away. Not gradually, but ... suddenly ... But to where does this vortex snatch us? Into speech (*das Sprechen*), of which the poem is the linguistic construct. What sort of speech is that? Who speaks to whom with whom about what? We are forcefully drawn into a conversation (*Gespräch*) that language (*Sprache*) brings to speech (*Sprache*), and indeed not just any casual or accidental speech ... [but one that concerns] naming and speaking.

(GA 39: 45)

The poetic word has often been called 'divine', and Heidegger too represents the poet as a mediator between gods and mortals. 'Thunder and lightning are the language of the gods and the poet is he whose task is to endure and to gather up this language and to bring it into the Dasein of the people' (GA 39: 31). In the case of Hölderlin this mediating role is connected with the poet's preoccupation with the demi-gods (Dionysos and Herakles in the Greek world and the personified rivers of the German landscape), who are 'above' mortals but 'beneath' the gods: beings who thus have a certain formal analogy to Nietzsche's superman. However, they are not simply creators of their own universe of meaning, as the superman is, but bearers of a meaning and a truth that transcends their own understanding.

Referring to Hölderlin's line that 'hints are, from of old, the language of the gods', Heidegger adds that poetry itself speaks a hinting and allusive language. On the one hand, poetry is public diction, spoken for and before the people, yet it is also veiled, a sign rather than a statement (GA 39: 32). Playing on the double-meaning of the German term 'Wink' which means both 'hint' and 'wave' (as in waving farewell), Heidegger says that such a hint/wave is 'a holding on to closeness in the course of increasing distance and, conversely, the revealing of the distance still to be covered in the joyful proximity of the one arriving. The gods, however, hint just by *being*' (GA 39: 32).

Snatched away, abducted by the ravishing vortex of the poem, the reader is translated into the realm of the enigmatic, hinting divine thunder and lightning, experiencing simultaneously the presence and absence, the proximity and the distance of the gods. This, of course, parallels the dynamics of thinking itself, lured into being by what withdraws from it and, in withdrawing, calling for thinking. Recall that for Heidegger 'What must be thought about, turns away from man. It withdraws from him' (WCT: 8). But, pulled forward into the current generated by this withdrawal, we are not merely led on by hinting, ambiguous signs of what lies out there to be thought. As we ourselves are drawn into the slipstream of what calls for thought, we too become signs, pointers to what is to be thought.

> Man is not first of all man, and then also occasionally someone who points. No: drawn into what withdraws, drawing toward it and thus pointing into the withdrawal, man first *is* man. His essential nature lies in being such a pointer. Something which in itself, by its essential nature, is pointing, we call a sign. As he draws toward what withdraws, man is a sign.
>
> (WCT: 9)

However, because that to which the riddle of human existence points and of which it is a sign is necessarily absent (since its absence is the vacuum that generates the current of thinking and is therefore itself constitutive of humanity's sign-character), Heidegger can sum the situation up in words from Hölderlin's poem 'Mnemosyne': 'We are a sign that is not read / We feel no pain, we almost have / Lost our tongue in foreign lands' (WCT: 10). This 'we' Heidegger interprets as 'We the men of today' (WCT: 11). However, Hölderlin is not simply giving expression to the experience of displacement and confusion characteristic of a particular era, modernity for example, since, as we have seen, that would merely be to interpret the poem from an external standpoint. As poet, as the bearer of a poetic word that is the transposition into speech of divine lightning, Hölderlin's sign, Hölderlin as sign, is profoundly unreadable, in the sense that there is no final, univocal meaning, but rather an ever-withdrawing, ever-provocative 'food for thought' (WCT: 11). In relation to the self-concealment of the poetic word, the interpreter's task becomes the task of hearing (*hören*) or, more precisely, attending to (*horchen*; cf. *gehorchen*: obey) the poetic word. Such attentiveness is both a waiting (*warten*) and a willingness to risk oneself (*wagen*), since there can never be a guarantee either that there is anything worth attending to or that we have secured the 'correct' interpretation. Ambiguity, allusion, hinting goes all the way down. Every act of interpretation is and must be a leap into the unknown.

If the meaning of poetic production is in this way compressed into the single category of the enigmatic, hinting sign, and remembering that we ourselves are defined in the representative figure of the poet as a 'sign', the sign is what it is in and as language, as word. So, just as Heidegger identified the essence of the thinker with that single (unthought) thought that determines the whole orbit of his intellectual activity, the poem, despite its many words, is referred to as the 'poetic word' in the singular (GA 52: 33) – an assertion that highlights Heidegger's distinctive strategy of philosophising by meditating upon the 'basic words' that, in his view, define the course of thinking.

What is needed if we are to understand poem and poet, then, is neither historical nor literary nor any other kind of knowledge, but simple readiness to allow the word to speak to us and, in speaking, to reveal the time-space of its assigned domain.

In this regard we once more come close to the primordial doubling of experience in the intuitive experiencing of the world 'as' world. But this is not spoken of in this context in terms of a phenomenology of perception, as the irreducible doubling in the experienced encounter of, e.g., the eye and its object. For what is now being stressed is that the object, the thing, is only really *seen*, only able to stand out into the open space of perception, when and as it is named, when the word is spoken over it.

If the speaking of this word is supremely the task of the poet, we have to remember that poetry in the narrow sense preserves and condenses the essence of language as such. In other words, Heidegger's understanding of the poetic word is not offered as the resolution of a problem in aesthetics, but as an attempt to exemplify the essential nature of language. 'Language itself is poetry in the essential sense' (PLT: 74). Poetry is a way of speaking that lets the essence of language itself be seen.

These remarks are reminiscent of a way of thinking about poetry that goes back to early Romanticism and to the view that poetry was the original language of ancient peoples, that became profaned and degraded into the prose of everyday speech in the course of history. Heidegger revisits this idea a number of times. However, in contrast to some versions of it, he is neither attempting a historical argument nor arguing for the priority of poetry over the other arts. Instead his emphasis is on what poetry, as original language, tells us about language. Thus 'every genuine word is, as word, already poetic' (GA 52: 55). The continuing resonance – albeit for the most part unattended – of the poetic word in everyday usage thus becomes one of the guiding threads of Heidegger's whole hermeneutical strategy, as he rescues the essential meaning of words from their debased usage in idle, objectified talk.

But just as the question of poetry is not merely an issue in aesthetics, so too the question of language is not merely an issue in the philosophy of language, understood in the sense of an autonomous branch of philosophy.[3] For the question of language is not only tied up with the question of human existence (since we are ourselves, as language speakers, 'signs') but is also inseparable from the ever-decisive question of Being. This is spelt out by Heidegger in the 1934–5 lectures and establishes a position from which he never retreats. 'For in language man ventures furthest, putting himself altogether at risk by venturing out into Being. In language there occurs the revelation of beings ... In the power of language man becomes the witness of Being (*Seyn*)' (GA 39: 61–2). The poet, as the paradigmatic speaker of language is 'the founder of Being (*Seyn*)' (GA 39: 214).

Yet, paradoxically (although entirely in keeping with Heidegger's consistent view as to the interrelationship of Being and non-Being), language is, in a phrase of Hölderlin, 'the most dangerous of goods', because its potential for uncovering beings in their Being is inseparable from the dehiscence of Being accomplished in language. In other words, because human beings are human only in language and as speakers of language, it is language itself which separates them from the rest of nature, from the unspoken life of the animal kingdom and from biological and other forms of causality. Language itself is an ecstatic transcending of nature in the literal sense of the term ec-stasy, 'standing-out', and, as such, transports us into a dimension of relative non-being. Language is 'the most dangerous of goods' 'because it first creates and alone holds open the possibility of any kind of threat to Being' (GA 39: 62). A silent world is simply what it is; a world suffused with language, a world represented in language, is radically unstable, open to multiple and conflicting interpretations. 'Because man *is* in language he creates this danger and brings [upon himself and upon beings – GP] the destruction it threatens' (GA 39: 62). This danger may take one of two forms. In the mythological language of Heidegger's exposition of Hölderlin it may tempt us to blasphemy, to a presumption as to our own god-likeness, and our consequent destruction (as when we assume that our power of naming beings is itself creative and is the reason or ground for beings being as they are: Logos as reason). Or language may slip away from what it names and sink down into the superficiality of idle talk (GA 39: 63–6). Allowing our world to be shaped and defined by such idle talk, we slip into a way of life in which all our relationships are drained of any original, authentic relation to Being.

Now it might seem as if the course we have been following has involved a continual narrowing of focus. Beginning with art, we singled out poetry, and went on to isolate poetry in a stronger, more exclusive sense, 'the poetic', which was then, in its turn, defined as the unreadable sign that is the single, decisive word bestowed upon the poet by the gods; and in this single, decisive word the whole essence of language, the saying of Being, was, in turn, concentrated. This would not be entirely misleading – but it might lead us to ask what has happened to the promised feast? Hasn't Heidegger's procedure evacuated language of all its extensive riches and shrunk it down to a singular event? For all his protestations, doesn't such an approach rob poetry of its poetic expressiveness?

It is clearly not Heidegger's intention to undertake an exercise in reductionism. One element in his strategy is indeed to focus in on the singularity of the true poetic word, a word that is said to be foundational for the whole realm of language in all its manifold outworkings. Equally, however, he stresses that the poetic word exists only in the articulated structure of the poem as a whole. Each poem, each poet's poetic universe, may form a unitary whole under the impact of a single, decisive poetic word, but it is what it is and as it is as an internally differentiated composition or sequence of compositions. Furthermore, the word, the hinting sign, is never uttered except as a distinctive figuration of the irreducible fourfoldness of earth, sky, mortals and divinities.

Poetry and the fourfold

To see how this is worked out, we now turn to a closely interconnected complex of themes that Heidegger finds in Hölderlin's poetry: the 'Between', time, the rivers, wandering and place, the feast, measure, the event of appropriation, and remembrance. In the light of this we shall then go back to *What is called Thinking?* in order to see how this illuminates Heidegger's use of Hölderlin in that text in the context of his exposition of Parmenides and the Presocratics. In attempting to see these themes in their interdependence it is, however, necessary to remember three things. Firstly, that Heidegger does not himself present them systematically but only as they arise in the course of interpreting Hölderlin's poetry. Secondly, that the kind of interdependence concerned is that of fugal articulation rather than hierarchical construction, and that it would be misleading to single out any one as 'the' key to all the rest or as 'the' apex of Heidegger's exposition. Each is what it is and means what it means only by reference to all the others. Thirdly, that the themes chosen here are only a selection, and that the overall achievement of Heidegger's Hölderlin-interpretation is larger and more internally complex than it is possible to show in an introductory work. With this reservation, however, I believe that this group of topics does serve to convey something of the style, the tenor and the conceptual shape of Heidegger's view of Hölderlin and, through Hölderlin, of the nature of poetic language.

We have already seen that the place of the poet is, in one respect, that of mediator between gods and mortals. The site of this mediation, figured in the demi-gods, is named by Heidegger as 'the Between' (cf. GA 39: 285). This 'Between' can be envisaged in various ways. As the place where mortals and gods meet, it also marks the boundary that separates them, the extreme point of human possibility occupied by the poet, a point at which the question concerning the gods, the question of transcendence – i.e., the question as to what or who is to be found 'beyond' humanity – becomes pressing (GA 39: 167). As such it is also the 'Middle' of Being 'from out of which the whole realm of beings, gods, men, earth are to be newly brought out into the open' (GA 39: 183).

The middle of Being might also be spoken of as the 'Between' of

Being and non-Being, and as such equivalent to possibility, 'the possibility that belongs to actuality' (GA 52: 118) in the sense of that which does not exist in the manner of objects but has the potential to be realised in and through the freedom of action. This understanding of existential possibility is figured by Hölderlin in the image of the 'golden dream' – 'terrible but divine' (GA 52: 121).

The idea of possibility also points to the role of the 'Between' as the middle of time, the point of transition between past and future. What is to be shown forth in poetry is historicity in the sense of becoming in the midst of transiency: i.e., the movement of coming-into-being as the counter-movement to the flux of non-being and utter impermanence. It is what stays time, in the sense of restraining it, and thereby enabling a sense of presence to come to pass in the midst of ceaseless change (GA 52: 146). Throughout the realm of the transitional, of what exists as a process of passing from one state into another, the 'Between' establishes what is essential in the sense described above: of what abides (GA 52: 98).

When at the start of the poem 'The Ister' the poet invokes the divine fire, the lightning-flash of imagination, in the words 'Now come, fire', this is said by Heidegger to be the poet defining his place precisely in the 'now', the moment between past and future, that is also a moment of expectation. This present is metaphorically represented in the river itself, ceaselessly flowing, vanishing away in endless flux yet, in doing so, preserving its identity as just this river that it is.

In the light of Hölderlin's historical context, in an intellectual situation which, as described above, was shaped by a sequence of conflicting polarities, we might be tempted to see this privileging of the 'middle' as a poetic way of expressing what Hegel set out to do by means of dialectical logic and mediation. To do so, Heidegger insists, is not only to miss the point that poetic diction is not merely a sensuous or figurative expression for a non-sensuous idea, it is also to obscure the essential difference between Hegel and Hölderlin: namely, that whilst Hegel is fundamentally a metaphysical thinker, Hölderlin is not – a comment that throws further light on the relationship between Hölderlin and Nietzsche, 'the last metaphysical thinker of the West' (GA 52: 99).

Consideration of the 'Between' has led us to the river, the image of becoming-in-the-midst-of-flux, a tension most vividly captured in Hölderlin's comment on the Ister that it seems to flow backwards, towards its source.

Rivers were a recurrent theme in Hölderlin's poetry, and they are central to Heidegger's own remarks on Hölderlin. The river is itself a demi-god, a 'being-between' (GA 39: 163–4), originating in the mountains that are seen as the dwelling-place of the gods, and descending to water the land, making it habitable for mortals. Crucial to Heidegger's understanding of Hölderlin's rivers is his insistence that the river is not simply an image of Heraclitean flux. Remembering everything Heidegger has said about the nature of poetic language, the poetic figure of the river is not an image 'of' or 'for' anything else: it is itself the meaning it articulates. Consequently, the river itself exemplifies becoming-in-the-midst-of-flux, understood as the emergence of order, pattern and stability in and on the basis of flux. Take the Danube, which originates in the Southern German mountains but then seems abruptly to change course, and to veer off sideways, winding its way eastwards to the Black Sea. This may at first seem to be an example of sheer errancy, an aimless meandering across the face of the earth. Indeed, Heidegger says, 'The river is the state of wandering' (GA 55: 35). Yet such wandering is not aimless. For a start, the river only exists and only continues to be able to flow at all as long as it retains its connection with its source (as in the image of the river seeming to flow backwards). Therefore a memory or trace of the source abides throughout the whole course of the river. Even the sea into which it flows enters into this relationship, a point that Heidegger makes in connection with a line from the poem 'Remembrance', where Hölderlin figures poets as sailors seeking riches at sea. Such seeking is not in the spirit of those Heidegger describes as 'planetary adventurers' (GA 55: 59), who have lost all sense of home and of the distinction between belonging and rootlessness, for the riches that such sailor-poets seek belong to the origin. The river's connectedness to its source means that as it wanders across the surface of the earth it is able to shape the landscape, creating places where mortals can dwell (GA 39: 93). The river makes paths on the previously pathless earth. 'That state of wandering defines what it is to make oneself at home on earth' (GA 55: 36). 'The river bears "place" within itself. The river itself dwells' (GA 55: 36).

Once again warning us against a levelling, philosophical or allegorising approach to poetic language, Heidegger cautions against seeing the river as 'just' a symbol for time, and place as 'just' a symbol for space, as though we could achieve a higher level of understanding by translating the figures into abstract ideas. More decisive is the identification of the rivers with the poet himself: 'the rivers are the poets who establish the poetic as the basis upon which man dwells' (GA 55: 183). As such, and in the sense of what was said in *What is Called Thinking?* about humanity as a sign pointing towards that which calls for thinking, the poets are a sign: 'the sign, the demi-god, the river, the poet – all this poetically names the one and only basis of historical humanity's making itself at home and its being founded by the poets' (GA 55: 192).

The poetic word is only possible by virtue of the heavenly fire, the lightning, and is thus an ecstatic word. But, as in the case of the river, ecstasy should not be taken as implying anything aimless or random. The poet 'founds what abides in the midst of flux' (GA 4: 45f.). 'The poet is the founder of Being (*Seyn*)', i.e., of the people, the *Volk*, existing as the historical unity of gods, earth, humans and beings as a whole (GA 39: 214). The poetic is not boundless but 'The poetic is the measure of all things that remain constant' (GA 52: 164).

If Heidegger seems to be affirming Shelley's view that the poets are the unacknowledged legislators of mankind, and if the poet seems in this regard to be pulling ahead of the statesman, we should not lose sight of the enormous tension that is involved in the destiny of the poet. For if the poet exists as one who retains a memory of the source in the midst of life's temporal meanderings, that source is never available in any immediate or simple way. The poet's path leads through darkness and remote places, and only one who has been a wanderer far from home will be able to bring home the message concerning what lies at the place of origins (GA 4: 23–4). The way to the source is difficult, and means going against the stream (GA 52: 170). The source can only be named poetically, and that means only in the ambiguity of the hinting sign. The gods are present in memory, only as having-been (GA 39: 107). For the journey away from the source is not simply a mistake but is the precondition for the coming into existence of gods and mortals in their interrelatedness. 'What this means is that humanity in its historicity is from the very beginning not at home, but because its thinking and meditation (*Sinnen*) seeks what is homely its supreme concern is joy' (GA 52: 189). For the poet of the West, the evening land (i.e., modernity), it is axiomatic that the gods have fled. We are in Germany, not Greece.

This insistence on the inescapability of homelessness not only distinguishes Hölderlin's position from that of naive Romanticism, it also marks off Heidegger's strategy from a simple valorisation of poetry, Greece and the world of origins over against the wasteland of modernity. The errancy of modernity is not the fault of this or that error in philosophy, still less is it an accidental by-product of industrialisation, for it is a destining that comes from Being itself (understanding Being, of course, in the twofoldness of its nominal and verbal aspects, Being in beings).

Nevertheless, in the midst of flux, in the midst of ontological homelessness, in the face of the absence of the gods, the poetic word reaches out, transcending the consciousness of the poet himself, into the 'Between', creating a space and a time wherein, in the figure of the poetic word, gods and mortals meet in their mutual boundedness. Poetry, at its most elevated, is therefore essentially festal, for the feast is precisely and fundamentally the event in which Gods and mortals encounter one another and acknowledge, affirm and order their respective domains. Of course, the festival, too, is subject to the law of ambiguity. As an interruption to the routine of work it can be the occasion for mere idleness and escapism, but it can also be a time when we concern ourselves with what is most authentic and most fitting to humanity, 'which,' says Heidegger, 'is always out of the ordinary' (GA 52: 65). In this latter sense the festival is pre-eminently the wedding feast of gods and mortals (GA 52: 69) and therefore a time for play, for dance, for lighting up the darkness (GA 52: 66). The festival arouses rapture – not, however, in the sense of mere drunkenness, but in the sense of the elevation of feeling to what is highest, to the holy. Such rapture is modest and chaste; it does not dispel thought, but calls for thinking (GA 52: 146–7). Like poetry itself, the festival gives order and measure. The cycle of festivals determines the calendar, giving order to time (GA 52: 66). Therefore the festival is 'the ground and essence of history' (GA 52: 68).

It is in the context of the festival that we appropriate and make our own what is most proper to us. It is the event (*Ereignis*) in the double sense that this term has for Heidegger, of occurrence (its everyday sense) and appropriation (playing on the stem *eigen*: 'one's own', as in *eigentlich*: 'authentic'). This duality serves Heidegger's larger philosophical purpose of deconstructing the priority of the conscious individual subject, since although the element of appropriation (taking to oneself what is proper to one) does involve the subject, the aspect of event or happening suggests that, even in appropriating our own essence, we are not isolated from a larger context, from what simply happens. The logic is precisely analogous to that of destining, in Heidegger's special sense of something that is at one and the same time a destiny but also an adaptation of Being to the capacities of human beings. With specific regard to the festival this means that the elevation of the human subject to the rank of one who deals with the gods occurs only by the grace and favour of the festival itself and can only occur at the duly allotted time. 'The festival is that in which the initial event of appropriation occurs and that bears and permeates everything that is involved in mutual encountering in its encounter' (GA 52: 69). 'The event of appropriation is what is festal in the feast' (GA 52: 77).

Once again, however, Heidegger retains a note of reserve. This has two aspects. On the one hand, Heidegger notes that Hölderlin's characteristic theme is that of the 'eve', the night of celebration preceding the festival proper. As such it is the 'vigil of destiny' (GA 52: 92). At the same time, the festival occurs in poetry precisely under the condition of the poetic word being spoken now, in the godless time of the West and in the face of the need and destitution of planetary homelessness. The event of appropriation exists for us only in the mode of 'remembrance', as the title of one of Hölderlin's poems has it.

We are now in a position to see the significance of Heidegger's references to Hölderlin towards the end of *What is Called Thinking?* in the context of his interpretation of Parmenides and, particularly, of Parmenides' term *chrē*, 'useful'. The first reference is to 'The Ister' and runs

> It is useful for the rock to have
>   shafts,
> And for the earth, furrows,
> It would be without welcome,
>   without stay.

To this Heidegger comments that

> There is no welcome where no meal, no food and drink can be offered. There is no stay here for mortals, in the sense of dwelling at home. If mortals are to be made welcome and to stay, there must be water from the rock, wheat from the field … Shafts pierce the rock. They break a path for the waters … Shafts are no more necessary to the rock than furrows to the earth. But it belongs to the essence of welcome and being at home that it include the welling of water and the fruits of the field … The home and dwelling of mortals […] is not determined first by the pathless places on earth. It is marked out and opened by something of another order. From there, the dwelling of mortals receives its measure.
>
> (WCT: 190–1)

This giving of measure, as we have seen, is precisely the task of the poetic word itself, the word that names beings and allocates to them their place, their office, their meaning. Analogously – yet more than analogously, because we are talking about 'shafts' and 'furrows' as represented in a poetic word – the shafts, the rock and the furrows are not mere brute facts, items of geological information, but hang together with the whole complex of meanings that constitute human being-in-the-world (as Heidegger might have put it in 1929) or 'mortals dwelling on earth' (as he was putting it by 1950). The poetic saying does not itself create beings. Poets do not bring rocks, etc., into being. What they do do, however, is to set up and order the fugal articulation by which beings are brought into a mutually limiting yet mutually respecting order that is an order of a quite different kind from that of causality.

This is also the burden of a quotation from Hölderlin's poem, 'The Titans'.

> For under the firm measure,
> The crude, too, is useful,
> That the pure may know itself.

In this case Heidegger identifies the 'firm measure' with 'the face of the sky' as 'the place where the unknown God conceals himself' (WCT: 190). Left to itself, the earth would be shrouded in perpetual obscurity, but the fact that the earth lies open beneath the clearness of the sky makes it possible for a world to come into being. As so often, it sounds almost as if Heidegger himself is mythologising here, but he is not really concerned with what we might call cosmogony. For the measure given by the sky, the alternation of day and night, of summer and winter, seed-time and harvest, only becomes a measure for human dwelling by virtue of the festival, and, as we have heard, the meaning of the festival, its essential nature or truth, is revealed exclusively in the poetic word.

Now whether or not he is successful in persuading us of this, it is important for Heidegger that this poetic word is not to be understood in the perspective of pure subjectivity, along the lines of Nietzsche's creator-artist, as if the world itself were empty of meaning unless or until human artistry stamped a subjective meaning upon it. Nor is it to be taken in the sense of Romantic immediacy, as if the poet simply received his vision in a kind of unconscious or preconscious trance. The poetic word comes to us only in and as the appropriating event, the destining in which we come into possession of what is proper to us, namely, to dwell on earth, as mortals, beneath the open vault of the sky, before the face of the gods.

If in expounding Heidegger's reading of Hölderlin we seem to be moving in circles, that is perhaps inevitable, both in the light of Heidegger's fundamental commitment to hermeneutical circularity, and of his understanding of the co-implication of the manifold elements that are fugally articulated in the order-bestowing speaking of the poetic word. Heidegger himself speaks of this circularity in 'The Thing', when he writes of the fourfold that

The fouring presences as the worlding of world. The mirror-play of world is the round dance of appropriating. Therefore, the round dance does not encompass the four like a hoop. The round dance is the ring that joins while it plays as mirroring. Appropriating, it lightens the four into the radiance of their simple oneness. Radiantly, the ring joins the four, everywhere open to the riddle of their presence.

(PLT: 180)

That this invocation of the round dance flows from Heidegger's meditation on the jug points to the fact that, of course, the Hölderlin-interpretation is not itself separable from the other themes that make up the thought world of the later Heidegger. Whether we begin with the poetry of Hölderlin, the temple, or the jug, each in their own way gives us a way of envisaging the world as the fourfold of earth, sky, mortals and gods and in that way restores to us a genuine sense of what it is to be at home in the world. This vision of what it could mean to dwell on the earth offers an alternative to the nihilistic planetary adventure of technology. But this poetic vision also converges with the task of thinking and, above all, with the task of thinking what it is for beings to be. As such – and Hölderlin's own relation to the Greeks is paradigmatic here – poetry also brings us to that place of primordial saying that is found at the very first beginning of Western thought, in the Presocratic naming of one-and-all, of being-and-becoming, being and Logos (word). And this, to say it again, is not intended as some kind of philosophical primitivism, but as an insight into possibilities of saying, possible modes of language, that are both chronologically and ontologically prior to language as conceived by logic, i.e., as a means of asserting propositions. This is the place of seeing-as, understood as a linguistic event: the recognition that 'there is' ('it gives') Being, and the appropriation of that recognition as what is most proper to thinking.

And so the spiral could continue, turning back upon itself in ever larger, ever more inclusive revolutions, until it has taken in all of Heidegger's manifold exegeses, meditations and analyses, saying the same thing in different ways and in different combinations, as winding and endless as a forest path or the meandering of a great river.

But what does it all mean? Is this still philosophy in any recognisable sense? Or is the later Heidegger no more than a literary critic, or even a kind of poet? Or perhaps (and perhaps still worse, from the standpoint of philosophy) a mystic or the prophet of new epiphanies and new gods? Or does his talk of mountains, rivers, rocks and seas mark him out as the first thinker of deep ecology, an intellectual eco-warrior devoted to the destruction of the technological world order and preparing the way for that non-anthropocentric world order that will follow upon the end of technology? And if, finally, it is at all meaningful to talk of Heidegger as a philosopher, what kind of philosopher is he? And, no less importantly, how good a philosopher is he? And how, if we are able to understand it, are we to judge his philosophical achievement? It is to these questions that we now turn.

Chapter 8

What kind of thinker?

We have followed Heidegger along some of the paths that collectively constitute the map of his later thinking, although in each case we have only succeeded in going a little of the way and have merely touched on issues that have each generated their own ever-expanding secondary literature: the question of his Nazism, his critique of technology and the turn to art, his readings of Nietzsche and of the Presocratics as the beginning and end points of his grand renarration of the history of philosophy, his embracing of Hölderlin as a provi-dential gift to thinking in a destitute time – but what, in the end, does it all amount to? More specifically, what is there in this massive body of writing that makes it of interest to philosophers? Why should we not bracket it with the works of cultural commenta-tors like Spengler, Lewis Mumford or Arnold Toynbee? Such thinkers, masters of the 'vision thing', are respectable enough in their own terms, and, at one level, there would be no cause for shame if Heidegger were to be classed among them – perhaps, indeed, as the greatest of them. Counting against this, however, are Heidegger's own ceaseless polemics against the confusion of philosophy and 'world-view', and his constant pursuit of a path of thinking that is not constrained within nor predetermined by any actual or possible world-view. Heidegger is not, as such thinkers are, offering a 'philosophy for our time'. Heidegger repeatedly insists that his are ways, not works, and that the aim is not the revelation of a new view of life but the most adequate formulation of a question. We are, of course, perfectly free to refuse Heidegger's own self-interpretation and to regard what he calls his questions as merely the rhetorical form of a doctrine. And even if we do accept the genuineness of his questioning, we may still regard it as too imprecise, too general, too unscholarly to count as philosophical in any significant sense.

But if Heidegger did not want to be read as the proponent of a visionary system, can we thereupon conclude that he wanted to be read as a philosopher? After all, one of the central claims made over and over again in his later thought is that everything we have known as philosophy, from Plato to Nietzsche (and taking in Christian theology) is but one way of enframing truth and, indeed, a way that has led us to the dangerous situation of virtually forgetting Being. So isn't the whole movement of his later thought a movement away from philosophy as we have known it towards a new kind of thinking, albeit a kind of thinking that must, for now, remain enigmatic? Answering such questions affirmatively, wouldn't we want to say that, whatever else it may be, Heidegger's later thought just isn't philosophy?

Such a conclusion, however, would obscure the fact that, whether we finally agree to call it philosophy or not, the later Heidegger situates his thought in a constant and decisive relation to the history of philosophy. His programme of overcoming metaphysics is not a simple repudiation of the philosophical tradition, and it is typical of Heidegger's method that he prepares the way for the advent of a new kind of thinking by reading the tradition anew. To be sure, the thinking that is to come is not simply one more development in the history of ideas, a 'higher' stage of consciousness à la Hegel, since there is a significant break or moment of discontinuity. On the other hand, this does not mean that it is entirely unconnected to what has gone before. The history of Being does not progress in the manner of a step-by-step linear development but by a series of leaps, yet Heidegger claims that these leaps are not random or arbitrary and have their own inner fittingness to the situation in which they occur; they are events of appropriation in which the subjective act of appropriation is inseparable from the self-giving of Being.

Even without subscribing to Heidegger's own grand narrative, it would not be hard to argue that philosophy today is in a state of crisis. Its status in the university and its very nature are matters of intense debate, and the general picture is both extraordinarily pluralistic and extraordinarily fluid. The great traditions of 'continental' and 'Anglo-Saxon' philosophy continue on their separate ways, but they are each continually challenged by the claims and counter-claims of other disciplines (e.g., science, social science and literary theory) and the demands of new or newly reconceptualised issues (e.g., gender, genetics and post-Marxist politics). It is even happening that some 'continental' philosophers are taking lessons from the Anglo-Saxons, and, even more improbably, some Anglo-Saxons are engaging with continental philosophy (and sometimes even reading Heidegger). In this situation it is extremely difficult to pretend to any kind of authority in declaring what philosophy 'is'. Different philosophical cultures, in which diverse questions are being pursued by diverse methods, co-exist with greater or lesser degrees of mutual understanding and respect. Whether Heidegger is to count as a philosopher, then, might seem to be simply a matter of where one is coming from. For some he is the only modern philosopher of whom it can be said with certainty that he will come to rank alongside Plato, Aristotle, Kant and the other greats. Others suspect him of having been a charlatan, a Wizard of Oz figure whose awesome fireworks cannot finally conceal the pettiness of the man behind the curtain.

Is it then simply a question of consumer choice in the global hypermarket of ideas? That those who like this kind of thing will go for it, and others won't?

That is tempting, but glib. For even those who like that kind of thing ought to be capable of giving further thought to what exactly it is they like (and why), whilst those who don't should be able not only to say why not (and that, minimally, means taking the trouble to read those they wish to exclude) but also to acknowledge the possibility that they might, after all, be overlooking something of value. Both, then, ought to be able to unite in asking whether Heidegger is, in any significant sense, a philosopher, and, if so, in what sense. But that also means being willing to face the question that Heidegger himself put to the philosophical tradition: a question that calls the very existence of philosophy into question. What, then, do we mean by philosophy? What is it to philos-ophise? Or, simply, to think? These are questions posed by Heidegger himself, and they are questions we must address if we are to take seriously the question as to Heidegger's own philosophical status.

My procedure in this chapter will be that of a *via negativa* in that, before asking directly what is genuinely philosophical in Heidegger's later thought, I shall look at a number of other ways in which we might categorise it: as poetry, as mysticism, as deep ecology. In each case we shall see that there are some grounds for seeing Heidegger as, respectively, a poet, a mystic or a deep ecologist, but also that none of these really get to the heart of the matter. Finally, then, I shall suggest why only an appreciation of the philosophical intentions of the later Heidegger provides a point of view from which adequately to evaluate his way of thinking.

Poetry

There is a certain plausibility in seeing the later Heidegger as essentially a poetic thinker. His own lectures on Hölderlin repeatedly draw attention to the kinship between poetry and thinking, even asserting that 'thinking is a co-poetising' – and, of course, the lectures on Hölderlin themselves demonstrate Heidegger's view that philosophy has important business amongst the poets. Not only this, but Heidegger's own thinking becomes increasingly 'poeticised', as in his description of the jug that, in the act of pouring, makes present the fourfold. In 'The Thinker as Poet' (from the collection *From the Experience of Thinking*) Heidegger presents some of his characteristic thoughts in poetic form:

> In thinking all things
> become solitary and slow
> (PLT: 9)

writes the thinker, in words that once more provoked Adorno's sarcasm (Adorno 1986: 52).

Also relevant in this context is Heidegger's translation of the Parmenides fragment, and the concern expressed in his discussion of its grammatical form to make us aware of modes of speaking and writing that elude the net of propositional logic (yet which, Heidegger claims, are not thereby unthinking or lacking in rigour).

In a very broad, sense, then, it might seem justifiable to see the later Heidegger as a poetic rather than as a narrowly philosophical thinker, whose genius (if genius it is) is to evoke, to suggest, to hint and to lure rather than to argue or to assert. Ambiguity and inconclusiveness are, in this perspective, not so much signs of Heidegger's failure to think clearly as part of the script. Two comments from Gerald L. Bruns nicely capture the quality I am trying to suggest.

> His writings on language and poetry do not represent the unfolding of a theory. They are rather a lingering with a subject matter, where lingering means holding back, not seeking advancement or mastery, refusing to determine the subject conceptually, acknowledging Parmenides' judgment 'that everything that lies before us is ambiguous'.
>
> (Bruns 1981: 150)

> The folly of trying to follow closely ... his later writings, comes out very forcefully when you try to stop, because there is no natural stopping place, no place of arrival, where everything falls into place and you can say, 'Well now that's done: and I'm glad it's over'.
>
> (*Ibid.*: 174)

If that judgment stands it will, of course, put Heidegger beyond consideration for some philosophers, and bring him into the orbit of deconstruction (as Bruns in fact argues).

Yet if the later Heidegger not only concerns himself *with* poetry but also lectures and writes in a way that is, however loosely, describable as 'poetic', this does not mean the simple neglect of philosophy. It is not as if Heidegger has given up philosophy in order to devote himself to poetry. Rather, the move to a more poetic subject matter and form of expression is itself positioned by his understanding of the history and crisis of philosophy.

Does it follow from this that we must now change tack and, instead of categorising Heidegger as a poet, charge him with subordinating poetry to philosophy? Is Heidegger, after all, simply re-enacting the Hegelian trope of seeing in art the 'merely' external or sensuous form of inner, spiritual truth? Or, more subtly, the Schellingian approach that, whilst elevating the aesthetic intuition above all form of ratiocinative reflection, nevertheless turns art itself into a kind of philosophy? In other words, does positioning art philosophically inevitably mean deciding in advance on the question as to whether art and art's figurative mode of expression are simply another way of expressing the same thing as philosophy?

Heidegger, however, consistently refuses to adopt any kind of hierarchisation. The poet is not 'higher' than the thinker or the statesman, or vice versa. All are equal but different. How, then, can we articulate that difference?

Heidegger's way is, at this point, characteristically circular. Art may, at first, seem to be the more original, since it is art that, as active bringing-forth, first gives thinking its matter, i.e., something to think about. Language is the matter of thinking and the aim of thinking is to let language itself speak, but the essence of language, language's own primordial speaking, is to be heard precisely in poetic diction. Yet – and this is where the argument turns back upon itself in a self-supporting circle – poetic diction is what it is as *thought*, since we could never say that there was a kind of poetry that was not already thinking. Poetry is never thoughtless in the manner of an animal or a stone, although, as we have seen, the full meaning of the poetic word overreaches the poet himself. It is not something he possesses but is something spoken by him. In this respect the thinker has the possibility of understanding the poet better than he understands himself.

Heidegger, we know, had no problems with circular procedures in thinking, so we may not be able to hold out much hope of getting out of this particular circle. Nevertheless, we may take it to another level by recalling how, for Heidegger, thinking is always governed by what is unthought, and this in two ways. Firstly, all serious thinking is an attempt to reach beyond that with which we are already familiar, that which we already know, and to grapple with what we have not yet understood. Thinking, in other words, is aroused by puzzlement, by aporia. But, secondly (and this may be regarded as a particular application of the previous point) the unthought is what governs interpretation, in that the thinking interpretation of a great thinker does not seek merely to extract and reformulate the content of the work under consideration, but to look beyond the work itself to the original puzzlement that inflamed the thinker's own passion for thought. So, too, in the case of poetry. The thinking interpreter is not concerned solely with what the poet says nor even the how of its being said. What matters is the attempt to think what the poet himself did not think and did not say in the poem, what overreaches the poet's self-consciousness and the formal content of the work.

It might be objected that, even if this does not lead to a subordination of poetry to thinking à la Hegel or Schelling, it may nevertheless end by giving philosophy the last word. This is how Véronique Fóti, a stern critic of Heidegger's approach to poetry, sees it. '[Heidegger's] insistence on the essential unsaid as the unitary source of textual configuration repudiates unreadability, the antidote to totalisation' (Fóti 1992: 46). For Fóti it seems that the poetic element in poetry has to do precisely with the way in which poetry challenges our assumptions about meaning and 'readability'. This is why, for example, poetry is the best language we have for addressing the tragic and for posing the possibility of the radical and irreconcilable rupture in consciousness highlighted by tragedy. It is for such reasons that she sees Heidegger's failure to rise to the challenge of Auschwitz as symptomatic – a failure epitomised in his non-meeting with Paul Celan. Heidegger's totalising view, she says, insures in advance against any such fatal rupture in meaning.

Her remarks are, intentionally, hostile; but, looking at it from the side of philosophy, might we not argue, by analogy with Kant's assumption concerning the intelligibility of the world as a whole, that philosophy does indeed have a duty to humanity and to itself to press the claims of readability and to refuse the opt-out of allowing in advance for any lacunae, any moments of sheer nonsense in discourse? And if this conjures up the shades of rationalistic hubris, we should not immediately conflate this insistence on meaningfulness with totalising rationalism in a narrow sense. To insist on the principle of wholeness and to claim to have comprehended the totality are two very different things.

In this connection it is important once more to note that Heidegger's distinctive way of defining the role of the thinker in relation to poetry focuses on the thinker's search for what is unthought in the work, and this already puts a block on any simplistic reduction of the complexity and ambiguity of the work to any determinate system of meaning, idealistic or materialistic as the case may be. For the unthought, as we have heard Heidegger claim, is immeasurably deep, and, as he also insists, every revealing is at the same time also a concealing: truth is untruth. The process of interpretation, then, cannot be brought to a halt by producing a final philosophical 'truth' as the 'true' meaning of the work. Every interpretation is provisional, but – and this, I think, expresses Heidegger's philosophical commitment in a positive sense – the infinite delay in reaching an end to interpretation does not mean that we simply surrender the possibility of meaning. Thought is led ever onwards by the guiding conviction that there is something to be thought, something to understand in each and every poem or human production, in every experience of the world. Philosophy in the narrow sense of what is currently practised in university departments of philosophy, will not, of course, be able to do all the work of interpretation, which will inevitably devolve upon the various disciplines, especially the interpretative disciplines of the humanities. Philosophy can, however (and, arguably, must) seek to stimulate the conscience, the will to meaningfulness, of the interpretative disciplines, to say 'never give up on the effort to make sense, to understand, no matter how obscure, how uncharted, how tedious, or how impossible the search may seem'.

Seeing it like this brings Heidegger close to deconstruction, with its practice of breaking open any and every closed system of meanings, but it also suggests why Heidegger cannot be counted as a simple deconstructionist (and, perhaps, why deconstruction itself, or any theory or practice of sheer difference, cannot dispense with some kind of relation, however polemical, to the principle of meaningfulness). As Bruns puts it, if the later Heidegger is closer to Derrida than we often suspect (particularly when Heidegger is caricatured as the oracle of a colossally inflated principle of Being), Derrida is also closer to Heidegger than many Derridians allow (Bruns 1981: 198).

Mysticism

A second 'charge' (if one sees it that way) is that the later Heidegger is simply indulging in mysticism, trading in the clarity of argument and definition for a mystical rhetoric in which Being (under erasure) plays the role of the hidden God of negative theology, and the 'gods' play the part of that God's fleeting epiphanies.[1] Or it might be felt that, even if there is no specific doctrinal link-up, the overall mood of the later Heidegger is 'religious', a religiosity without God or Church. Commenting on Heidegger's reflections on the history of Being and the various 'destinings' bestowed by being upon humanity (and, more specifically, on our situation in this time of destitution between the departure of the old gods and the coming of the new), Karl Löwith saw this as a rewriting of the Christian myth of Creation, Fall and Redemption, with Heidegger's account of our present situation modelling itself on the theological understanding of the Church between the Ascension and the Second Coming. Löwith – writing in the 1940s, when relatively few of the works that make up the later Heidegger had been published – saw Being as having supplanted Heidegger's earlier focus on Dasein to such an extent that the parameters of finitude and temporality had all but vanished. Despite Heidegger's own protestations against identifying Being with 'the Supreme Being' of metaphysical theology and against seeing it as in any way 'personal' like the theistic God, Löwith argued that it was virtually impossible not to compare Heidegger's Being with the Judaeo-Christian God, periodically revealing Himself to mortals for purposes that are both inscrutable and, as yet, unfulfilled. Whereas in *Being and Time*, Being 'is' only as long as Dasein is, Dasein itself now exists only by the grace and favour of Being. But, asks Löwith, 'how should one be able not simply to wish, hope, believe, but to know, that the Being of all beings is essentially interested in us humans, not to mention in the Europeans?' (Löwith 1995: 57–8). How, he asks, can Being both be and do all that Heidegger ascribes to it – giving itself, revealing itself, withholding itself – unless it is personal? And surely it is a fundamentally important question whether this giving is a mere occurrence or the gift of a loving, personal deity? Although this latter possibility is consistently disallowed by Heidegger Löwith comments that 'In the end, Heidegger the thinker … is today not at all far removed from the religious writer Kierkegaard' (1995: 62). Like Nietzsche, Heidegger claims not to be directing us towards anything 'super-sensuous', but what is more super-sensuous than Being (Löwith 1995: 126)? And what is Heidegger's *Seinsverlassenheit* ('abandonment by Being') but a transcription of Nietzsche's proclamation of the death of God (Löwith 1995: 115–16)?

Now Löwith is undeniably justified in drawing attention to the strong analogy between aspects of Christian theology and modern religious thought, on the one hand, and the very grand narrative that seemingly constitutes the thought of the later Heidegger. However, it does not follow that they are simply 'the same', nor that Heidegger is not justified, in his own terms at least, in holding them apart.

How might he do that?

To answer this question we need to retrace the story of Heidegger's involvement with religion. It is now clear that his early intellectual development was inseparable from his immersion, firstly, in Catholic theology, with special emphasis on the mystical philosophy of the Middle Ages and scholastic theology, and, secondly, the theology of Paul, Augustine, Luther and Kierkegaard (see Kisiel 1993). This second group of influences played a particularly important part in the formation of *Being and Time*, as it offered an account of human existence that focused on the anguished individual, challenged to take upon himself the burden of his finitude and mortality, living 'between the times', cut off from the naiveté of an original paradisal absorption in the world but not yet arrived at a final, eschatological resolution, and orientating himself in the meanwhile by 'moments of vision' in which time is seized resolutely as the possibility of authentic existence.

Important as these religious sources are, Heidegger is consistent in his evaluation of them. He acknowledges that they provide the material, the ontic evidence upon which the ontological analysis will build. However, such analysis is alien to the religious thinker, and a Luther or a Kierkegaard, no matter how acute their psychological observations on the human condition, remain at the level of the ontic or *existentiell*. Their question was never the question of Being but such individual, personal questions as 'How can I find a gracious God?' or 'How can I become a Christian?' *How* they addressed such questions shows us, their readers, what resolute confrontation with finitude, guilt and death might mean, but they themselves never understood the ontological meaning of their works. It takes the advent of the ontological thinker to think what is unthought in their own works. Heidegger does not therefore regard himself as having to affirm or even take a position on their religious faith, since he is interested in something else entirely. Nor need this disinterest be regarded as anti-theological. Heidegger's Marburg colleague, Rudolf Bultmann (a leading New Testament scholar who used Heidegger's existential analyses to translate the anthropology of the New Testament into modern terms), agreed that the central concern of theology was not metaphysical speculation but faith, and the call to faith and the explication of faith did not need to appeal to ontological categories. When the would-be convert asks what is necessary for salvation, the answer is not an ontological description but an *existentiell* challenge: 'Repent and be baptised!' The religious appeal always occurs in the context of a unique and concrete I and Thou, speaking the particular language of their time and place. It was thus possible for Heidegger and Bultmann, from their very different perspectives, to agree an admittedly unstable truce (see Pattison 1999: 140–4).

If the existential analyses of *Being and Time* are strongly analogous to the *existentiell* analyses of Kierkegaard, they not only leave out the theological orientation that permeates Kierkegaard's whole authorship, they also, more specifically, pass by Kierkegaard's Christological works: i.e., his appeal to the Incarnation as a way out of the situation of *existentiell* estrangement. Strangely, perhaps, the later Heidegger comes close to Kierkegaard in this respect, since there is a very strong analogy between Kierkegaard's account of the Incarnation as the paradoxical encounter between God and humanity that offends reason, is incognito and hidden under the 'sign of contradiction', and Heidegger's account, via Hölderlin, of the poet as the bearer of the heavenly fire that is hintingly and ambiguously articulated in the poetic word. The poet no more makes the divine immediately present than does Kierkegaard's incognito Christ, who is accessible only to faith – and in each case understanding is arrived at only on the basis of a leap.

This might seem to strengthen Löwith's charge that what we are dealing with here is a covert theology. Yet here too the earlier distinction between the ontic and the ontological can be applied. The mere fact of a formal analogy does not explain what kind of analogy it is, still less does it mean that Heidegger's later thought is in some way controlled or determined by the Christian myth. Even if this myth is in play, in a Kierkegaardian or in any other form, it need not be regarded as more than an ontic, *existentiell* testimony to that which is to be thought, which, in turn, is also what is unthought in the myth itself.

Now although Heidegger seemed willing, at one point at least, to conclude a truce with theology of an existential orientation, he had a far more hostile view of the God of philosophical theology. In his view the Christian tradition, through Augustine's Christian Platonism and Thomas Aquinas' adaptation of a Latinised Aristotle for Christian purposes, had allowed its God to be absorbed into the Supreme Being of metaphysics. In Heidegger's own terms, the Christian Creator God had become identified with onto-theology. The result of this was that theology had become incapable of speaking of God's radical otherness, since, by construing God metaphysically, it had placed him on a continuum with beings and trapped him within the reifying system of enframing. Is this charge justified?

Insofar as Aquinas does acknowledge that we cannot know God as He is in Himself, he would seem to have a basis for rebutting Heidegger's accusation of conflating God with the Supreme Being. Nevertheless, he goes on to argue that human language *is* capable of speaking truthfully (or 'properly') about God. Following Augustine, Aquinas regarded it as axiomatic that God is that being in whom essence and existence coincide, that God's Being is to be what He is. A biblical warrant for this claim was adduced from Exodus Ch. 3, verses 13–14, when God tells Moses that His name is 'I am who I am'. Augustine and Aquinas interpreted this as meaning that ' "He who is" is the most appropriate name for God' (*Summa Theologiae* 1a. 13.11). For this name signifies existence itself and, as such, is universal and establishes an implicit relation to every possible entity, since the existence of all entities must, according to Aquinas' logic, derive from the supreme existence of God. It is, moreover, uttered in the present tense and therefore bespeaks the abiding, constant presence of God – i.e., of Being-Itself – in and to all creatures/beings. In the derivation of beings from God and in God's constant presence to beings resides the possibility of an analogy of Being, whereby, despite every difference between Creator and creature, infinite and finite, eternal and temporal, every being *qua* being is implicitly related to every other being – and this includes the Supreme Being, who is thereby brought within the compass of a general ontology. Whether this is regarded as a good or a bad thing, and whatever consequences flow from holding this position, Heidegger's case would seem to be vindicated.

But if Heidegger's charge that all theology is onto-theology may indeed apply to a theology that incorporates the kind of mongrel Platonic-Aristotelian doctrine of Being characteristic of medieval scholasticism, is he justified in asserting that all theology is metaphysical? After all, Heidegger was very well aware of the Lutheran repudiation of metaphysics, and of thinkers like Kierkegaard in the nineteenth century and Karl Barth in the twentieth century who insisted on the 'wholly other' nature of God and the 'infinite qualitative difference' between God and humanity. He was also aware of Jewish traditions that preserved a theology of otherness, traditions of which thinkers like Rosenzweig and Buber were prominent contemporary representatives. If, then, Heidegger may be correct in differentiating his own questioning of Being from those theologies that insist on the identification of God and Being, how does it stand with theologies that argue for an anti-metaphysical God, a God of radical alterity?

There is scarcely scope here to answer such a question, which is at the very centre of current debate in theology itself (see Summerell 1998), but we can perhaps hope to focus it a little more sharply.

In the first place we must remember that it is by no means self-evident that every theology that claims to speak for a God of radical otherness really does so. After all, even theology that claims to base itself solely on divine revelation and, in doing so, declares the impassable gulf between human reason and divine revelation, does so in human language, with grammar, syntax and vocabulary shared with other human language users. Even if religious life in general, and theology in particular, develops its own specialised vocabulary and idioms, it still has to make itself comprehensible to those who are being inducted into its belief-system, and if what the theologian or religious believer says is simply unintelligible, he will soon find himself ignored. The claim that religious belief is nevertheless comprehensible to a cognitive minority who are the beneficiaries of experiences or faculties denied to others is patently a piece of special pleading that may satisfy those who believe themselves to be so blessed but is as meaningless as any other private language to those outside the fold.

The problem, then, is how to communicate God's otherness (that is claimed as the foundation and guarantee of the godliness of the message) in language that is common, public, shared. Minimally, a theology that would want to accept Heidegger's critique of onto-theology would have to wrestle with this problem of communication. But is this problem resolvable at all? Heidegger himself, as we have seen, had recourse to poetry in order to speak of non-objectifiable Being, but can theology redefine itself as poetry without surrendering its distinctive truth-claims? And can it surrender its truth-claims and remain theology? And how could such a theology ground or promote any practical religious and moral imperatives? Wouldn't it be drawn towards the kind of quietism that some critics regard as typical of the later Heidegger?

But if, as these last comments suggest, Heidegger is justified in keeping his distance from theology (even if he falls short of being able to rule out absolutely the possibility of a non-metaphysical theology or way of thinking about God), what about the claim that Heidegger himself is some kind of mystic?

Mysticism is, of course, a word that means different things to different commentators, and for some it is no more than a term of abuse. Taking it here as implying the claim to some kind of direct experience of God, even if – especially if – that experience is described as entirely apophatic, negative and ineffable, the experience of noth-ingness or sheer otherness, we can once again see possible analogies with the later Heidegger. More broadly, the passive, quietistic attitude characteristic of much mysticism, and the demotion of will and self-assertion, also calls to mind Heidegger's repudiation of the dominatory aspect of technological thinking, understood as the supreme expression of the will-to-will. Heidegger's own deliberate adoption of the idea of 'abandonment' (*Gelassenheit*) from the writings of the best-known medieval German mystic, Meister Eckhart, points to his sympathy for the mystic's self-surrendering, letting-be, the abandonment of striving and self-assertion (see Heidegger 1966).

Nevertheless, it would seem to be impossible for Heidegger to go along with any claim to immediate intuition of God. At several points we have discussed his appeal to categorial intuition, but, firstly, such intuitions are not separable from the appearance of beings in the world. They do not give us a pure contemplation of Being, but of beings in Being. Categorial intuition does not, and by its nature cannot, leave the world or get behind the fourfold fugal articulation of Being in earth, sky, mortals and gods. The difference, the rift between beings and Being always intervenes. There is nothing to see, nothing to intuit beyond the world. But are there not mystical writings that also speak of this moment of nothingness or emptiness, of the incapacity of thought or image in the face of the divine abyss? There are well-known examples of this within the Christian tradition (and again Eckhart provides a particularly important example), and such an emphasis is even more characteristic of some Eastern traditions.

A certain affinity with elements of Buddhism (especially Zen) and also with Daoism have long been the subject of comment in connection with the later Heidegger. There is a substantial history of Heidegger-reception in Japan that explores these affinities (see Buchner 1989), and Heidegger's own essay 'Conversation with a Japanese' acknowledges that there was a possible rapport between his own thought and Japanese philosophy. At one point he also contemplated translating the Daoist classic, the *Daodeching* (see Parkes 1987: 93ff.).

The problems of dialogue between very diverse religious and philosophical cultures inevitably thrust themselves to the fore the moment we attempt to follow such hints further, and 'Conversation with a Japanese' is itself very preoccupied with the extent to which transcultural understanding is at all possible.

This concern is particularly acute when it comes to questions of religion. If Zen, for example, seems to speak of Buddhist enlightenment or satori as an 'experience of nothingness' or 'pure experience' (in the terminology of the influential twentieth-century Japanese philosopher Nishida Kitaro), how can that be related to Western concepts of religious experience, particularly if there is no personal God at the other end of the experience? For Zen, it would seem to make redundant the whole subject–object framework presupposed by Western models of an encounter between a human subject and a transcendent personal deity. But this is not only because Zen does not require belief in a deity, since it also refuses to ascribe any ontological significance to our sense of self. If Christian mysticism can speak of self-surrender as a moment, perhaps the consummatory moment of mystical experience, Zen asks us to recognise that there was never any self to surrender in the first place! As Nishida put it, pure experience is prior to the interpretation or constitution of experience as the experience 'of' an individual. '[I]t is not that the individual possesses feeling and the will, but rather that feeling and the will create the individual' (Nishida 1987 [1992]: 19). Similarly, the interpretation of religious experience as human experience 'of' God is undermined, since in pure experience there is no separation of human and divine. In such experience there is a direct relation to or identification with Being-*sive*-Nothingness, to reality itself. But this 'reality itself' is not conceived along the lines either of 'real' objects, nor of Kantian 'things-in-themselves' hidden behind the sensuous veil of experience. Being-*sive*-Nothingness is not the 'object' of experience, but the place, the topos (Japanese: *Basho*) that undermines the duality of subject and object, being and Nothingness.

It almost goes without saying that there are philosophers (and theologians) in the Western tradition who will not find any of this any more illuminating than what they regard as the confusion of categories in the later Heidegger, and who refuse to allow any sense to a concept of experience that bypasses or undercuts the assumption of a unitary subject of experience. No matter how difficult it may be to define this subject or explain how it relates to the known world, simply declaring the whole subject–object, self–world, divine–human structures to be illusory or unfounded would seem to be too easy a solution.

Again we cannot follow the argument further here, and it is not my intention to embark upon an apologia for Zen experience or its philosophical interpretation (see, however, Pattison 1996: 108–37). The point I am making here is limited to noting the analogies to Heidegger, analogies that include the attempt to think past the conceptualisation of the experience in terms of dualistic categories, the relativisation of Being and Nothingness, and the concern for the 'place' or 'site' of thinking and experience. It is also striking that both in Zen and in Heidegger we encounter the recognition that all of this has immense implications for communication, and in both we see, for example, the use of everyday objects, like Heidegger's jug or the implements of the Zen tea-ceremony, as means of awakening us to the truth of how things are.

And there is a further point. If Zen enlightenment seems to be proffered as the answer to an individual's religious quest, a quest provoked perhaps by intimations of mortality, it is not understood simply in personal terms. It does not just give an answer to the question 'How must I live?' but also to the question 'How is it with the world?' In this regard, Zen experience is understood as ontological disclosure. Here it relates itself both to Buddhist concepts such as dharma (or universal law) and to the Daoist concept of the Dao, or 'Way'.

Perhaps this latter concept is particularly fruitful for exploring the affinities between Heidegger and Eastern thought. For the Dao is a category that has both cosmic and human aspects. It is both 'how things are', the way the universe hangs together in an ordered but non-causal fashion, and, in response to that, the way in which humans should conduct themselves. Daoist philosophy is also generally regarded as allowing for a more temporalised understanding of the world than classical Western metaphysics: if the Way abides in the midst of change, it is not conceived of as other or separable from the world of change in the way that, e.g., Platonic ideas are (at least popularly). The Dao cannot be known or represented by means of abstract thought, but can only be interpreted concretely and figuratively. There is a particular resonance with Heidegger's lectures on Hölderlin in the prominence of water imagery in Daoism, a feature that led one commentator to subtitle his introductory book on the Dao 'The

Watercourse Way' (see Watts 1979). As in Zen experience, there is a certain relativisation of subject and object, human and non-human, Being and Nothingness, and yet, whereas Zen tends to emphasise the moment of enlightenment or satori and thus to highlight personal liberation, the tone of Daoist philosophy is more one of detached contemplation, corresponding to Heidegger's own category of 'abandonment', of adapting oneself to the way things are in their ceaseless, flowing becoming.

In all of these ways, Daoist thought fits well with what I have spoken of as Heidegger's concern with the fugal articulation of beings in Being, and with his understanding of the Parmenidean *chrē*, 'useful'.

If there is scope for exploring the connections between Heidegger and East Asian thought at greater length, it is important to keep both a sense of proportion and a certain reserve. Reinhard May, for example, has spoken of Daoism as a 'hidden source' of Heidegger's thought, and it is certainly likely that, like other German-speaking intellectuals of his generation, Heidegger may well have encountered the *Daodeching* in translation quite early in his career. However, it is probably more fruitful, and certainly adequate for any attempt at a philosophical interpretation, simply to note the affinities without attempting to track down their sources, especially as the elements that link Heidegger, Zen and Daoism also relate to other currents in his thought (e.g., the Presocratics). In any case, we should be clear that Heidegger did not subscribe to any religious programme based on Eastern philosophy, and there is nothing that hints at his promoting any particular course of meditation or spiritual training or of raising the prospect of some kind of enlightenment. Still less is there any overt orientalism. Neither Heidegger's nor our interests here are with the exotic aspect of East Asian thought, but with the real, if imprecise, affinities between the one and the other.

It is noticeable that, whereas Heidegger seems to have been relatively at ease in acknowledging these affinities, he was always very explicit about the difference between his own thought and anything 'religious' or 'theological' in the Christian sense. Perhaps the biographical background of this difference in attitude is readily understandable. However, this is arguably more than a merely personal issue, since Heidegger's personal animus against the Judaeo-

Christian tradition may have led him to overlook real elements in his own thought that do connect with the theological tradition and also to misread that tradition itself. Certainly Heidegger's own words should not lead us into overemphasising the Eastern tone of the later Heidegger at the expense of his Western roots. And, as was also the case with regard to Heidegger's reading of Hölderlin's relation to the Greeks, we should not forget that the time and place of Heidegger's encounter with the East is that of the modern, Western crisis of metaphysics. *This* is the site of *our* destiny, and we cannot circumvent it by applying the insights of other traditions in an uninterpreted, unqualified way.

Deep ecology

One of the dominant themes of the later Heidegger is the critique of technology. Tracing the danger of contemporary technology back to its essence in the enframing mind-set of metaphysics, his figuration of the fourfold of earth, sky, mortals and gods might seem to offer a way of envisaging the world that could break the grip of technological thinking and prepare us for a post-technological era. Yet although Heidegger's rhetoric clearly invokes many of the anxieties aroused by the contemporary environmental crisis, his concern with the essence rather than with the fact of technology might seem to result in a situation parallel to that of his relation to religion – i.e., that his is a policy of deliberate non-involvement in the 'merely' ontic, the level on which the day-to-day decisions of societies as well as individuals operate. Even if there are passages that suggest that his preoccupation with the essence of technology was in the cause of preparing humanity to face the challenge of assuming responsibility for technology, the very fact that many of his reflections on technology come from the period of his inner emigration and his retreat from the public world of political decision-making makes it all the more difficult to see how what he has to say might help us in the face of environmental degradation and devastation.

There is a real difficulty here, both in understanding the exact thrust of Heidegger's argument and in relating his insights to what we might regard as the needs of the present. If one of his complaints against Nazism was that it finally failed to confront the issue of technology, doesn't his own refusal to engage with the practicalities of technology also amount to failure? Heidegger himself liked to quote Hölderlin's line 'Where danger is, grows also that which saves', and is it not the case that, if technology itself is creating a danger for humanity and for the whole bio-sphere, only science and technology can save us? Indeed, isn't it geographers, biologists, chemists, botanists and other scientists who have done most to alert us to the catastrophic potential of many current industrial practices? And isn't it precisely a better scientific understanding of what is going on that will best prepare us for the most appropriate technological response? Solar panels, wind farms, insulation systems, cleaner cars and other 'green' initiatives all depend on the application of science, rather than its abandonment. Surely the further development of such technologies is more important than musing about the metaphysical foundations of enframing?

Looking at it like this, we might conclude that Heidegger's strategy is, bluntly, one of intellectual surrender, a failure to engage with what is most existentially pressing in the concrete reality of our contemporary destiny. Don't we, as in the case of religion, have to say that actual life is lived on the plane of the ontic, and involves wrestling with particular decisions and accepting particular responsibilities?

It might be objected that, whether we are talking about religion, politics or technology, the distinction between the ontic and the ontological does not of itself involve neglecting the former. It doesn't have to be a matter of either/or. We don't have to stop being religious in order to reflect on the ontological structures disclosed by the religious life, and many theologians have chosen to follow Heidegger in, as they see it, seeking an ontological anchor for the exigencies of the religious life as it is lived. Similarly, it would not seem necessary to suspend our efforts to solve particular environmental problems until we have succeeded in refiguring the world in a post-technological way. So, Heidegger need not be construed as saying that there is no point in doing what we can while we can to improve things in the here and now. Isn't his position rather one of giving unto Caesar's that which is Caesar's – i.e., of warning against assuming that the immediate problems of today and tomorrow are the *only* things that should concern us?

But if Heidegger's aim is neither to decry nor to promote the actual world of technology but simply to ask us to reflect critically on the limits of technology by considering its essence, does it follow that his strategy has *no* relation to the concrete, *no* practical significance or application?

One way of answering this question would be to acknowledge that Heidegger was no more of a practical environmentalist than he was a Christian preacher or a teacher of Buddhist meditation. He will not give us concrete answers to concrete problems (although which modern philosopher *has* given us any real help in the face of the environmental crisis?), and the one occasion when he tried to do so, in 1933, simply demonstrated the gulf separating his way of essential thinking from everyday reality. Nevertheless, the nature of the crisis confronting us today is so all-encompassing, permeating every level of society and culture, that its solution cannot be left to the scientists and technologists alone. For science and technology will necessarily direct their best efforts to particular problems, but, over and above the question of how to maximise renewable energy sources or how to take countermeasures against ozone depletion, we also need to be considering the kind of life-style, the kind of society we want to be living in. No matter how sophisticated our science, it will never be able to achieve more than crisis management so long as we go on living in an acquisitive, self-assertive society of individuals pursuing the maximisation of their personal autonomy, in moral, financial and political terms, and for whom the earth itself is nothing but a resource for human self-realisation. So long as this is how we choose to live, we will continue to degrade our environment in a cycle of ever more total crises. Unless we change at the fundamental level of values and of vision we will find ourselves, later if not sooner, passing the point of no return and rendering our planet humanly uninhabitable.

On this line of reasoning, we not only need technical solutions, we also need the vision thing. Alongside ecology we need 'deep ecology', a spiritual re-orientation that will make us fit custodians of planetary good.

The later Heidegger's turning away from self-assertion, his vision of humanity as 'shepherds of Being' and his invocation of the four-fold, may seem to mark him out as the pre-eminent thinker of such deep ecology. Perhaps the most eloquent proponent of this view is Bruce V. Foltz, for whom 'dwelling poetically upon the earth' (in, as Foltz understands it, Heidegger's interpretation of these words of Hölderlin) 'constitutes the possibility for a genuine environmental ethic' (Foltz 1995: 170). As Foltz points out, much so-called environmental action is itself determined by the technological approach. Against the view that this is both inevitable and necessary, Foltz argues that 'Such efforts would serve only to enhance the reign of technology by increasing its range while obscuring its pervasiveness' (*ibid.*: 166). This does not mean that we have to give up recycling, but we must learn to think of it differently.

> Recycling can be a reminder that even the aluminium can bears the pliant yet sustaining character of the earth itself – and hence can be a saving of that character along with the metal. And wilderness areas may be genuinely saved as those places of the earth where the mystery of self-seclusion consorts in splendor with the wonder of self-emergence. Everything depends on whether the saving arises from dwelling, and thus whether it is founded on the poetic.
>
> (Foltz 1995: 166)

This is an appealing application of the later Heidegger, but some caution is needed.

Admittedly, the overwhelming weight of Heidegger's rhetoric, if not of his argument, suggests that although his attitude towards technology does not involve any engagement with practical decisions about environmental policy, it is not strictly neutral. For if the concern with the essence of technology, though not itself technological, results in a critical drawing of limits around the realm of applicability of technology, and points to dimensions of being that are closed off to science by virtue of science's own fundamental assumptions, then this alone would already conflict with the popular view of science that governs the actual development of research, development and application. In this view it is widely assumed that there are no final limits and that there is no problem in the whole realm of humanity's dealings with its natural environment that cannot be resolved by science and technology, even if we may have to wait until the next round of research before the particular problem under consideration gets definitively sorted out.

Let us take a concrete example, the introduction of genetically modified crops. Government policies in this area are determined by various considerations such as: what is scientifically possible, what is economically advantageous, and what is politically acceptable. This last is generally assumed to be dependent on the previous two, so that if it can be shown that the scientific issues relating to the introduction of such crops have been adequately dealt with and if they are likely to provide cheaper food, then, sooner or later, the public will come round. Public fears are only 'legitimate' so long as scientific questions remain unresolved. If these questions are resolved, then those who go on being fearful are consigned to the realm of fringe politics.

How different things would be if, with Heidegger, we were to say that there was a prior question as to whether, in any particular case, the scientific view should count as decisive, and whether the licensing of new technologies was a matter on which governments should give most heed to scientific advisers. What if, instead of the now standard procedures, the outcome of each new round of technological innovation were to be decided by public debate (leaving aside the complexities of how this might be managed)? What if at the centre of such debate was the question as to the kind of beings we wished to be?

Such a way of responding to new technology would not necessarily lead to a negative result, although the fear that it would do so doubtless influences the institutions of science, government and industry in keeping to the present course of careful information management. But although it would not necessarily mean opposing technology, there is no doubt that over a period of time there would be a shift in the burden of proof and that the proponents of innovation would have to make a more powerful case than they are used to doing.

If such an imaginary scenario might be envisaged as one practical way of applying the later Heidegger's critical reserve towards technology, this would be something different from proclaiming him to be a deep ecological visionary, preparing us for the advent of a post-technological society. And against seeing him in such terms, we have to set his own insistent distinction between philosophy and world-view. Rather than seeing philosophy as the 'vision thing', Heidegger insists on its questioning character. As we saw in his account of Hölderlin, even the poet who mediates between gods and mortals exists and speaks under the shadow of ambiguity and mystery. Homecoming is no longer feasible as homecoming to a particular place, and even Meßkirch is bristling with television aerials. Home-coming is not possible for us except as a counter-movement to global homelessness, by attending to the mystery of the word that speaks to us from language itself. Even the fourfold is not so much the first sketch of a new cosmology, but a figuring of the anti-reductive, fugally articulated encounter with beings in Being and beings as a whole, which, as we heard Heidegger say, is always a matter of facing up to the questionableness of our own being and thus a preparation for decision.

The deep ecological interpretation of Heidegger may seem attractive, and it may even prove fruitful in the very specific need of our time. But to see it as the determining thrust of the later Heidegger would, I suggest, be to miss his fundamental philosophical intentions. If we can draw a deep ecological vision from Heidegger, then we must recognise that we are thinking beyond Heidegger's own word to what he himself did not think. We therefore turn now to some final reflections on the philosophical intentions of the later Heidegger.

Philosophy

We have tried seeing Heidegger as a poet, a mystic and a deep ecologist. In each case there have been good reasons for doing so, but none of them proved just right. Of course, if the question 'was Heidegger a philosopher?' is simply a dispute about words, such that the answer given depends on what we, variously, mean by philosophy, then it is not particularly worth asking. We can agree or disagree or agree to disagree, and it makes no difference either to our view of Heidegger or to our understanding of philosophy. The question is only interesting if it confronts us as a philosophical question concerning the nature of philosophy itself.

But if we are to conclude that, finally, it is as a philosopher that Heidegger is to be read and judged, we have to acknowledge at the outset that he is a philosopher of a peculiar kind. It can scarcely be otherwise with a thinker who set himself to question the history of philosophy in such a way as to bring the whole of that history into question. The distinctiveness of Heidegger's relation to the history of philosophy can fairly easily be highlighted by a comparison with two very different thinkers, Karl Marx and A.J. Ayer. In each case there is a thorough-going rejection of the metaphysical assumptions of the philosophical tradition, as there is in Heidegger. But, for all the differences between Marxism and logical positivism, they would agree that, once the errors of metaphysics have been exposed, it can safely be consigned to what Marxists liked to call the dustbins of history (before they were themselves consigned to them!). Now, despite Heidegger's many-sided conservatism, there is something in this modernist critique of metaphysics with which he can go along, but his final view is far more complex. For, as he saw it, metaphysics was not simply a mistake. Metaphysics too was a destining of Being, an unconcealment of truth, and, conversely, whatever comes 'after' metaphysics will also have to live with the situation that truth is also error and every unconcealment is also a concealment. What we move on to from there is neither a more correct view nor the result of previous history (in the sense that the classless society arises as the result of the self-contradictions of capitalism), but simply a new response to a new destining of Being. Moreover, despite the very different ways in which they viewed science, both Marx and Ayer would have agreed that it was science itself that showed the futility of metaphysics, whereas for Heidegger science, too, was a fruit from the metaphysical tree.

Heidegger, then, insists on the limitations of metaphysics no less stringently than thinkers of very different casts of mind. But, at the same time, he believes that metaphysics remains a potent force in contemporary science and, no less importantly, that because of the truth in metaphysics we can only free ourselves from it by thinking through the history of philosophy from its beginning to its end in a never-ending hermeneutic spiral. It follows that, even if Heidegger turns out to have been mistaken in everything he said about Parmenides, Plato, Aristotle, Descartes, Nietzsche, etc., the attempt to show how and why he was mistaken will have to engage with philosophical questions on the ground of philosophical texts. Even the attempt to show that Heidegger was not a good philosopher would have to involve a philosophical confrontation with his work.

Now, whatever the detail of Heidegger's many readings in the philosophical tradition, I should like to suggest that he was exemplary in this: that the modern critique of the tradition cannot itself be appropriated as a 'result' and incorporated as a datum of future philosophising. This alone already makes Heidegger more philosophically interesting than Marx or Ayer (which may, of course, not be saying much). For whether it, or any of its representative figures, is 'right' or 'wrong', fruitful or dangerous, the philosophical tradition exists for us today only as it lives in the light of sustained and ongoing interpretation. Another side of this is that even in moving beyond metaphysics (if that is what we are doing), we need to be clear as to what we are moving beyond, and this can only be established by constant reference to the texts that define metaphysics in its own terms. Heidegger's is in one respect a hermeneutic of suspicion, in that he finds in the texts of the tradition a different meaning from that which their authors themselves intended. However, the interdependence of truth and error, concealment and unconcealment is such that to expose the truth of a thinker as error is, paradoxically, to bring what is concealed in the thinker's thought into unconcealment and thus into truth. Heidegger does not simply rubbish the tradition, he interprets it.

Perhaps more importantly, even the furthest reaches of Heidegger's path of thinking are themselves governed by intellectual imperatives that Heidegger shares with many post-Kantian philosophers of various traditions. In particular, even when it seems most poetic or mythological, Heidegger's thought is critical in the sense that he is fundamentally concerned with determining the boundaries of the various specialised sciences and seeking to ground the unity that, nevertheless, in assigning these boundaries, constitutes the field of possible knowledge.

This may seem like an odd claim, given Heidegger's overriding preoccupation with the question of Being, since this is precisely what Kant's own critical philosophy excludes. Yet, as previously noted, if the question of Being is indeed the single decisive unifying factor in Heidegger's entire body of thought, from the very beginning the question was posed with a note of reserve. In *Being and Time* already it is not 'Being' that is the subject of interrogation but the *meaning* of being. Later on, Being is radically distinguished from the 'Being' of Christian Aristotelianism, it is respelt *Seyn* or placed under erasure – all pointing to the fact that, for Heidegger no less than for Kant, Being is not the object of possible knowledge 'in-itself'. Appropriated in the event, the happening of the round dance of the fourfold, Being is never identifiable with any particular entity or aggregate or level of entities, divine or mortal, earthly or heavenly. Only in the process of binding and dissolving the interrelationship of the fourfold 'is' there being, 'are' there beings in Being. The proximity of such assertions to Daoist conceptions of the Way, suggests that we can ascribe to Heidegger the reticence so concisely defined in the opening lines of Lao Tse's great work: 'The Way that can be spoken of / Is not the constant way; the name that can be named / Is not the constant name.'

In the steps of Kant, Heidegger's apophaticism goes all the way down.

Heidegger himself spoke of the importance of the tone of philosophy and of the necessity of hearing how the philosopher speaks his word. I am suggesting that we need to hear in the later Heidegger a tone that is at once critical, questioning and reserved. Heidegger himself remarked that in reading Nietzsche we should not substitute blinking for thinking, no matter how dazzling Nietzsche's intellectual pyrotechnics. We need to exercise a similar caution with regard to Heidegger himself if we are to think *with* Heidegger rather than simply talk about him, and we should not be seduced by his own rhetoric into thinking that he is saying more than he actually is.

This suggests a further point: that if we do wish to try philosophising in the manner of Heidegger, we will not do so by simply repeating Heidegger's own words or showing our proficiency in using Heideggerian terminology. For, if we were to be truly faithful disciples, we would need to go beyond what Heidegger thought to what Heidegger didn't think, to what remained unthought in Heidegger's thinking, and that means to the original impulse, the enticing puzzlement that first stung Heidegger himself into thinking. Can we say what that is? Perhaps Heidegger himself tells us. In the early pages of *What is Called Thinking?* Heidegger makes a remark that he then takes up as a kind of refrain throughout the text: 'Most thought-provoking in our thought-provoking time is that we are still not thinking' (WCT: 6).

Everything depends here on how we hear Heidegger's 'we'. Does this 'we' include Heidegger himself? If not, then we must understand the sentence and the text as a whole, and perhaps the entirety of the later Heidegger, in terms of what I have called the rhetoric of superiority: that Heidegger is putting himself forward as a master of thinking, offering to instruct those who cannot think or who are not yet thinking in this most difficult task. Or should we take Heidegger at his word and allow his 'we' to include himself: 'we, I included'. In this case Heidegger would himself be one of those who are not yet thinking, and would stand before us as one seeking to learn thinking, seeking to learn what it is to think, seeking to fathom what it is that has aroused this passion for thinking in him. If by the end of the lectures he has named 'what calls for thinking' as 'beings in Being', this is not the definition of an object amongst objects, not something we can ever possess, but a way of indicating a duality that is not an answer but 'what is most worthy of question' (WCT: 244). To say that the heart of the later Heidegger is the thinking of Being, then, is not to define the content of this body of writing but, precisely, to name what remains unthought within it, what Heidegger himself could not have claimed to think, but the question, the puzzle, the wonder that provokes thinking.

One further, concluding comment. Whatever else may be said for or against him Heidegger was a spellbinding teacher. Many of his works, perhaps the majority, come to us as the texts of lectures. His commitment to teaching and, especially, to university teaching, even if this became the occasion of his greatest miscalculation, distinguished him from many of the writers and thinkers who stamped his own thought: Kierkegaard, Dostoevsky, Nietzsche, Hölderlin and those early thinkers who lived before the foundation of the academy. In this connection, much of what Heidegger says about thinking, about philosophy and about hermeneutics need not, or need not only, be read as signposts pointing us towards the ontological heights, but as extremely pithy, quite practical and almost commonsensical instructions for students in any discipline. Take for example his insistence on the point that a great thinker thinks only one single thought: true or not, do we not, as teachers, continually encourage our students to seek a unitary, cohesive approach in their study of any great thinker, rather than merely listing 'twelve important points' in the teaching of Plato, Kant or Heidegger? Is this so very far from being a practical expression of what Heidegger proposes as a fundamental principle? And – just maybe – expressing it as a fundamental principle might actually be the best way to get students to adopt it as a practical directive.

Perhaps Heidegger's pedagogical instructions culminate in the maxim that we should never settle for second-hand opinions but should learn to think, slowly, carefully and in dialogue with the great thinkers of the past, yet also to think for ourselves: and this, of course, is above all true when we are faced with a teacher as imposing as Heidegger.

Notes

1 Is there a later Heidegger?

1   This raises the kind of problems that bedevil
    Heidegger's translators. William J. Richardson, for
    example, reverts to the Anglo-Saxon 'beon' for the occa-
    sions when Heidegger adopts the 'Seyn'-spelling
    (Richardson 1963). However, this is misleading, since
    'Seyn' was still in use in philosophical works in the nine-
    teenth century and would be seen and heard by
    Heidegger's contemporaries as a variant of 'Sein',
    whereas 'beon' would be incomprehensible without
    further explanation to most contemporary English
    speakers. In such ways Heidegger-in-translation is often
    made to appear perhaps more obscure than he really is –
    however, this doesn't help the translator who has to face
    the lack of any obvious English equivalent!

2   *Beiträge zur Philosophie* was only published in German
    in 1989 and, at the time of writing, its first English
    translation is still in preparation. *Besinnung* appeared in
    German only in 1998.
        Because these are texts that are not likely to enter into
    the mainstream of English-language philosophy
    teaching for some time, I have not addressed them
    extensively here. However, the issues with which they
    deal overlap at many points with those we shall be
    discussing.

3 'Besinnung' itself is another term that defies easy translation. The easiest options, 'reflection' or 'recollection', are problematic in a philosophical context because of the very specific connotations of these terms, connotations that 'Besinnung' is precisely intended to avoid. What Heidegger means is a kind of thinking that is reflective, recollective, somewhat introverted, like the 'remembrance of things past' that comes upon us when we revisit a childhood scene and recall the vanished voices and faces.

2 1933 and after

1 Wolin gives an excellent anthology of primary sources relating to Heidegger and Nazism. Also useful is Ott 1994. Influential in starting the contemporary debate was Farias 1989, although this last is highly tendentious and has been subjected to an incisive critique by Lacoue-Labarthe 1990. Many commentators include passing discussions of Heidegger's Nazism, and extensive treatments are also to be found in de Beistegui 1998, Ward 1995, Young 1997, Zimmerman 1990 and, of course, Safranski 1998. Heidegger's remark about the Holocaust and the East Germans echoes a frequent complaint in post-war Germany – compare with more recent equivalences such as Russia in Chechnya = NATO in Kosovo.
2 See Tanabe 1986 and Pattison 1996.
3 On Heidegger's non-meeting with Celan see Safranski 1998: 421ff. Also Fóti 1992.
4 Wolin's retention of 'Volk' (unitalicised) in his English translation undoubtedly serves to emphasise the Nazistic character of the speech as a whole. However, there is not a generally satisfactory English word that covers all the connotations of the German term.
5 See Rockmore 1992.
6 However, it is somewhat ironic that, having castigated Heidegger (who, after all, was actually acquainted with some farmers) for his 'sixth-hand' knowledge, Adorno goes on to say that 'Here we find an ignorance of everything we have learned about rural people', citing a series of French novels and stories from Balzac to Maupassant – hardly 'first-hand' knowledge, still less 'social research'!
7 A broadly similar approach is taken in Zimmerman 1990. This is an excellent source for much of the material covered in this chapter and the next.
8 Young 1997, p. 21.
9 Although some argue that *Being and Time* itself endorses a technological-pragmatic view of the human subject. See, e.g., Haar 1993. Haar's view is summed up in his comment that in *Being and Time* Heidegger is 'blind to the earth' (1993: 19). Zimmerman, however, emphasises that Heidegger was already privileging the world of the craftsman's shop over against factory production in *Being and Time*.

10   See the discussion of Van Gogh in Chapter 4 below.

3 Technology

1   A more extensive discussion of these passages will follow in Chapter 4 below.
2   Here is another way (not Heidegger's) of making the point. Imagine you are to make a photographic record of a stained-glass window. What would be the 'best' image you could produce? Would it be the image produced by removing the window from its frame, placing it over a light-box in a studio, thereby ensuring equal and standard illumination across the whole surface of the glass? That might seem the most correct, least subjective view. But that is not how anyone ever actually *sees* the window. What people see is far more complex, and the interaction of light and shade is crucial to such 'normal' perception.
3   For a further discussion of Heidegger's use of the verbal form 'wesen', see Chapter 7 below.
4   See Stiegler 1998 for a discussion of the priority of technology in relation to humanity, a point that he argues with reference not only to Heidegger but also to the possible influence of early tool-making and tool use amongst prehominids on human evolution itself.
5   For a good discussion of Jünger, see Zimmerman 1990.

4 Seeing things

1   This may be translated 'Forest Paths'. However, it means more specifically the kind of path that turns out to lead nowhere, petering out or running into thick undergrowth.
2   It will be clear from what follows that I do not accept the view that Heidegger's turn to art reflects the aestheticism of Nazi politics, interesting as that idea is – partly, because, as will become clear, Heidegger's concern is, at one level, not with 'art' at all.
3   See Pöggeler 1994: 110ff.
4   See Derrida 1987.
5   In the best-known of such auctions of impounded works, held in Lucerne, Switzerland on 30 June 1939, a self-portrait by Van Gogh was the most expensive work on sale.
6   We shall attempt to grasp the full significance of this point later, in discussing Heidegger's reading of Hölderlin (see Chapter 7 below).
7   Heidegger does not pause to discuss this, but he will have been very well aware that, even when the material substratum of art is acknowledged and given its place in aesthetic theory, it was usual for the different forms of art to be hierarchically graded according to the extent to which this materiality was sublimated and subordinated to the 'meaning' element. Hegel's aesthetics is an outstanding example of this.

8   It is characteristic that Heidegger mixes such philosophical-sounding properties as 'extension' and 'heaviness' with 'lack of shape' and 'dullness'.

9   The justification for turning back to the 'early' Heidegger at this point presupposes a positive position on the question of continuity between early and later works. The text we are about to consider itself shows how we can relate the sometimes startling procedures of the later Heidegger back to methodological principles that he embraced very early in his career.

10 As it is not immediately relevant, I shall not pursue here the further question which Heidegger discusses as to whether it is also possible to have what he calls ideational intuition: i.e., intuition in which I intuit one-ness, unity itself, as such and apart from its manifestation in, e.g., the row of trees or flock of ducks.

11 A comment that, in the light of Heidegger's notion of presumptive intentionality should not be heard as simply moral condemnation.

5 Nietzsche

1   Cf. Löwith 1995: 127.

2   Cf. 'The thinker needs one thought only' (WCT: 50). Derrida has brought attention to the peculiar audacity of Heidegger's reading Nietzsche as the thinker of a single decisive thought, asking rhetorically 'Next to Kierkegaard, was not Nietzsche one of the few greatest thinkers who multiplied his names and played with signatures, identities, and masks?' (Derrida 1995: 63)

3   Indeed, Heidegger says, if we are truly to understand Nietzsche it may be necessary for us first to study Aristotle for ten or fifteen years! (WCT: 73).

4   Whether or not this works as an interpretation of Descartes, Laurence Lampert has vigorously rejected it as an interpretation of Nietzsche, asserting that 'making the song of eternal return a hymn to machinery runs counter to everything that Nietzsche himself said about it ... [Eternal return] does not express a secret desire to achieve permanence but celebrates the impermanent. It is not a song of dominance but of sheltering and letting-be ... not a work song but a song of play and playfulness' (Lampert 1986: 262). To decide such an argument would, of course, take us away from Heidegger into the realm of Nietzsche scholarship – a task for another day perhaps.

5   Whereas they see the call to liberation from the closure of the past and the opportunity to become radically free for the future as always a matter for the concrete individual, Heidegger turns away from that towards the underlying (as he sees it) question of Being. See Pattison 1999: 134–8, 142–4 for a discussion of Heidegger and Bultmann.

6   Cf BT: §76 and §77, which, when juxtaposed with Heidegger's Nietzsche interpretation, once more points to the significant continuity between the early and the later Heidegger.

6 The first and second beginnings of philosophy

1   I say 'approximately', because Heidegger is not always consistent as to when exactly the 'fall' of thinking into metaphysics occurred. For the most part it is clear that this fall becomes virtually irreversible with the translation of philosophy from Greek into Latin and its subsequent Christianisation. However, Aristotle himself, despite Heidegger's undoubted admiration for him, is the wrong side of the divide. As we shall see, it is not even clear that the so-called 'Presocratics' are themselves entirely pure. See Rosen 1993, Chapter 1.

2   For a fuller account of the various revisitings of Ancient Greece in modern German thought see Butler 1958 (1935).

3   Cf. the analogous comments in *What is Called Thinking?*, where Heidegger comments that we do not speak of Kant as a pre-Hegelian (WCT: 184).

4   Heidegger's point works better in German than in English. In German a present participle, e.g. 'laufend' ('running') can readily be adapted as a substantive, such that 'Der Laufende' means 'the man who is running', or, in the present example, 'Das Blühende' means 'that which is blooming'. The nearest English equivalent might be in expressions like 'the running one'.

7 Hölderlin

1   For a good introduction to Hölderlin, see Constantine 1988.

2   If we are disposed to be generous to Heidegger, we might hear in this remark a critical downplaying of the claims made on behalf of the Nazi revolution to define the future of Germany on the basis of a particular event in chronological time.

3   Indeed, it is striking that, even when Heidegger himself gives a lecture entitled 'Language', he expounds language by interpreting a poetic work. In this respect I have tried to follow Heidegger's own example by embedding the account of his understanding of language in the exposition of his remarks on Hölderlin's poetry.

8 What kind of thinker?

1   Not everyone sees this as a fault, however. Quite different attempts to incorporate Heidegger into a postmodern form of mysticism are represented by, e.g., Don Cupitt (see Cupitt 1998) and David Levin (see Levin 1988).

Bibliography

Works by Heidegger

Texts in German

All references are to the *Gesamtausgabe*, Frankfurt am Main: Vittorio Klostermann, 1978– (continuing).

Texts in English

(1962) *Being and Time*, tr. John Macquarrie and Edward Robinson, Oxford: Blackwell.
(1966) *Discourse on Thinking*, tr. John M. Anderson and E. Hans Freund, New York: Harper & Row,
(1975) *Early Greek Thinking*, tr. David Farrell Krell and Frank Capuzzi, New York: Harper & Row.
(1995) *The Fundamental Concepts of Metaphysics: World, finitude, solitude*, tr. W. McNeill and N. Walker, Bloomington: Indiana University Press.
(1991) *Nietzsche: Volumes one and two*, tr. David Farrell Krell, San Francisco CA: HarperCollins.
(1991) *Nietzsche: Volumes three and four*, tr. David Farrell Krell, San Francisco CA: HarperCollins.

(1998) *Pathmarks*, ed. W. McNeill, Cambridge: Cambridge University Press.

(1971) *Poetry, Language, Thought*, tr. Albert Hofstadter, New York: Harper & Row.

(1977) *The Question Concerning Technology and Other Essays*, tr. and ed. William Lovitt, New York: Harper & Row.

(1974) *The Question of Being*, tr. W. Kluback and Jean T. Wilde, London: Vision.

(1967) *What is a Thing?* tr. W.B. Barton Jr and Vera Deutsch, Chicago IL: Henry Regnery.

(1968) *What is Called Thinking?*, tr. Fred D. Wieck and J. Glenn Gray, New York: Harper & Row.

Heidegger, Martin, and Eugen Fink (1979) *Heraclitus Seminar 1966/67*, tr. Charles H. Siebart, Tuscaloosa AL: University of Alabama Press.

Secondary sources

Adorno, Theodor (1986) *The Jargon of Authenticity*, tr. K. Tarnowski and F. Will, London: Routledge & Kegan Paul.

Beistegui, M. de (1998) *Heidegger and the Political: Dystopias*, London: Routledge.

Bernasconi, R. (1985) *The Question of Language in Heidegger's History of Being*, Atlantic Highlands NJ: Humanities Press.

Bruns, Gerald L. (1981) *Heidegger's Estrangements: Language, truth, and poetry in the later writings*, New Haven CT and London: Yale University Press.

Buchner, Hartmut (ed.) (1989) *Japan und Heidegger: Gedenkschrift der Stadt Meßkirch zum hundertsten Geburtstag Martin Heideggers*, Sigmaringen: Jan Thorbecke.

Butler, E.M. (1958 [1935]) *The Tyranny of Greece over Germany: A study of the influence exercised by Greek art and poetry over the great German writers of the eighteenth, nineteenth and twentieth centuries*, Boston MA: Beacon Press.

Caputo, John D. (1993) *Demythologizing Heidegger*, Bloomington IN: Indiana University Press.

—— (1977) *The Mystical Element in Heidegger's Thought*, Athens OH: Ohio University Press.

Constantine, David (1988) *Hölderlin*, Oxford: Clarendon Press.

Cupitt, Don (1998) *The Religion of Being*, London: SCM.

Derrida, J. (1995) 'Interpreting Signatures (Nietzsche/Heidegger)' in Sedgwick (ed.) (1995).

—— (1987) *The Truth in Painting*, Chicago IL: Chicago University Press.

Farias, Victor (1989 [1987]) *Heidegger and Nazism*, tr. G.R. Ricci, ed. J. Margolis and Tom Rockmore, Philadelphia PA: Temple University Press.

Foltz, Bruce V. (1995) *Inhabiting the Earth: Heidegger, environmental ethics, and the metaphysics of nature*, Atlantic Highlands NJ: Humanities Press.

Fóti, Véronique (1992) *Heidegger and the Poets: Poiesis, sophia, techne*, Atlantic Highlands NJ: Humanities Press.

Guignon, Charles (ed.) (1993) *The Cambridge Companion to Heidegger*, Cambridge: Cambridge University Press.

Haar, Michel (1993 [1987]) *The Song of the Earth: Heidegger and the grounds of the history of being*, tr. R. Lilly, Bloomington IN: Indiana University Press.

Harries, Karsten, and Christoph Jamme (eds) (1994) *Martin Heidegger: Politics, art and technology*, New York: Holmes & Meier.

Hegel, G.W.F. (1977 [1807]) *Phenomenology of Spirit*, tr. A.V. Miller, Oxford: Oxford University Press.

Hüneke, A. (1991) 'On the Trail of Missing Masterpieces' in Barron, Stephanie (ed.) *'Degenerate Art': The fate of the avant-garde in Nazi Germany*, New York: Harry Abrams and Los Angeles CA: County Museum of Art.

Kisiel, Theodore (1993) *The Genesis of Heidegger's Being and Time*, Berkeley and Los Angeles CA: University of California Press.

Kockelmans, J. (ed.) (1972) *On Heidegger and Language*, Evanston IL: Northwestern University Press.

Lacoue-Labarthe, Philippe (1990 [1987]) *Heidegger, Art, Politics*, tr. Chris Turner, Oxford: Blackwell.

Lampert, Laurence (1986) *Nietzsche's Teaching: An interpretation of Thus Spake Zarathustra*, New Haven CT: Yale University Press.

Levin, David Michael (1988) *The Opening of Vision: Nihilism and the postmodern vision*, New York and London: Routledge.

Löwith, Karl (1995 [1984]) *Martin Heidegger and European Nihilism*, tr. Gary Steiner, ed. R. Wolin, New York: Columbia University Press.

Marx, Werner (1987 [1983]) *Is there a Measure on Earth? Foundations for a non-metaphysical ethics*, Chicago IL: University of Chicago Press.

May, Reinhard (1996 [1989]) *Heidegger's Hidden Sources: East Asian influences on his work*, tr. Graham Parkes, London: Routledge.

McCann, Christopher (ed.) (1996) *Critical Heidegger*, London: Routledge.

Nishida, Kitaro (1987, 1992) *An Enquiry Into the Good*, New Haven CT: Yale University Press.

Ott, Hugo (1994 [1988]) *Martin Heidegger: A political life*, tr. A. Blunden, London: Fontana.

Parkes, Graham (ed.) (1987) *Heidegger and Asian Thought*, Honolulu: University of Hawaii Press.

Pattison, George (1996) *Agnosis: Theology in the void*, Basingstoke: Macmillan.

—— (1999) *Anxious Angels: A retrospective view of religious existentialism*, Basingstoke: Macmillan.

Pöggeler, Otto (1994) 'Heidegger on Art', in Harries and Jamme (eds) (1994).

—— (1987 [1980]) *Martin Heidegger's Way of Thinking*, Atlantic Highlands NJ: Humanities Press.

Richardson, William J., SJ (1963) *Heidegger: Through phenomenology to thought*, The Hague: Martinus Nijhoff.

Rockmore, Tom (1992) *On Heidegger's Nazism and Philosophy*, London: Wheatsheaf.

Rosen, S. (1993) *The Question of Being: A reversal of Heidegger*, New Haven CT: Yale University Press.

Safranski, Rüdiger (1998 [1994]) *Martin Heidegger: Between good and evil*, tr. E. Osers, Cambridge MA: Harvard University Press.

Sallis, John (ed.) (1993) *Reading Heidegger: Commemorations*, Bloomington IN: Indiana University Press.

Schama, Simon (1995) *Landscape and Memory*, London: HarperCollins.

Sedgwick, Peter R. (ed.) (1995) *Nietzsche: A critical reader*, Oxford: Blackwell.

Sikka, Sonya (1997) *Forms of Transcendence: Heidegger and medieval mystical theology*, Albany NY: State University of New York Press.

Spanos, William V. (ed.) (1979) *Martin Heidegger and the Question of Literature: Towards a postmodern literary hermeneutics*, Bloomington IN: Indiana University Press.

Steiner, George (1978) *Heidegger*, London: Fontana.

Stiegler, Bernard (1998 [1994]) *Technics and Time 1: The fault of Epimetheus*, Stanford CA: Stanford University Press.

Summerell, Orrin F. (1998) *The Otherness of God*, Charlottesville VA: University of Virginia Press.

Tanabe, Hajime (1986) *Philosophy as Metanoetics*, Berkeley and Los Angeles CA: University of California Press.

Ward, James F. (1995) *Heidegger's Political Thinking*, Amherst MA: University of Massachusetts Press.

Watts, Alan, with Al Chung-liang Huang (1979) *Tao: The watercourse way*, Harmondsworth: Penguin.

Wolin, Richard (1993) *The Heidegger Controversy: A critical reader*, Cambridge, MA: MIT Press.

—— (1990) *The Politics of Being: The political thought of Martin Heidegger*, New York: Columbia University Press.

Young, Julian (1997) *Heidegger, Philosophy, Nazism*, Cambridge: Cambridge University Press.

Zimmerman, Michael (1990) *Heidegger's Confrontation with Modernity: Technology, politics, art*, Bloomington IN: Indiana University Press.

Index

230